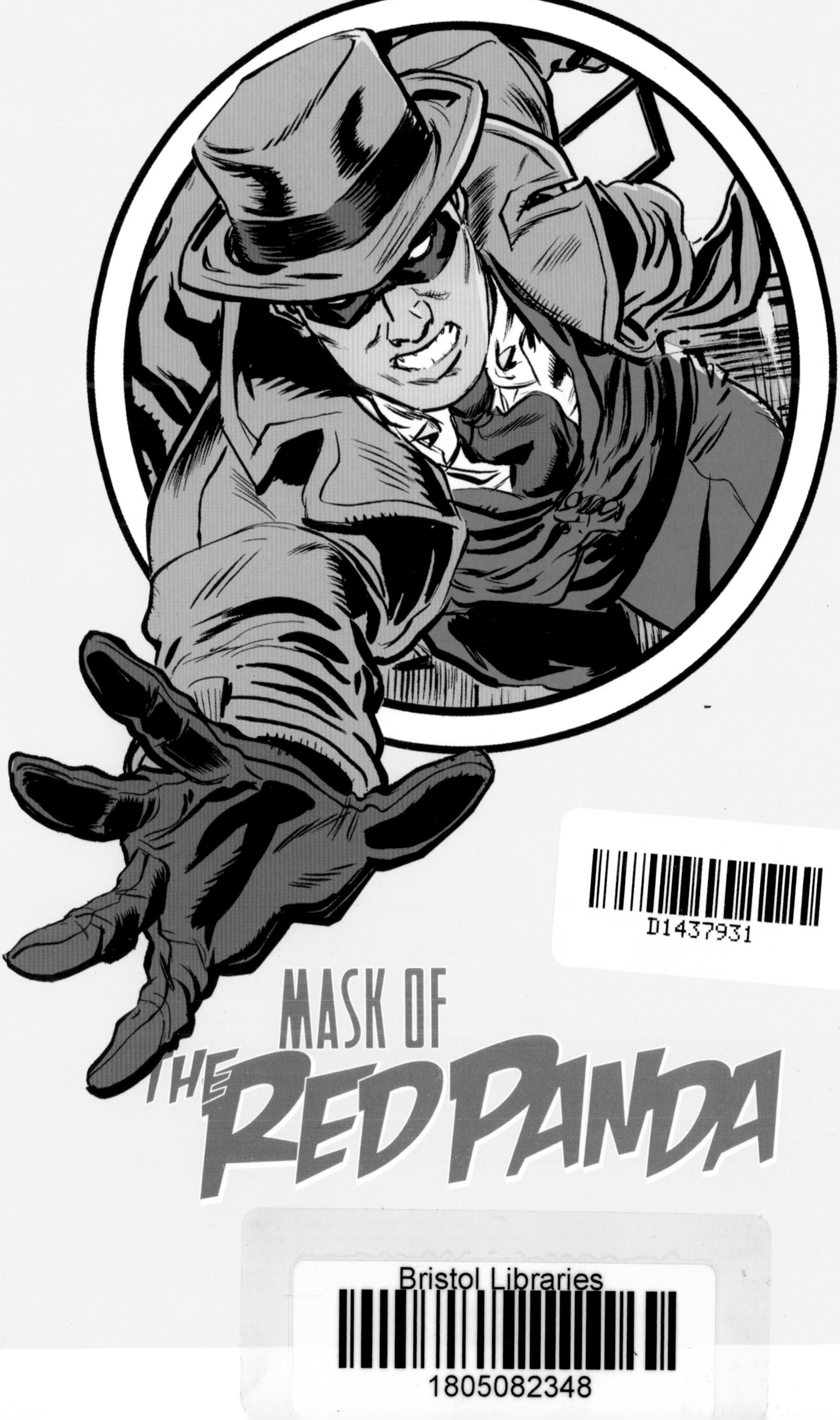

MASK OF THE RED PANDA

WRITTEN BY
GREGG TAYLOR

ART, COLORS, AND LETTERS BY
DEAN KOTZ

ORIGINAL COVER COLORS BY
JEREMY COLWELL

COVER BY
DEAN KOTZ

COLLECTION EDITS BY
JUSTIN EISINGER
AND
ALONZO SIMON

COLLECTION DESIGN BY
ROBBIE ROBBINS

monkeybrain COMICS

ISBN: 978-1-61377-871-5

17 16 15 14   1 2 3 4

Ted Adams, CEO & Publisher
Greg Goldstein, President & COO
Robbie Robbins, EVP/Sr. Graphic Artist
Chris Ryall, Chief Creative Officer/Editor-in-Chief
Matthew Ruzicka, CPA, Chief Financial Officer
Alan Payne, VP of Sales
Dirk Wood, VP of Marketing
Lorelei Bunjes, VP of Digital Services
Jeff Webber, VP of Digital Publishing & Business Development

www.IDWPUBLISHING.com
IDW founded by Ted Adams, Alex Garner, Kris Oprisko, and Robbie Robbins

Facebook: facebook.com/idwpublishing
Twitter: @idwpublishing
YouTube: youtube.com/idwpublishing
Instagram: instagram.com/idwpublishing
deviantART: idwpublishing.deviantart.com
Pinterest: pinterest.com/idwpublishing/idw-staff-faves

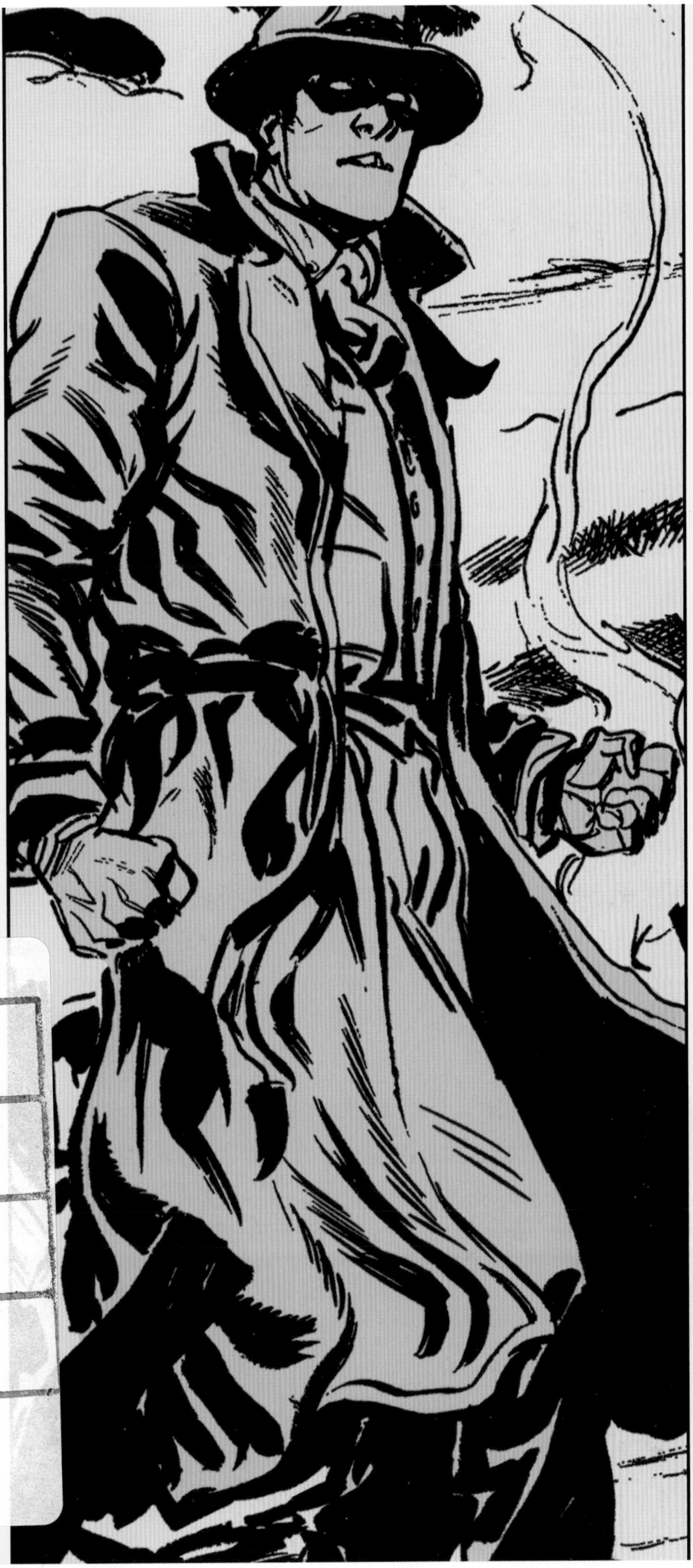

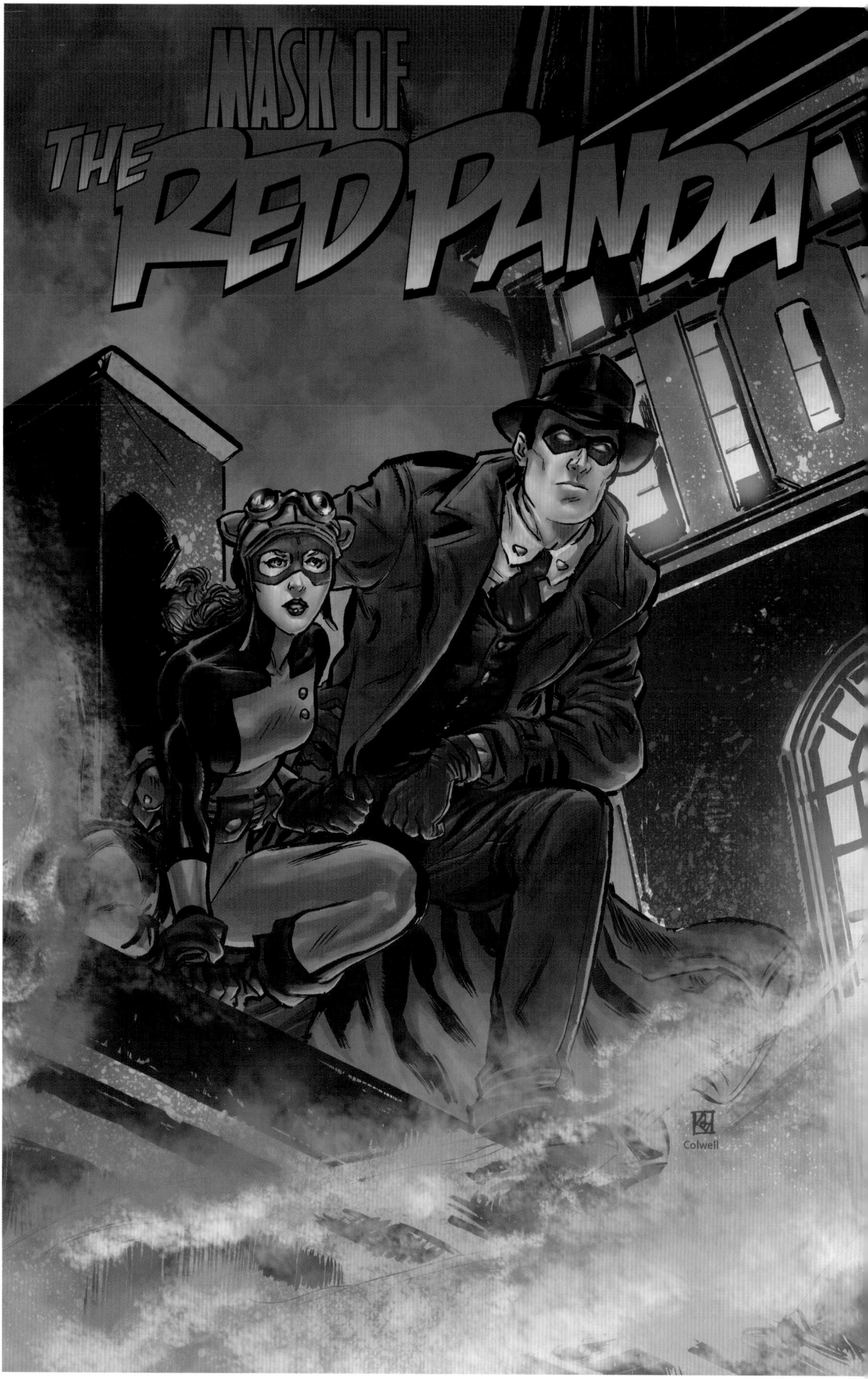
MASK OF
THE RED PANDA
Colwell

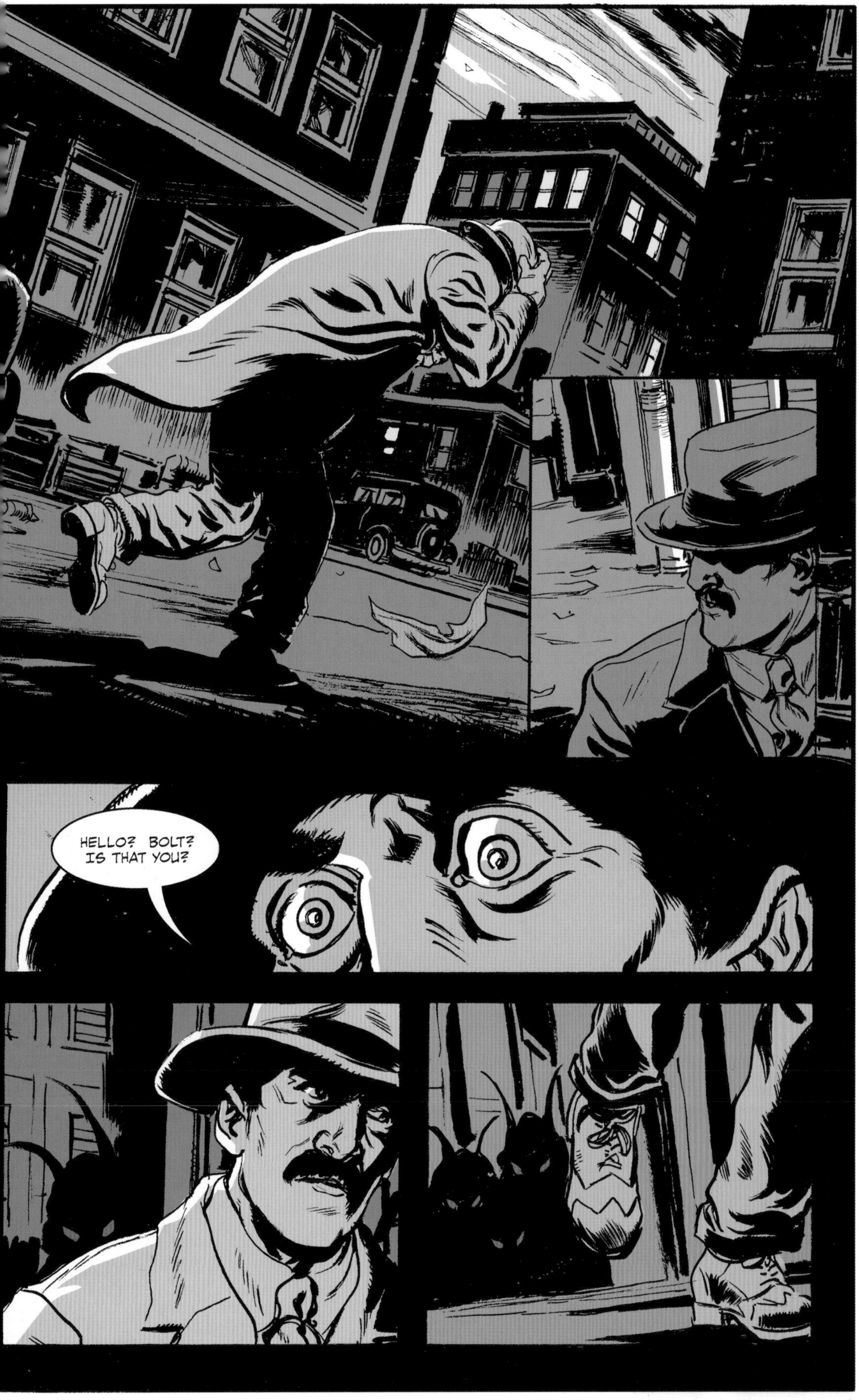
HELLO? BOLT? IS THAT YOU?

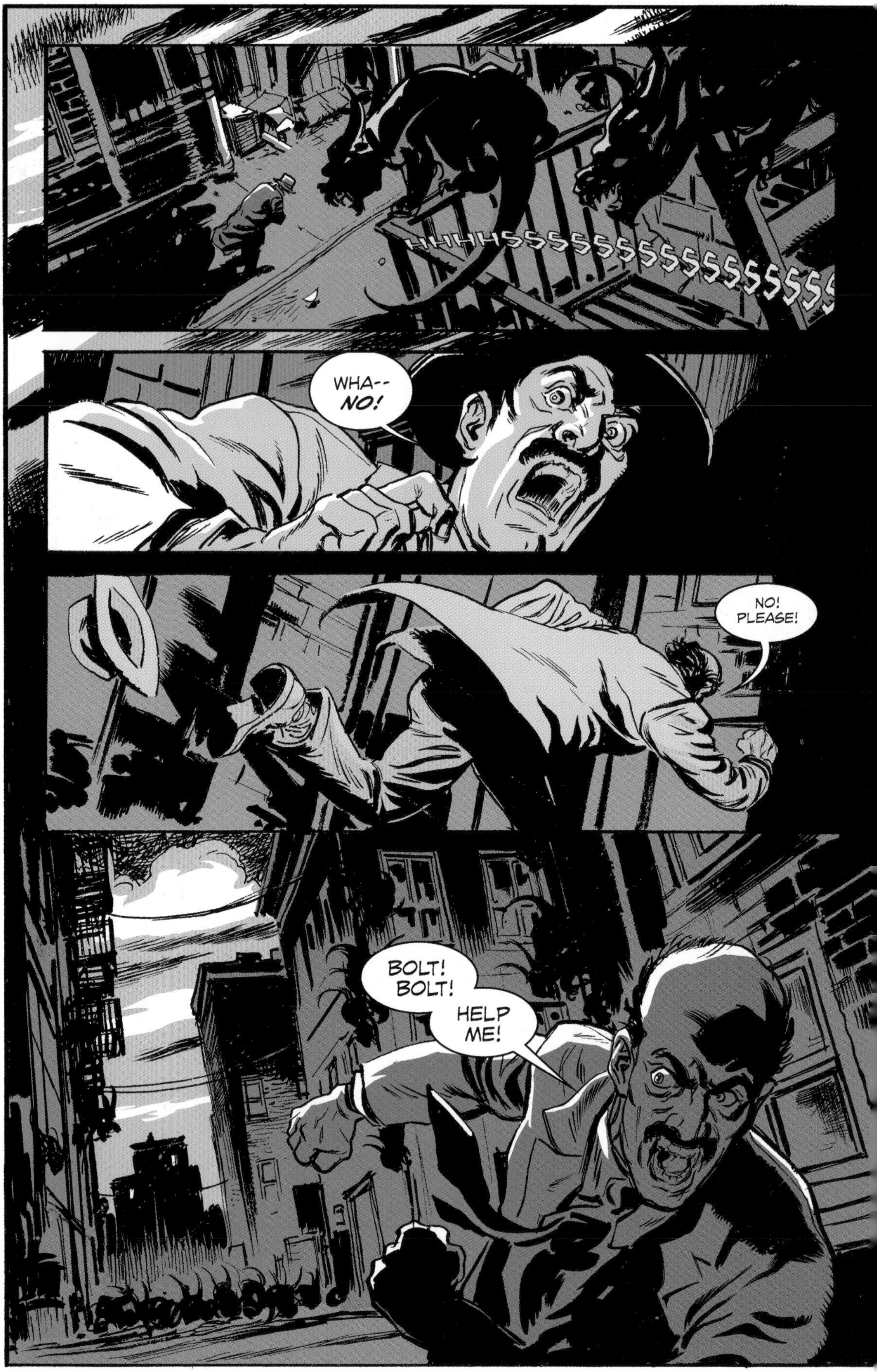
HHHHSSSSSSSSSSSSSSSSSS
WHA--
NO!
NO!
PLEASE!
BOLT!
BOLT!
HELP
ME!

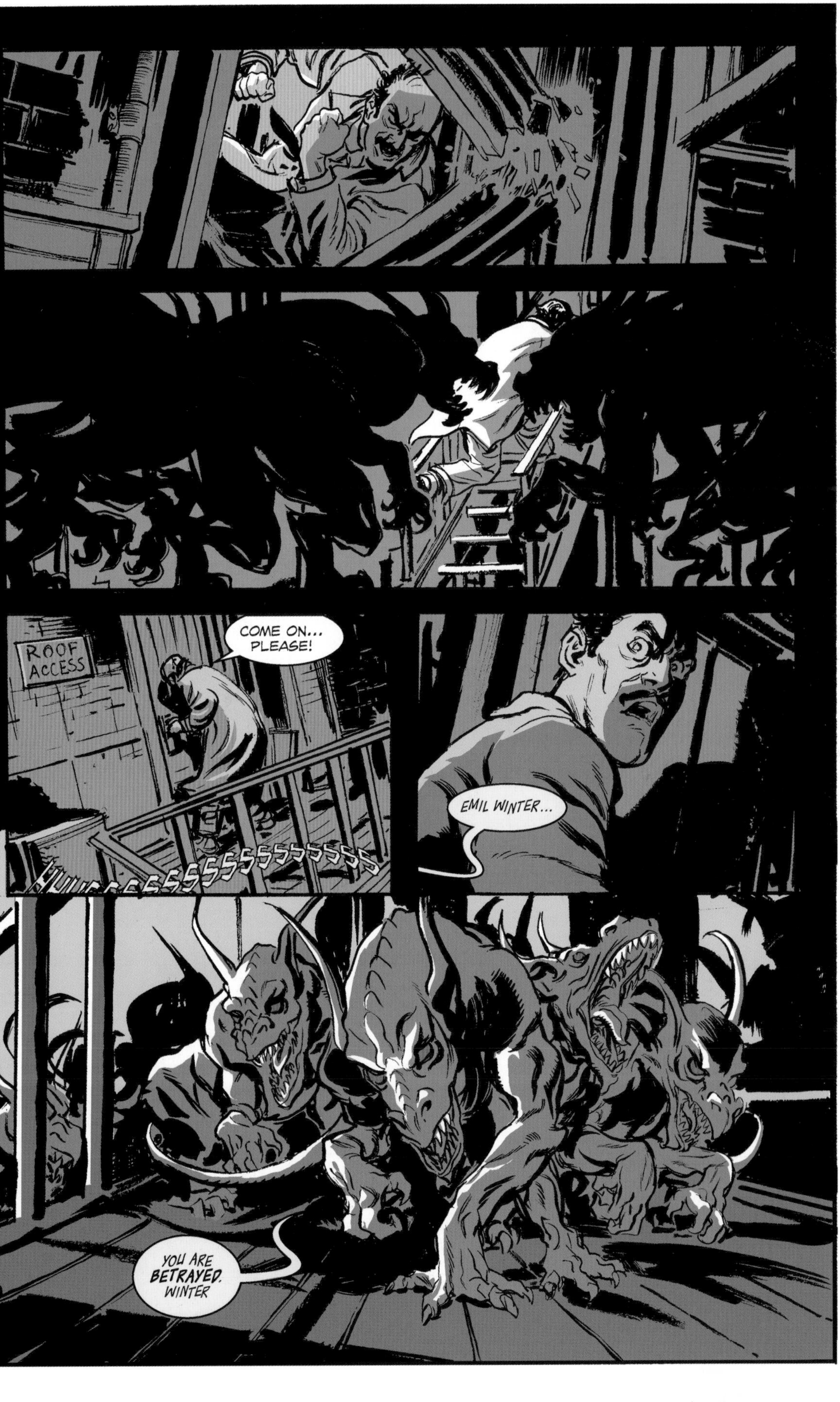
ROOF ACCESS
COME ON... PLEASE!
EMIL WINTER...
YOU ARE BETRAYED. WINTER

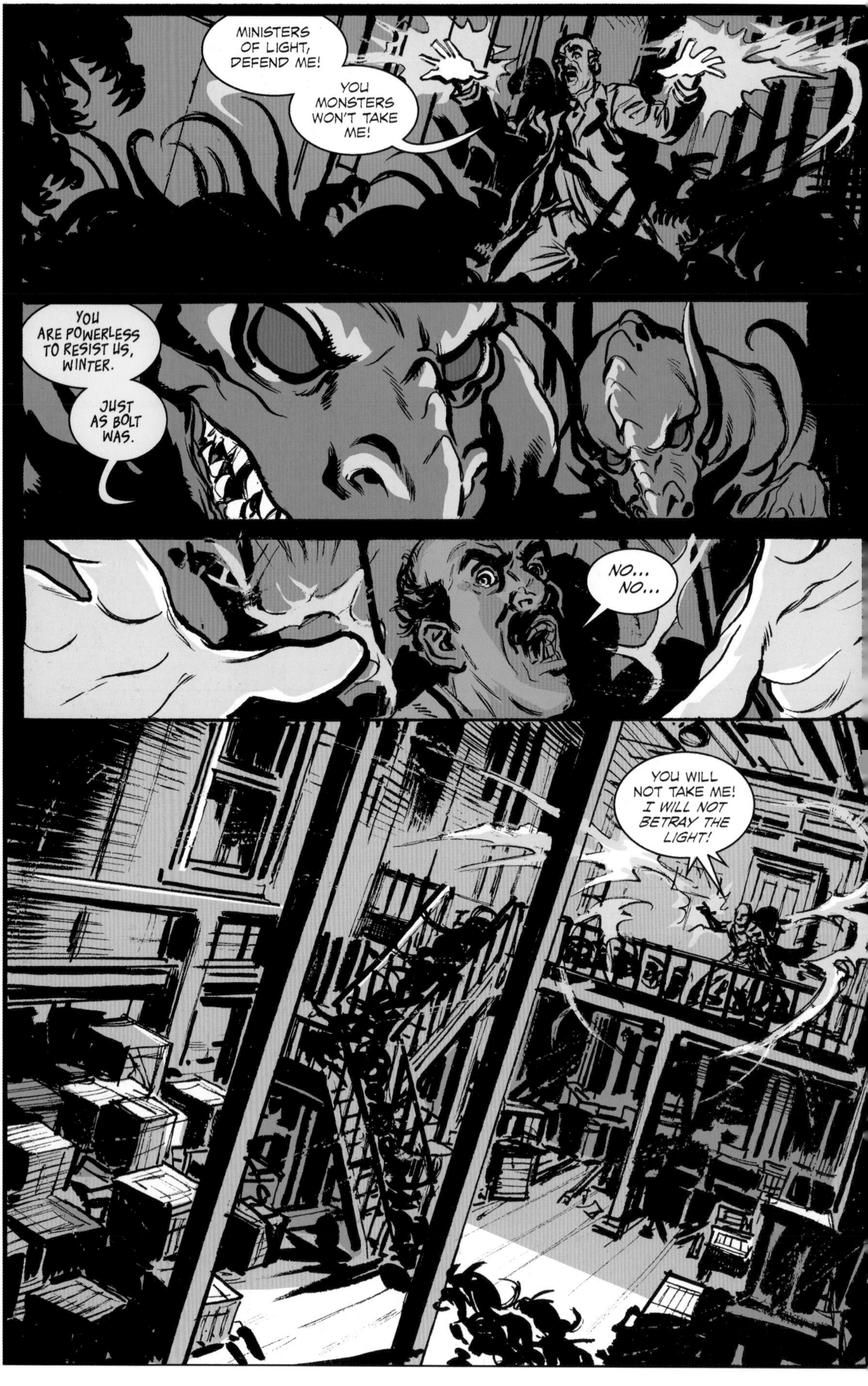
MINISTERS OF LIGHT, DEFEND ME!
YOU MONSTERS WON'T TAKE ME!
YOU ARE POWERLESS TO RESIST US, WINTER.
JUST AS BOLT WAS.
NO... NO...
YOU WILL NOT TAKE ME! I WILL NOT BETRAY THE LIGHT!

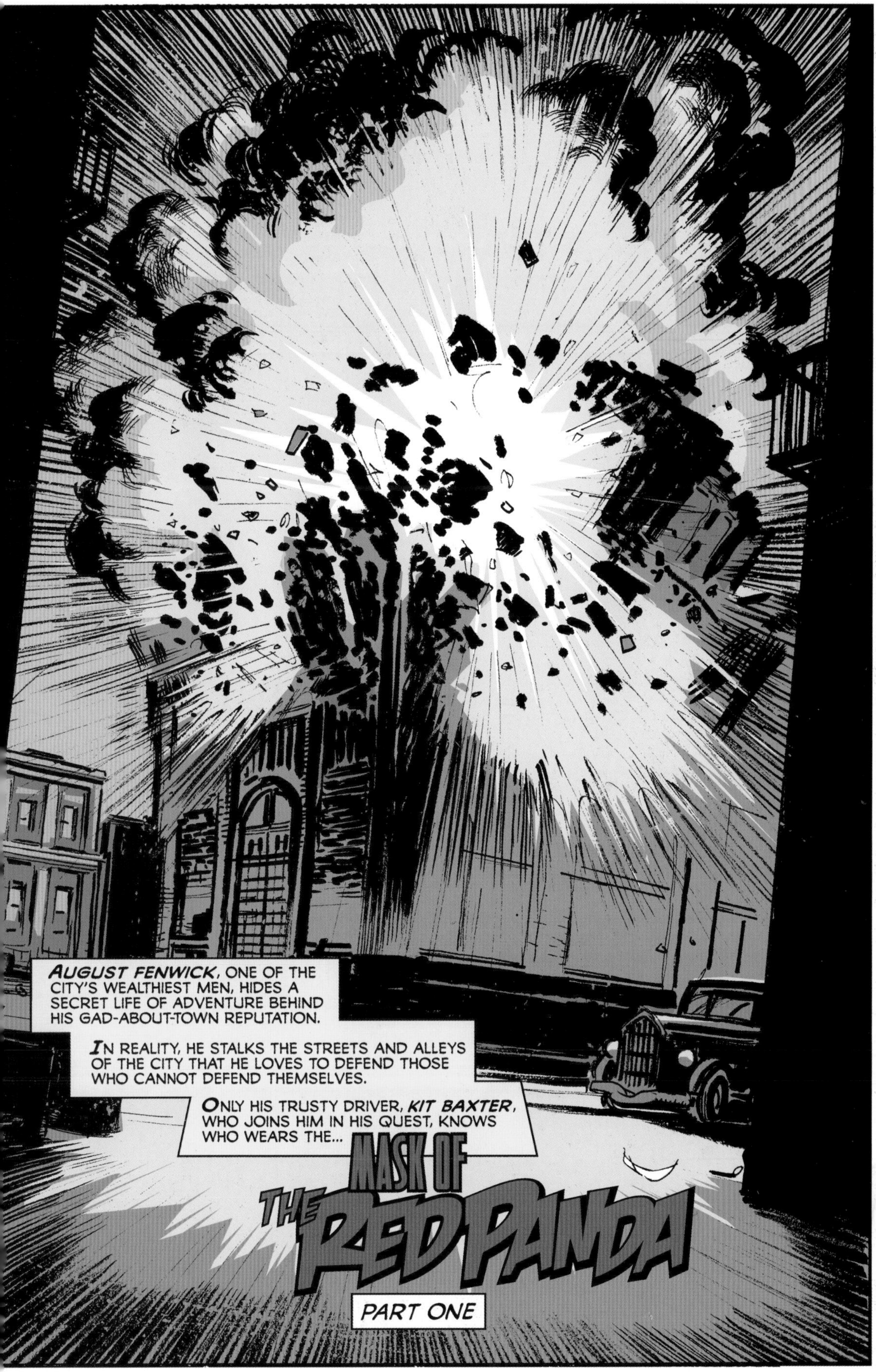
AUGUST FENWICK, ONE OF THE CITY'S WEALTHIEST MEN, HIDES A SECRET LIFE OF ADVENTURE BEHIND HIS GAD-ABOUT-TOWN REPUTATION.
IN REALITY, HE STALKS THE STREETS AND ALLEYS OF THE CITY THAT HE LOVES TO DEFEND THOSE WHO CANNOT DEFEND THEMSELVES.
ONLY HIS TRUSTY DRIVER, KIT BAXTER, WHO JOINS HIM IN HIS QUEST, KNOWS WHO WEARS THE...
MASK OF THE RED PANDA
PART ONE

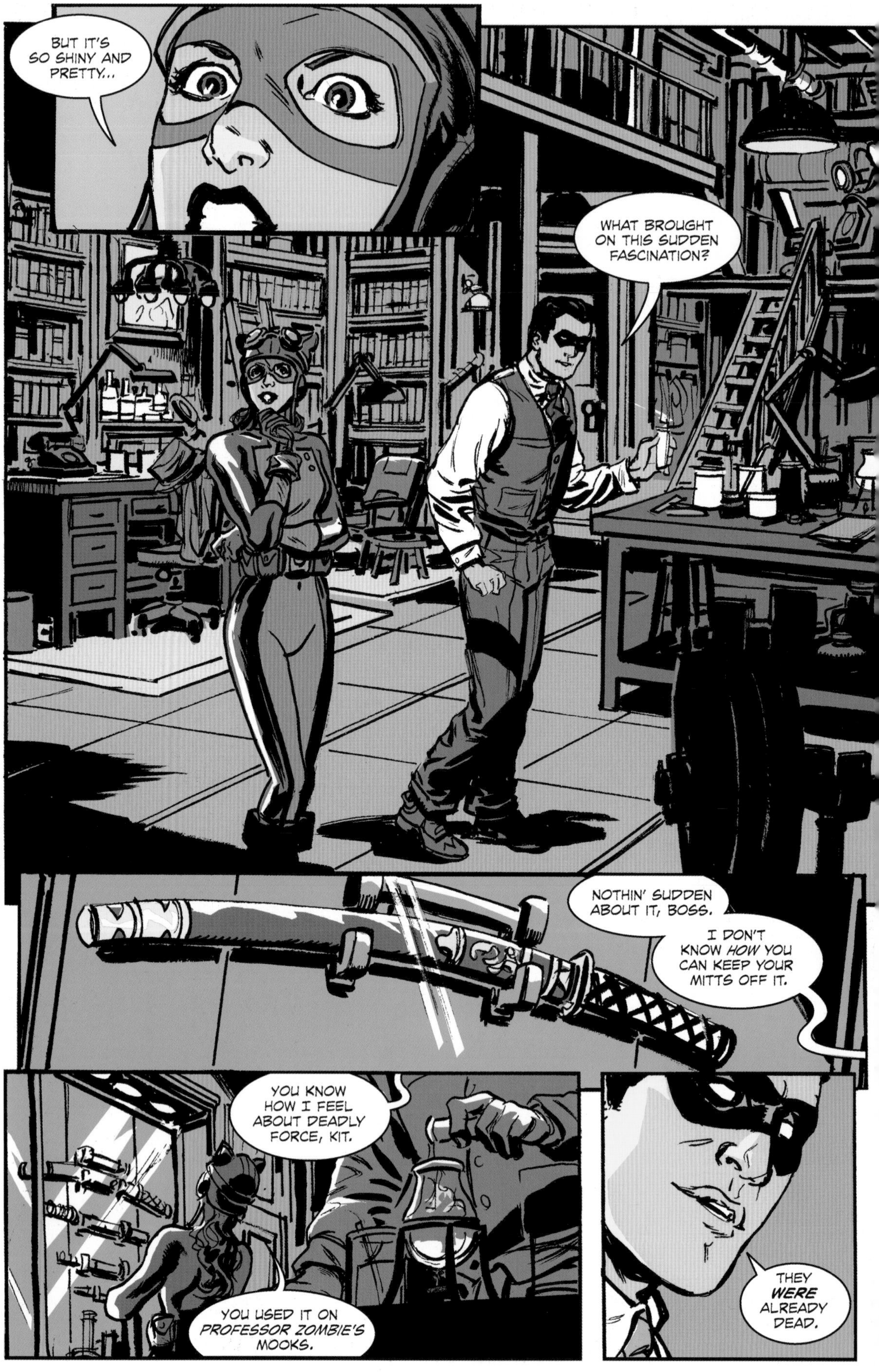
BUT IT'S SO SHINY AND PRETTY...
WHAT BROUGHT ON THIS SUDDEN FASCINATION?
NOTHIN' SUDDEN ABOUT IT, BOSS.
I DON'T KNOW *HOW* YOU CAN KEEP YOUR MITTS OFF IT.
YOU KNOW HOW I FEEL ABOUT DEADLY FORCE, KIT.
YOU USED IT ON *PROFESSOR ZOMBIE'S* MOOKS.
THEY ***WERE*** ALREADY DEAD.

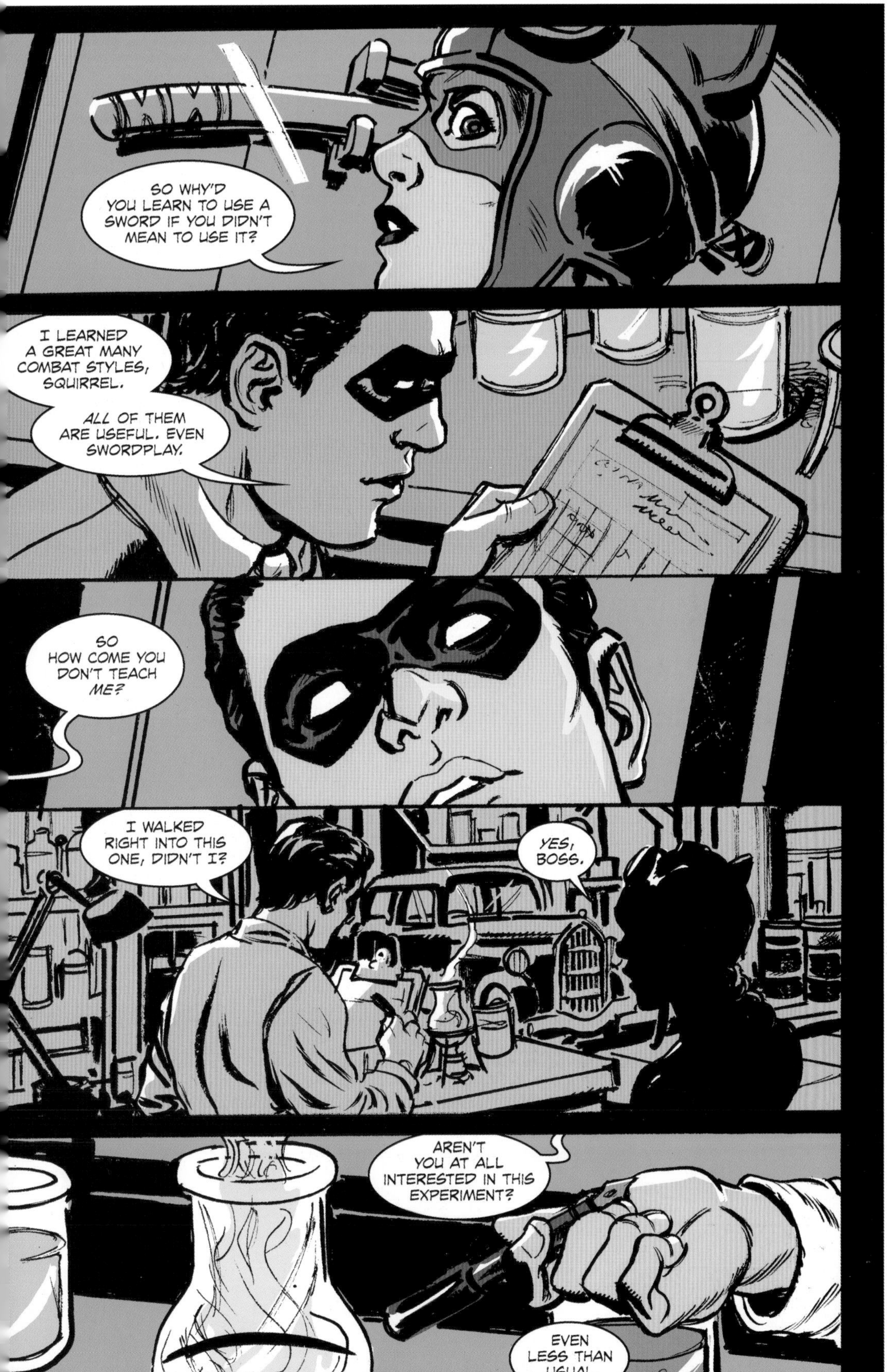
SO WHY'D YOU LEARN TO USE A SWORD IF YOU DIDN'T MEAN TO USE IT?
I LEARNED A GREAT MANY COMBAT STYLES, SQUIRREL.
ALL OF THEM ARE USEFUL. EVEN SWORDPLAY.
SO HOW COME YOU DON'T TEACH *ME*?
I WALKED RIGHT INTO THIS ONE, DIDN'T I?
YES, BOSS.
AREN'T YOU AT ALL INTERESTED IN THIS EXPERIMENT?
EVEN LESS THAN USUAL.

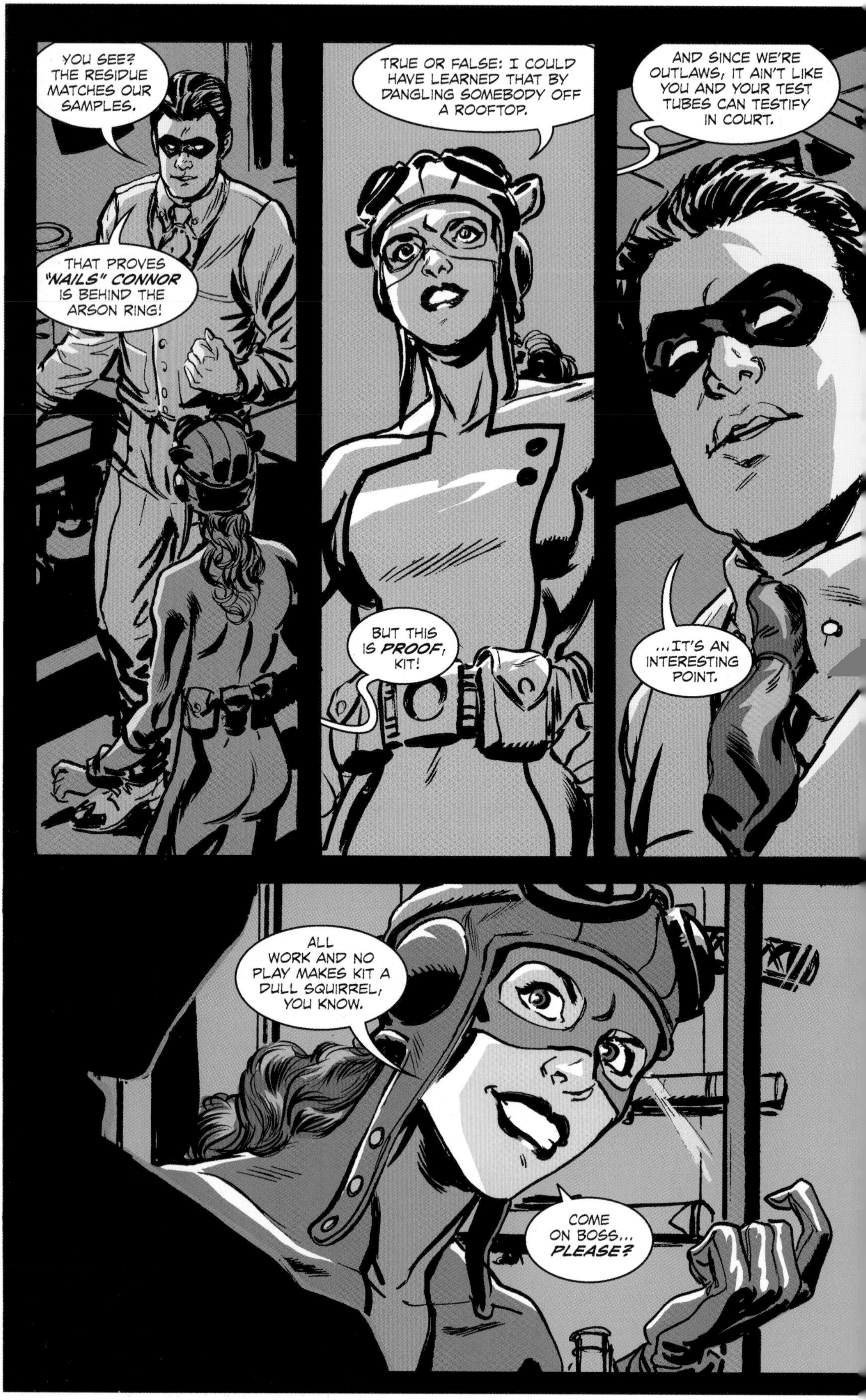
YOU SEE? THE RESIDUE MATCHES OUR SAMPLES.
THAT PROVES "NAILS" CONNOR IS BEHIND THE ARSON RING!
TRUE OR FALSE: I COULD HAVE LEARNED THAT BY DANGLING SOMEBODY OFF A ROOFTOP.
BUT THIS IS PROOF, KIT!
AND SINCE WE'RE OUTLAWS, IT AIN'T LIKE YOU AND YOUR TEST TUBES CAN TESTIFY IN COURT.
...IT'S AN INTERESTING POINT.
ALL WORK AND NO PLAY MAKES KIT A DULL SQUIRREL, YOU KNOW.
COME ON BOSS... PLEASE?

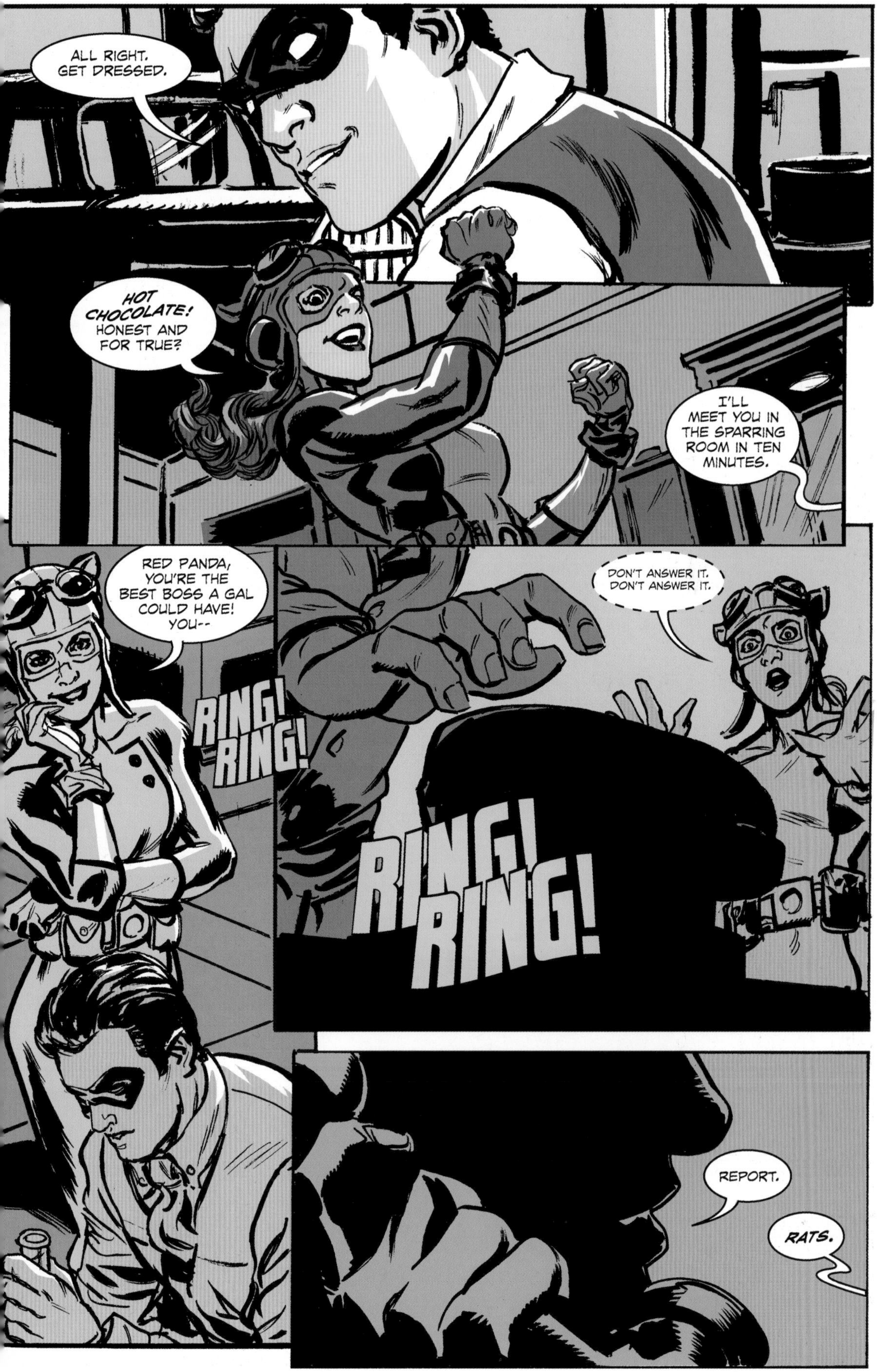
ALL RIGHT. GET DRESSED.
HOT CHOCOLATE! HONEST AND FOR TRUE?
I'LL MEET YOU IN THE SPARRING ROOM IN TEN MINUTES.
RED PANDA, YOU'RE THE BEST BOSS A GAL COULD HAVE! YOU--
RING! RING!
DON'T ANSWER IT. DON'T ANSWER IT.
RING! RING!
REPORT.
RATS.

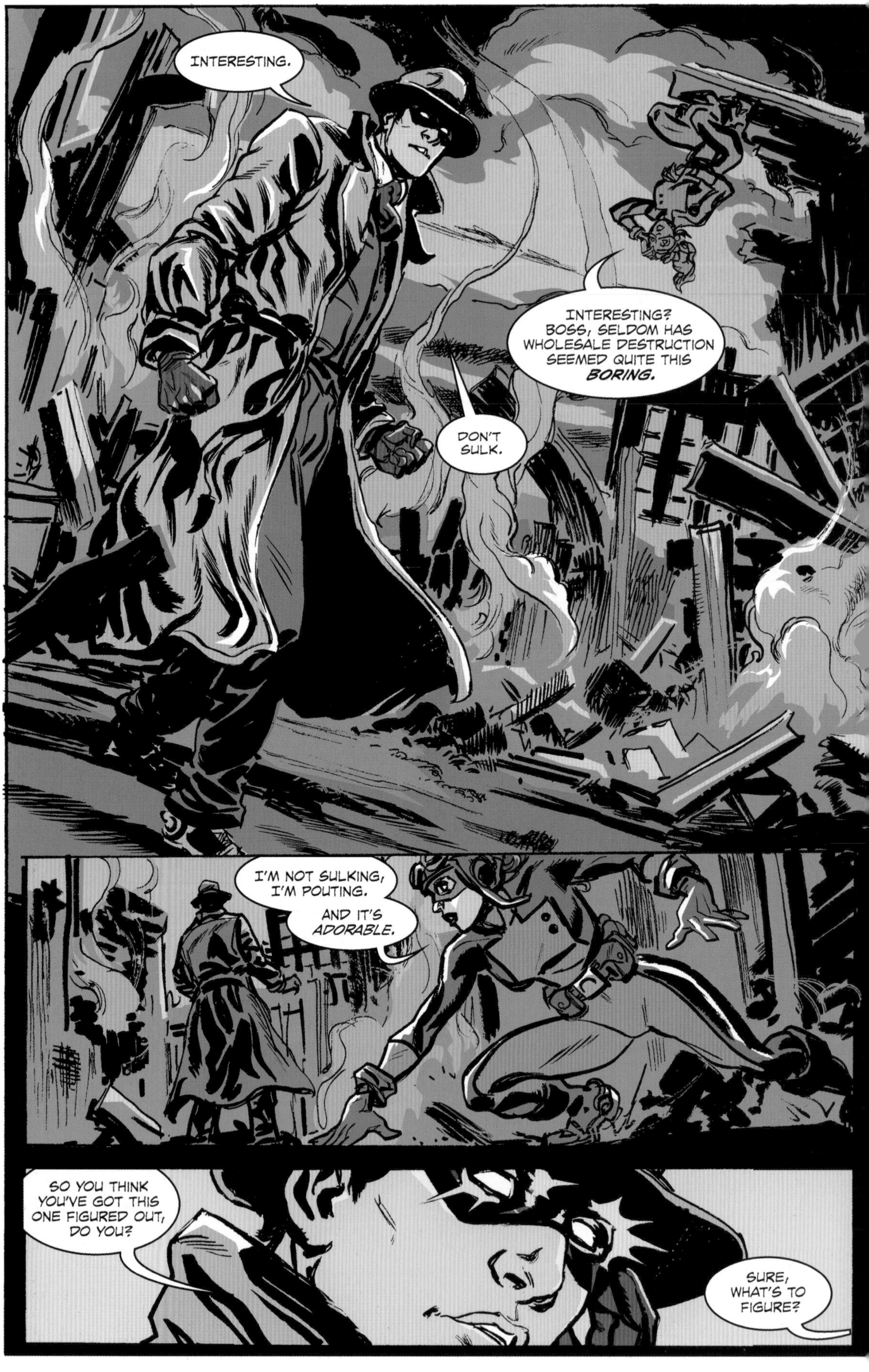
INTERESTING.
INTERESTING? BOSS, SELDOM HAS WHOLESALE DESTRUCTION SEEMED QUITE THIS BORING.
DON'T SULK.
I'M NOT SULKING, I'M POUTING.
AND IT'S ADORABLE.
SO YOU THINK YOU'VE GOT THIS ONE FIGURED OUT, DO YOU?
SURE, WHAT'S TO FIGURE?

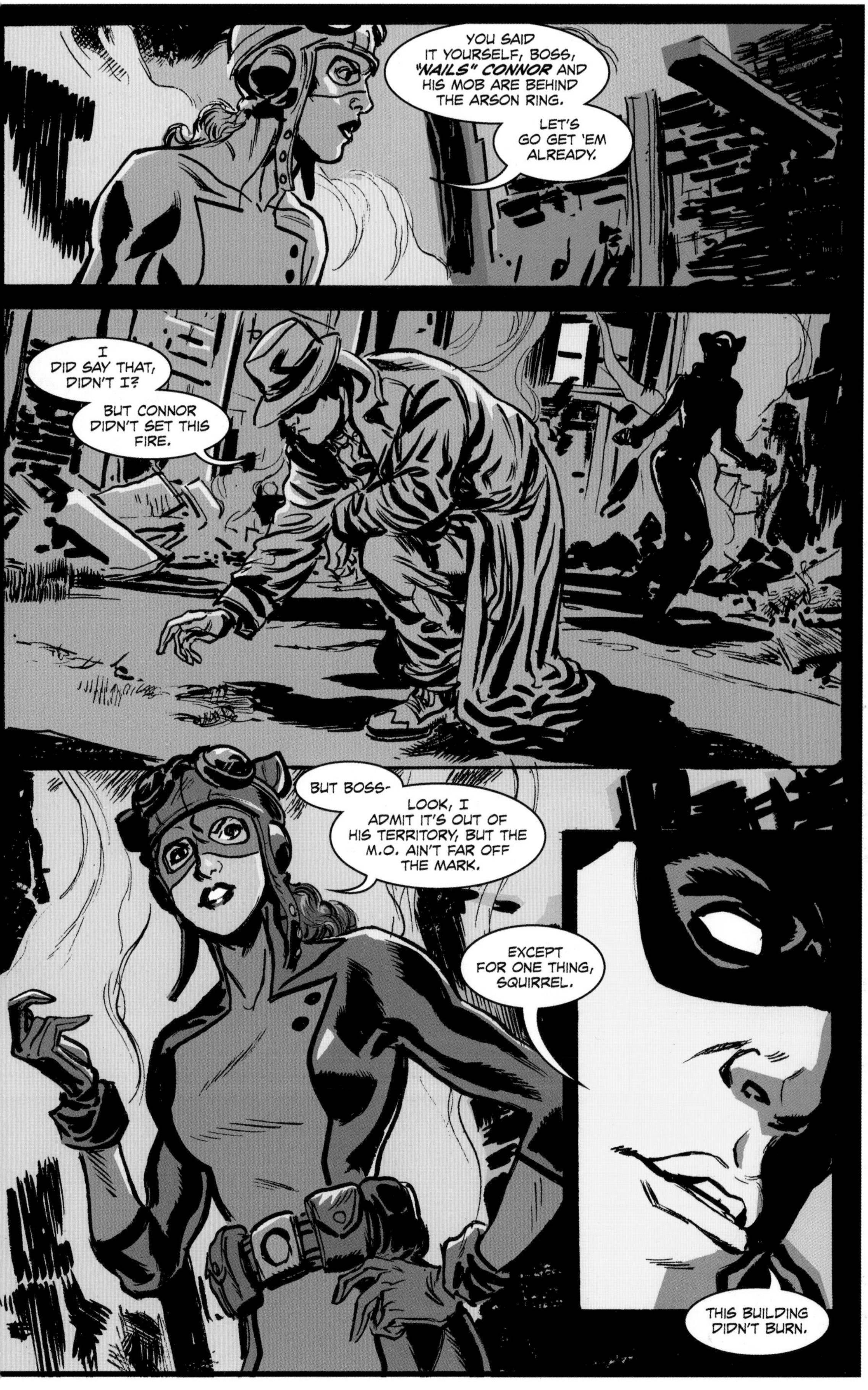
YOU SAID IT YOURSELF, BOSS, "NAILS" CONNOR AND HIS MOB ARE BEHIND THE ARSON RING.
LET'S GO GET 'EM ALREADY.
I DID SAY THAT, DIDN'T I?
BUT CONNOR DIDN'T SET THIS FIRE.
BUT BOSS-
LOOK, I ADMIT IT'S OUT OF HIS TERRITORY, BUT THE M.O. AIN'T FAR OFF THE MARK.
EXCEPT FOR ONE THING, SQUIRREL.
THIS BUILDING DIDN'T BURN.

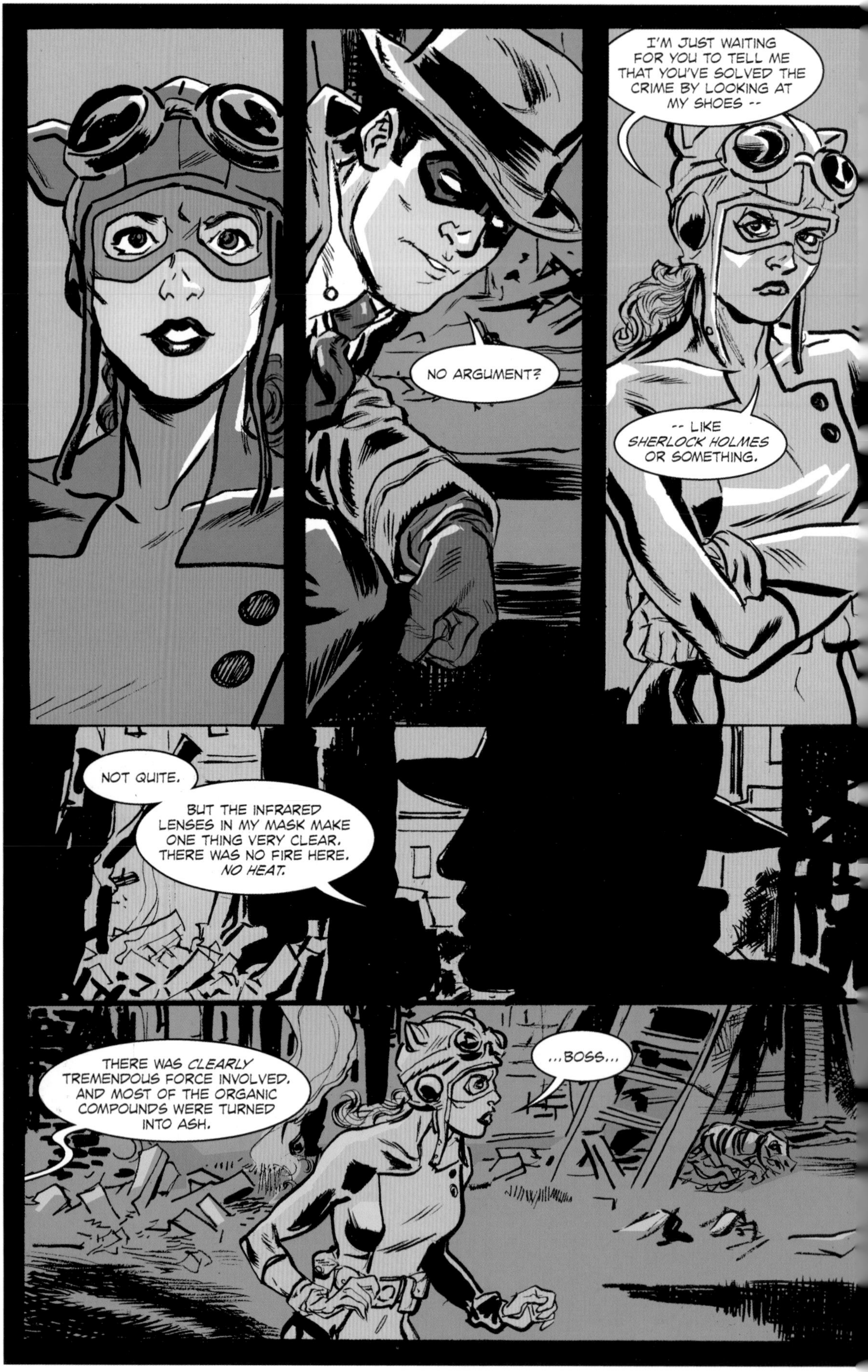
NO ARGUMENT?
I'M JUST WAITING FOR YOU TO TELL ME THAT YOU'VE SOLVED THE CRIME BY LOOKING AT MY SHOES --
-- LIKE *SHERLOCK HOLMES* OR SOMETHING.
NOT QUITE.
BUT THE INFRARED LENSES IN MY MASK MAKE ONE THING VERY CLEAR. THERE WAS NO FIRE HERE. *NO HEAT.*
THERE WAS *CLEARLY* TREMENDOUS FORCE INVOLVED. AND MOST OF THE ORGANIC COMPOUNDS WERE TURNED INTO ASH.
...BOSS...

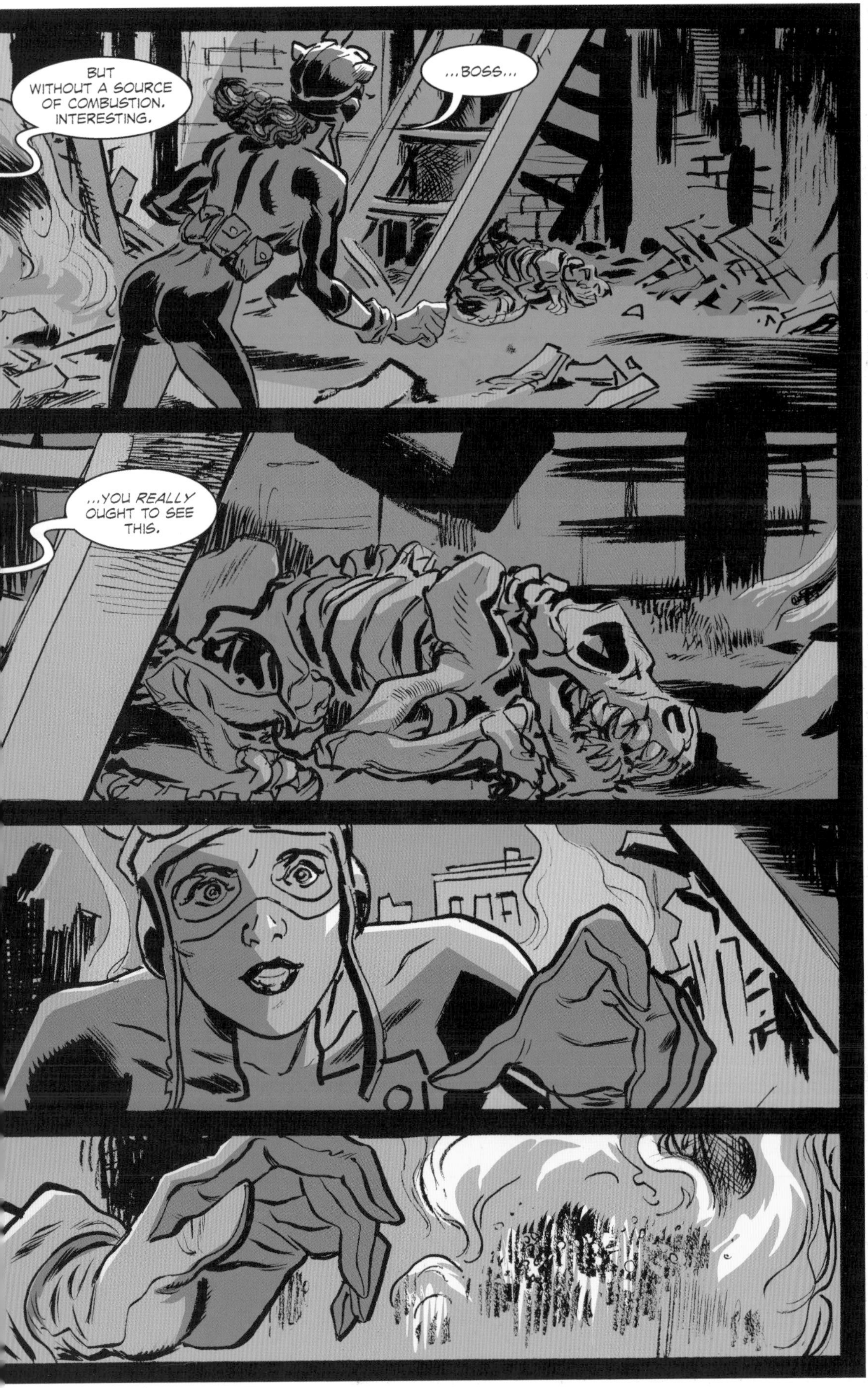
BUT WITHOUT A SOURCE OF COMBUSTION. INTERESTING.
...BOSS...
...YOU *REALLY* OUGHT TO SEE THIS.

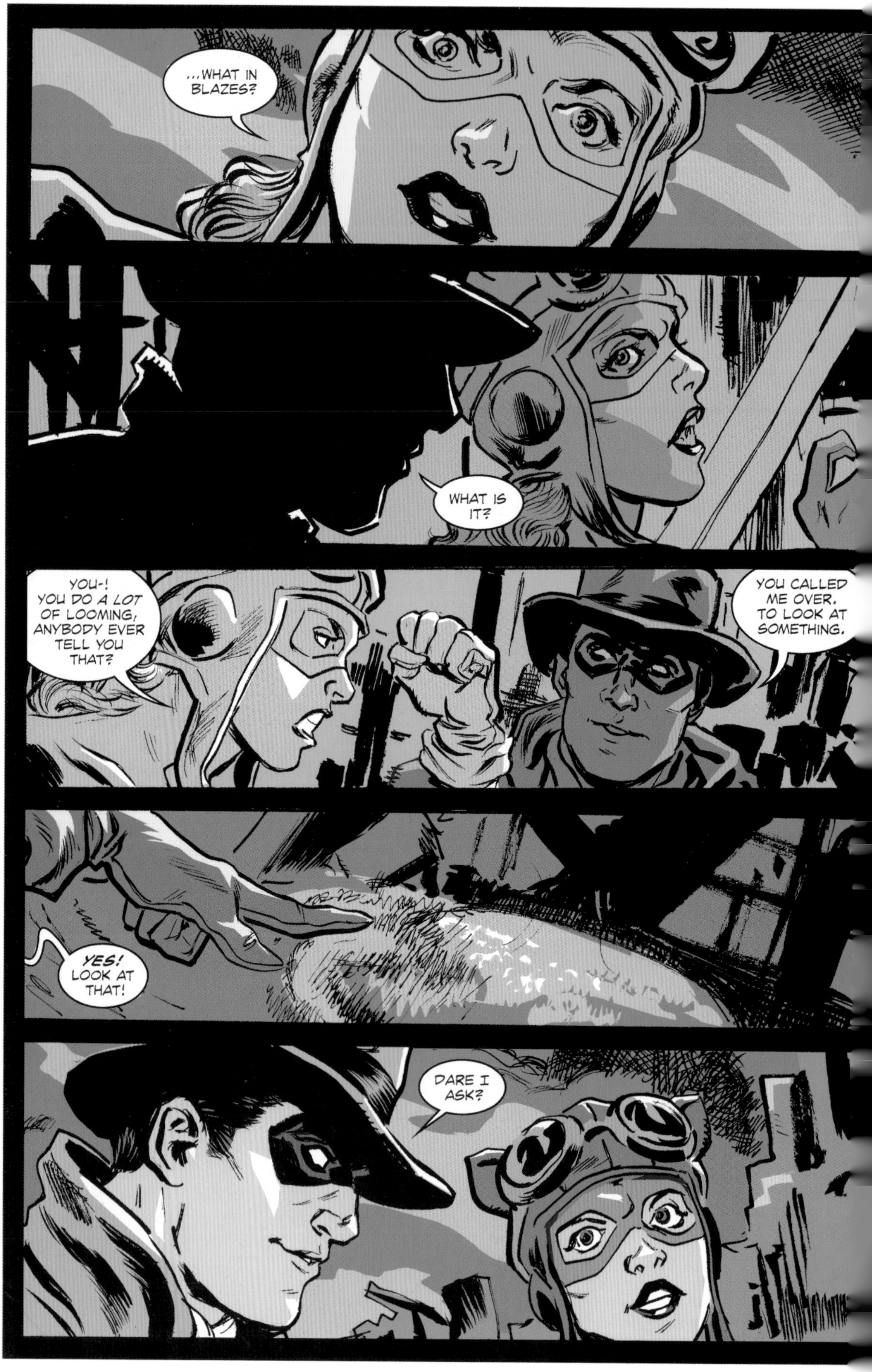
...WHAT IN BLAZES?
WHAT IS IT?
YOU-! YOU DO A LOT OF LOOMING, ANYBODY EVER TELL YOU THAT?
YOU CALLED ME OVER. TO LOOK AT SOMETHING.
YES! LOOK AT THAT!
DARE I ASK?

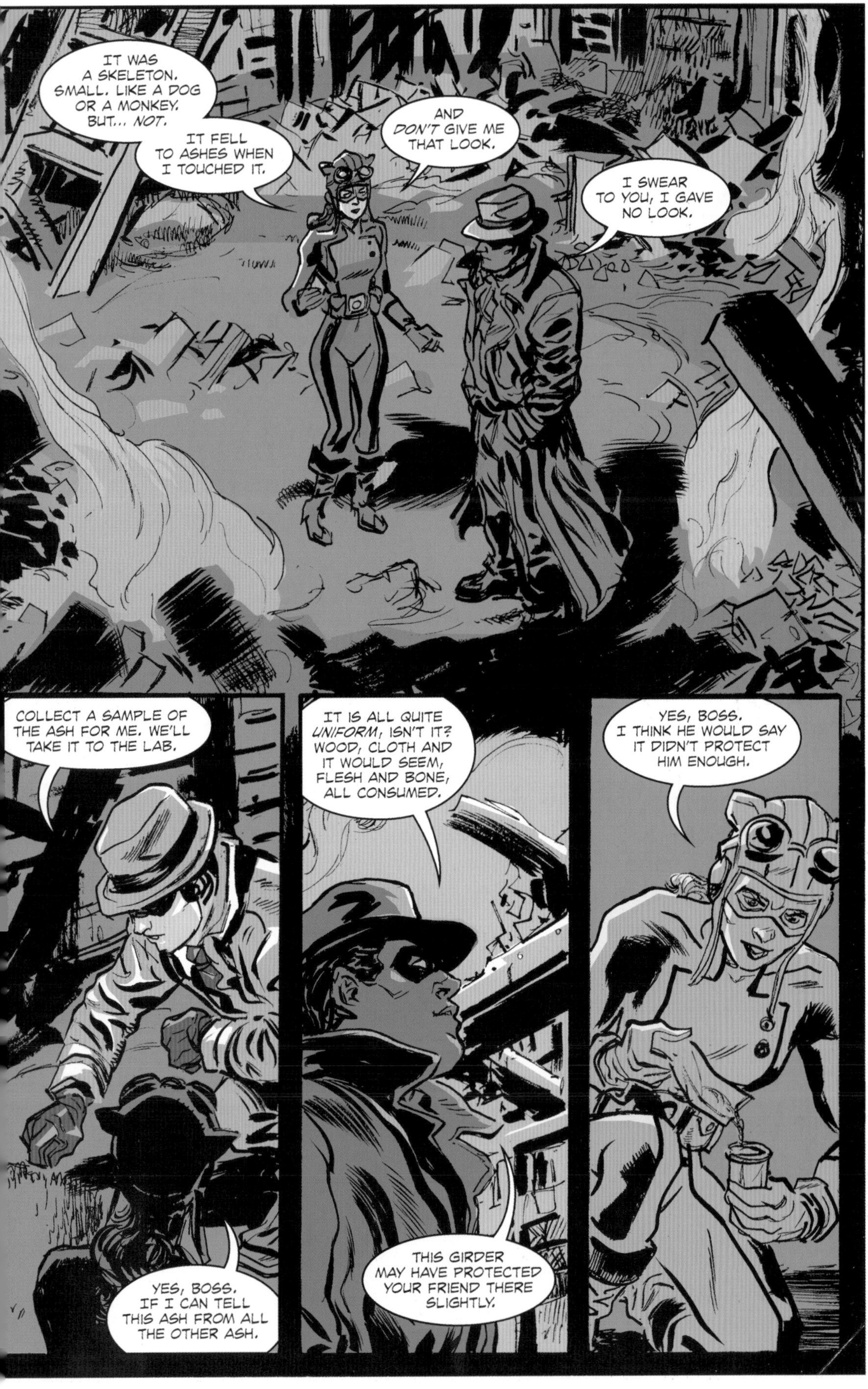

IT WAS A SKELETON. SMALL. LIKE A DOG OR A MONKEY. BUT... *NOT.*
IT FELL TO ASHES WHEN I TOUCHED IT.
AND *DON'T* GIVE ME THAT LOOK.
I SWEAR TO YOU, I GAVE NO LOOK.
COLLECT A SAMPLE OF THE ASH FOR ME. WE'LL TAKE IT TO THE LAB.
YES, BOSS. IF I CAN TELL THIS ASH FROM ALL THE OTHER ASH.
IT IS ALL QUITE *UNIFORM*, ISN'T IT? WOOD, CLOTH AND IT WOULD SEEM, FLESH AND BONE, ALL CONSUMED.
THIS GIRDER MAY HAVE PROTECTED YOUR FRIEND THERE SLIGHTLY.
YES, BOSS. I THINK HE WOULD SAY IT DIDN'T PROTECT HIM ENOUGH.

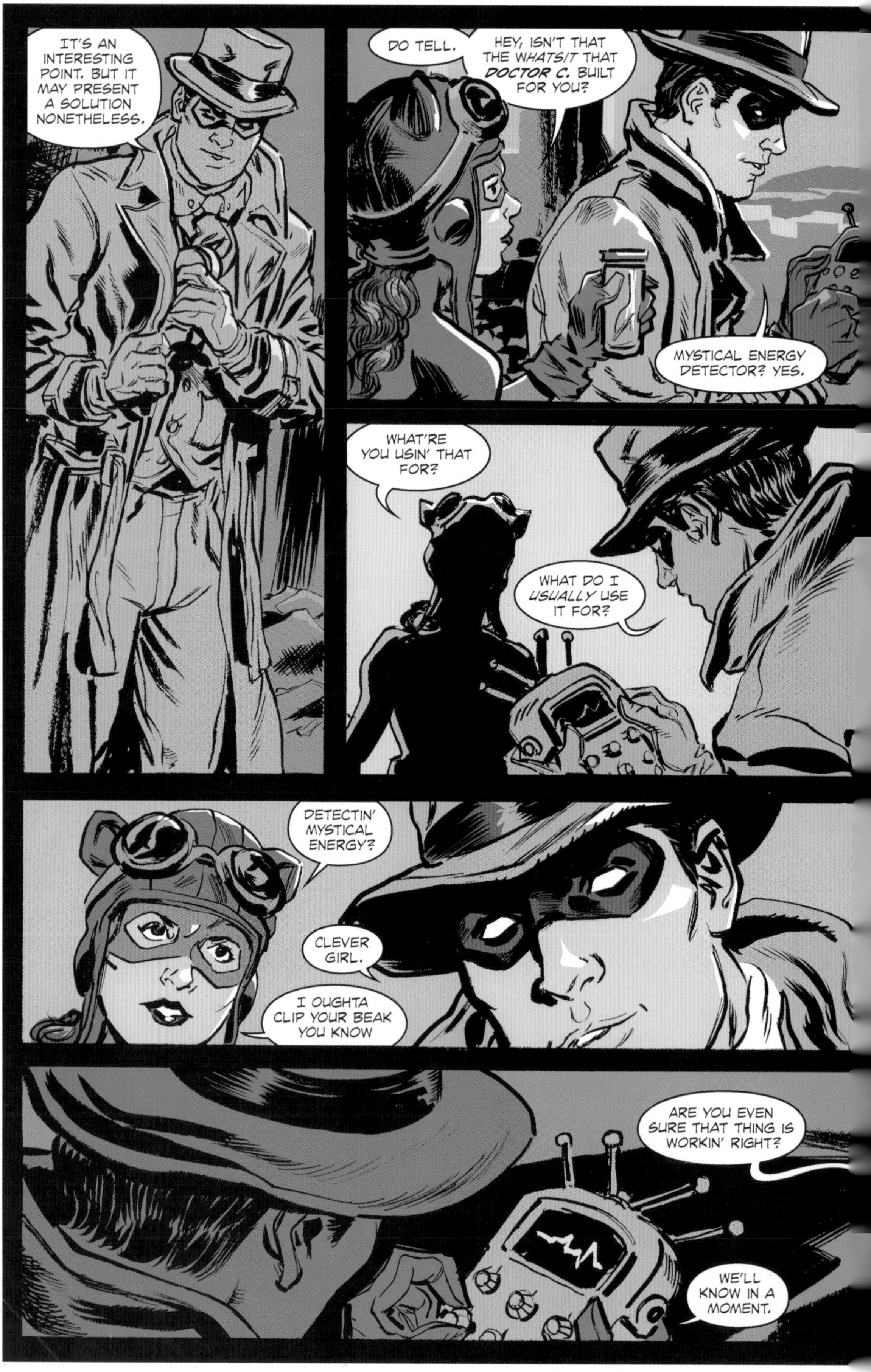
IT'S AN INTERESTING POINT. BUT IT MAY PRESENT A SOLUTION NONETHELESS.
DO TELL.
HEY, ISN'T THAT THE *WHATSIT* THAT ***DOCTOR C.*** BUILT FOR YOU?
MYSTICAL ENERGY DETECTOR? YES.
WHAT'RE YOU USIN' THAT FOR?
WHAT DO I *USUALLY* USE IT FOR?
DETECTIN' MYSTICAL ENERGY?
CLEVER GIRL.
I OUGHTA CLIP YOUR BEAK YOU KNOW
ARE YOU EVEN SURE THAT THING IS WORKIN' RIGHT?
WE'LL KNOW IN A MOMENT.

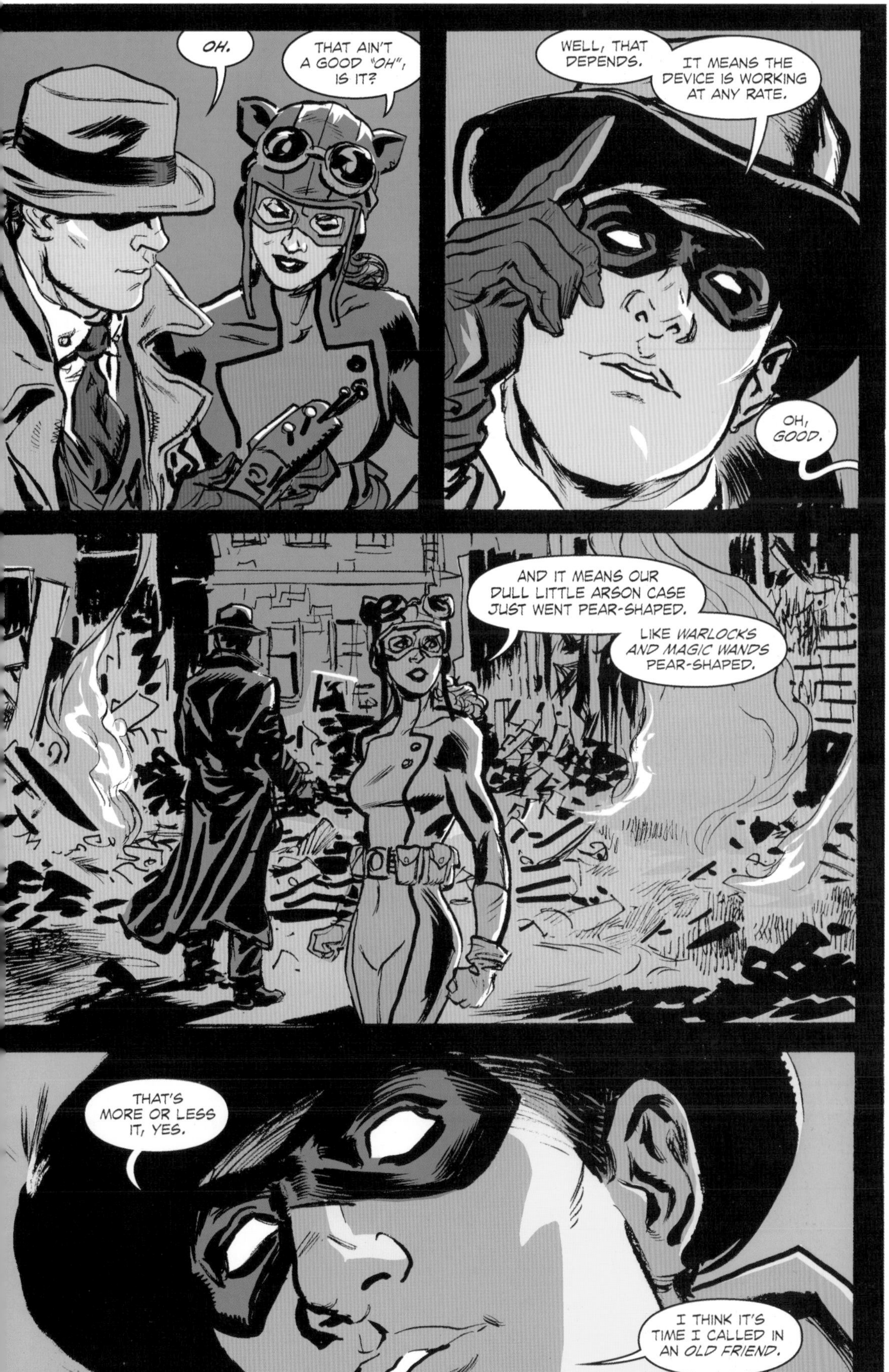
OH.
THAT AIN'T A GOOD "OH", IS IT?
WELL, THAT DEPENDS.
IT MEANS THE DEVICE IS WORKING AT ANY RATE.
OH, GOOD.
AND IT MEANS OUR DULL LITTLE ARSON CASE JUST WENT PEAR-SHAPED.
LIKE *WARLOCKS AND MAGIC WANDS* PEAR-SHAPED.
THAT'S MORE OR LESS IT, YES.
I THINK IT'S TIME I CALLED IN AN *OLD FRIEND*.

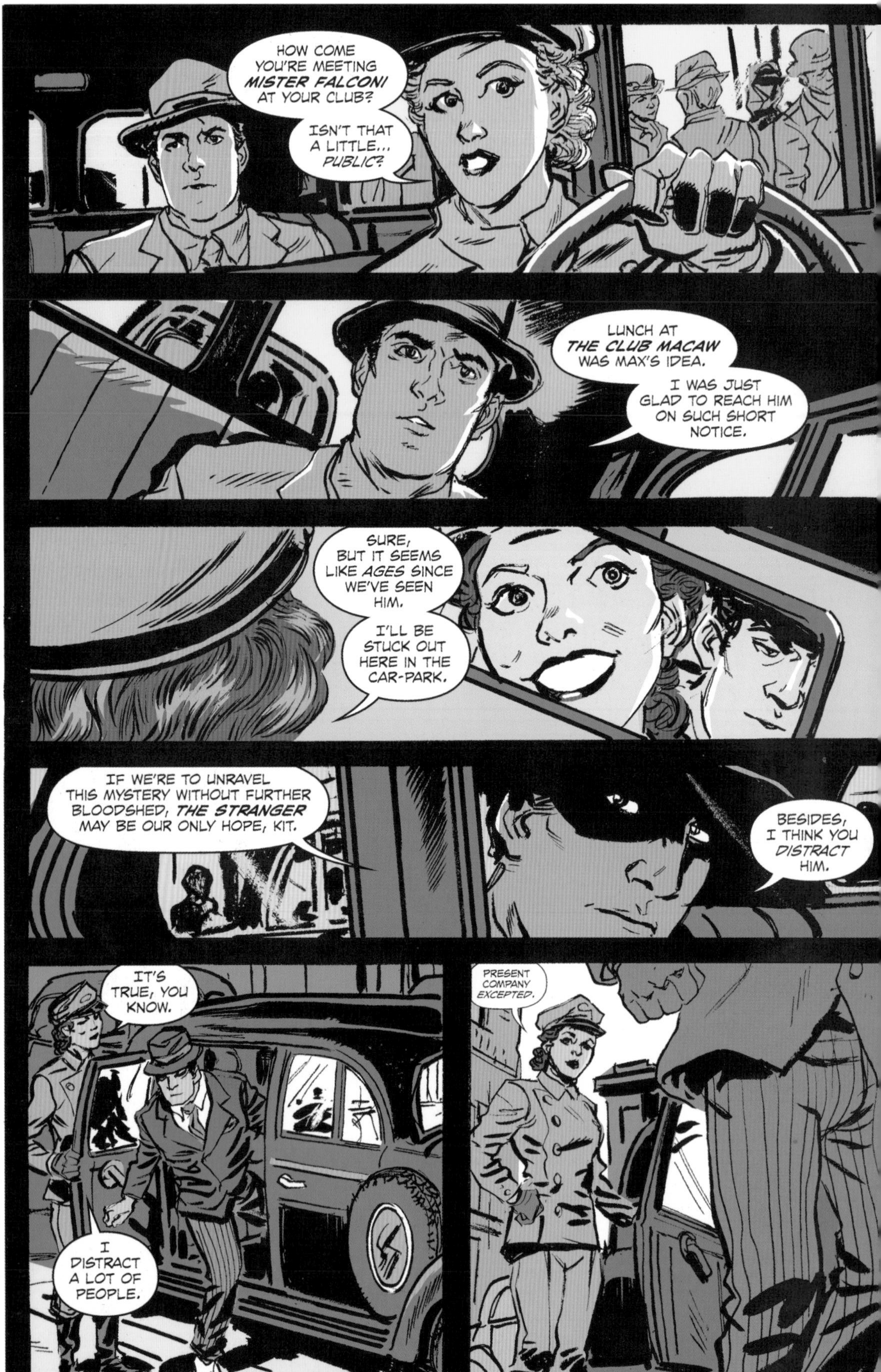
HOW COME YOU'RE MEETING MISTER FALCONI AT YOUR CLUB?
ISN'T THAT A LITTLE... PUBLIC?
LUNCH AT THE CLUB MACAW WAS MAX'S IDEA.
I WAS JUST GLAD TO REACH HIM ON SUCH SHORT NOTICE.
SURE, BUT IT SEEMS LIKE AGES SINCE WE'VE SEEN HIM.
I'LL BE STUCK OUT HERE IN THE CAR-PARK.
IF WE'RE TO UNRAVEL THIS MYSTERY WITHOUT FURTHER BLOODSHED, THE STRANGER MAY BE OUR ONLY HOPE, KIT.
BESIDES, I THINK YOU DISTRACT HIM.
IT'S TRUE, YOU KNOW.
I DISTRACT A LOT OF PEOPLE.
PRESENT COMPANY EXCEPTED.

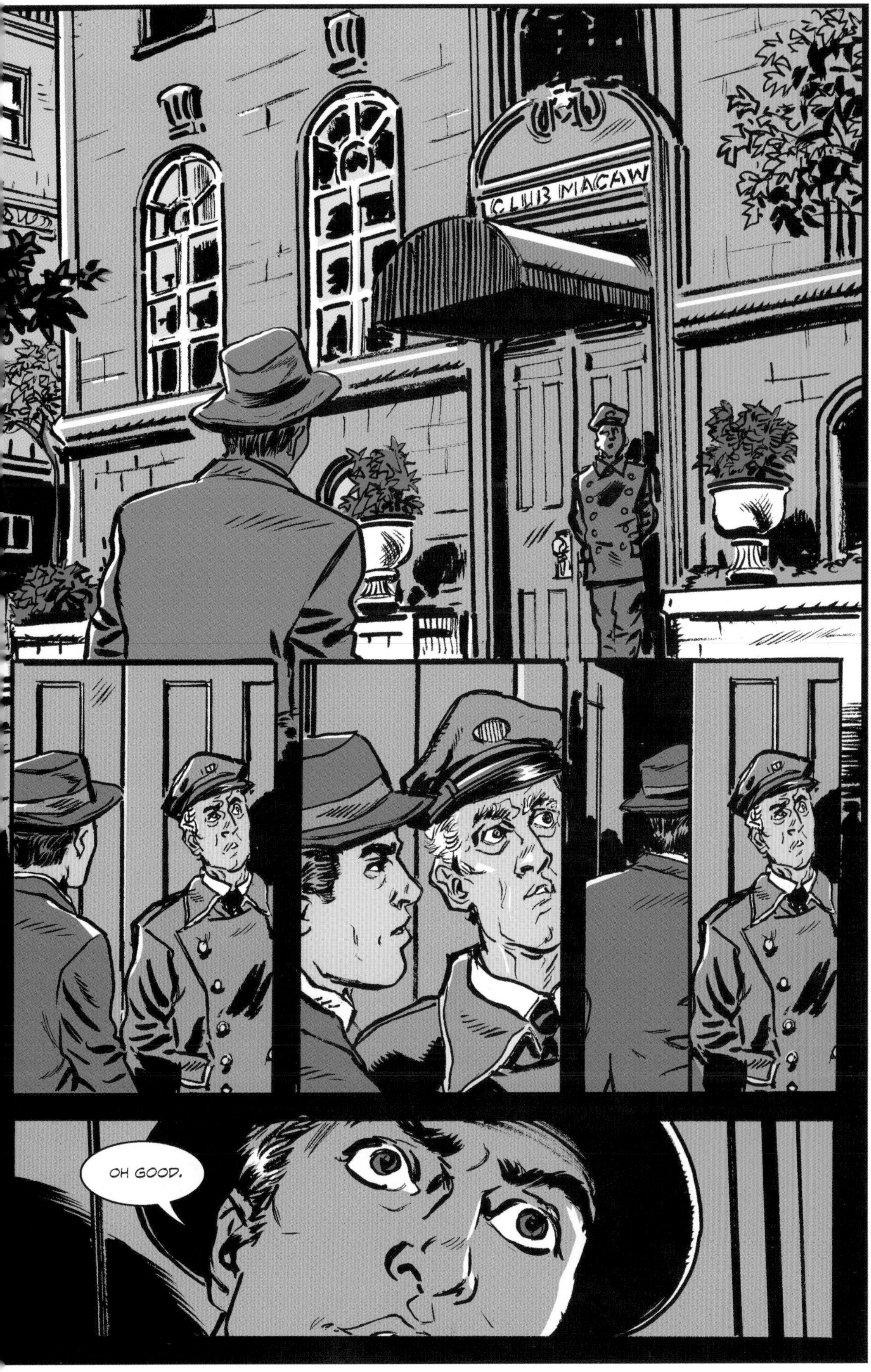
CLUB MACAW
OH GOOD.

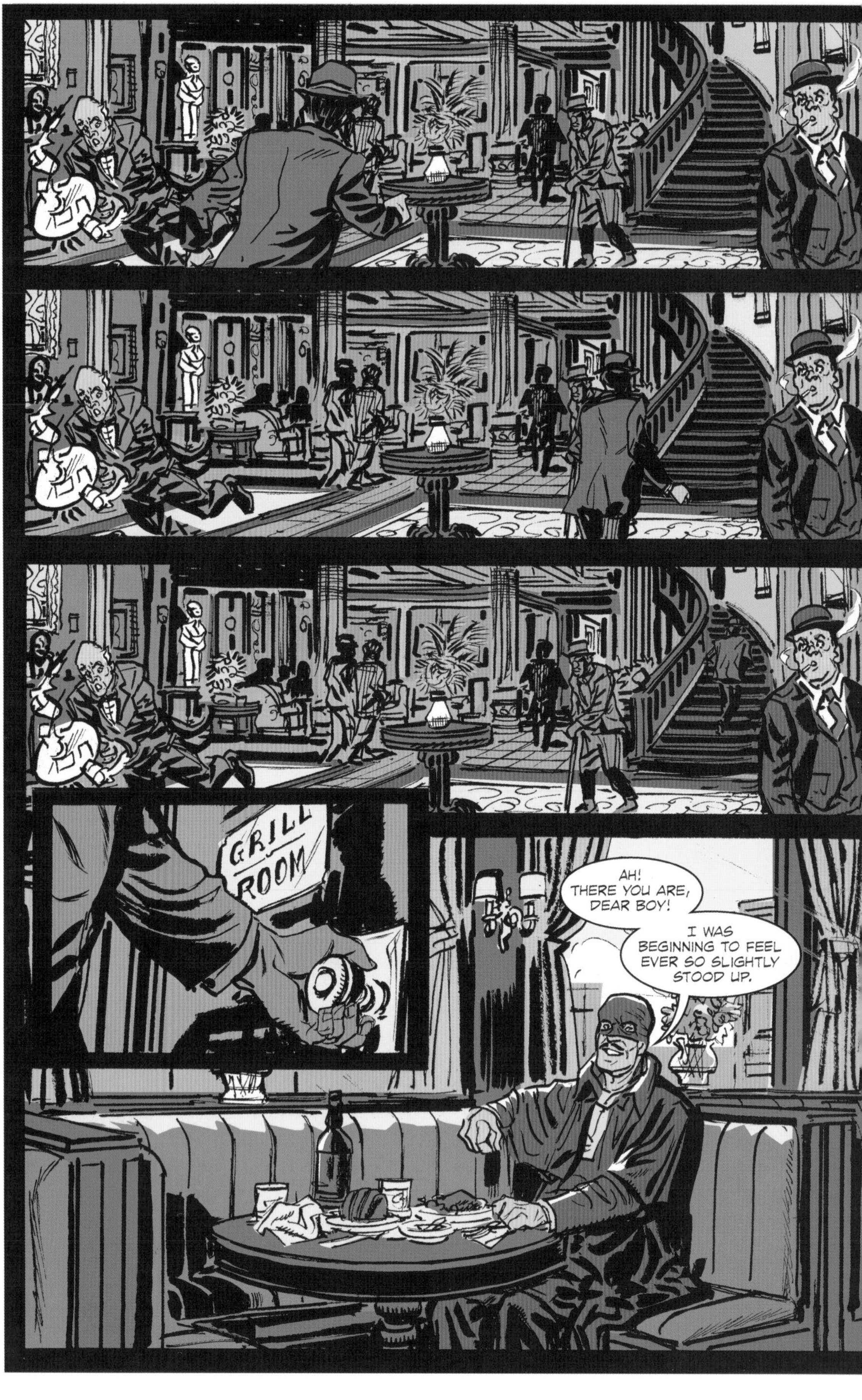
GRILL ROOM
AH! THERE YOU ARE, DEAR BOY!
I WAS BEGINNING TO FEEL EVER SO SLIGHTLY STOOD UP.

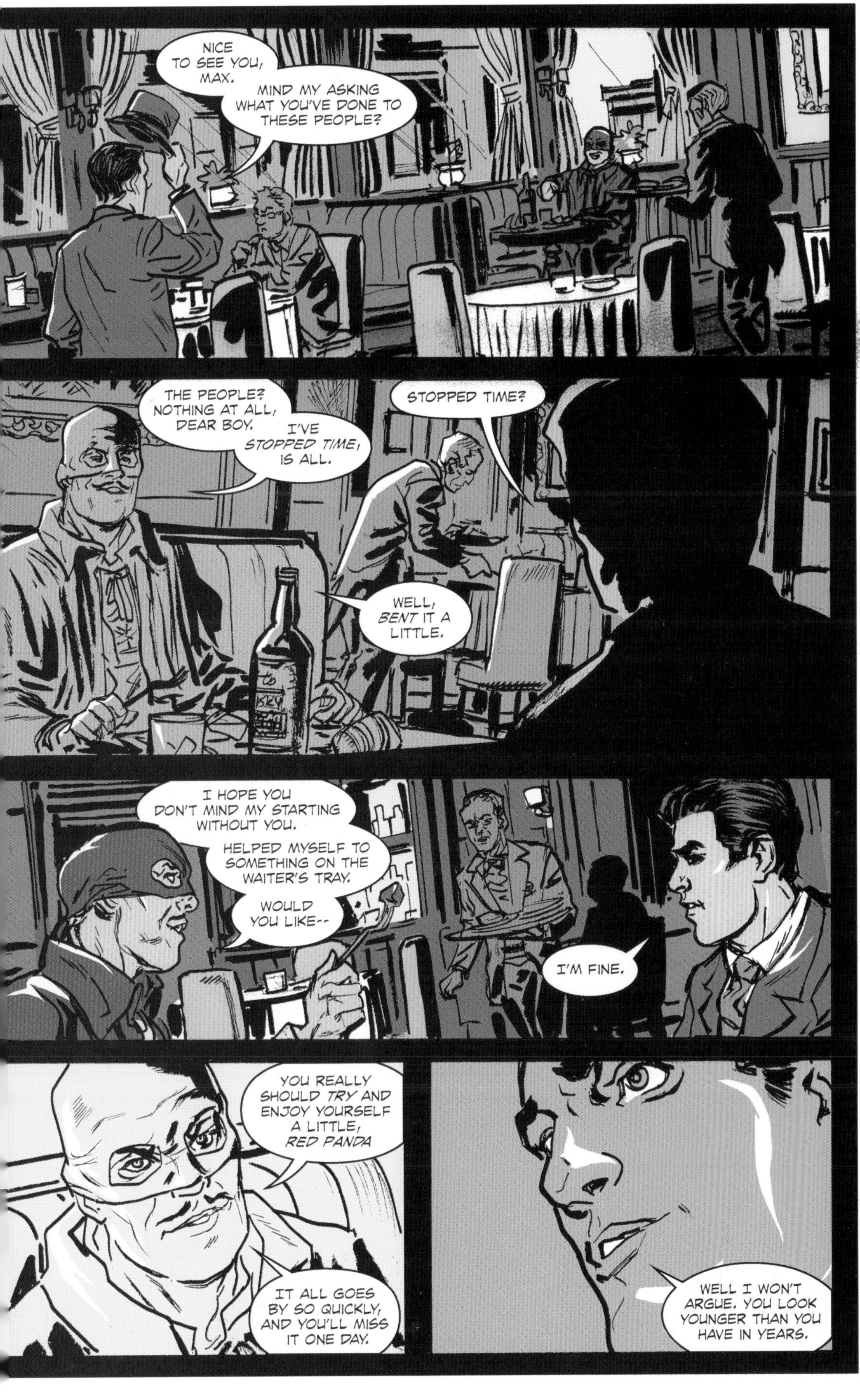
NICE TO SEE YOU, MAX.
MIND MY ASKING WHAT YOU'VE DONE TO THESE PEOPLE?
THE PEOPLE? NOTHING AT ALL, DEAR BOY.
I'VE *STOPPED TIME*, IS ALL.
STOPPED TIME?
WELL, *BENT* IT A LITTLE.
I HOPE YOU DON'T MIND MY STARTING WITHOUT YOU.
HELPED MYSELF TO SOMETHING ON THE WAITER'S TRAY.
WOULD YOU LIKE--
I'M FINE.
YOU REALLY SHOULD *TRY* AND ENJOY YOURSELF A LITTLE, *RED PANDA*
IT ALL GOES BY SO QUICKLY, AND YOU'LL MISS IT ONE DAY.
WELL I WON'T ARGUE. YOU LOOK YOUNGER THAN YOU HAVE IN YEARS.

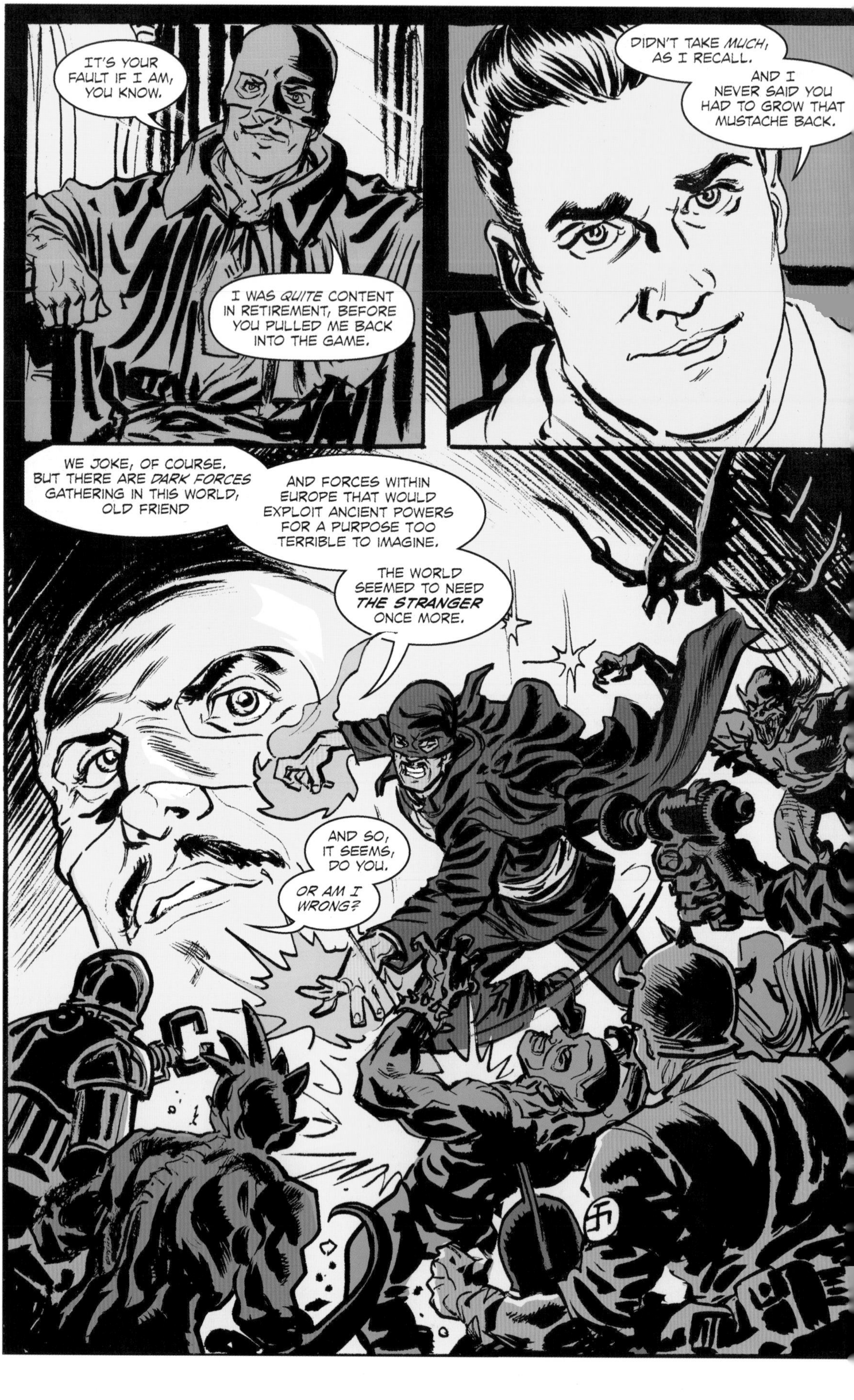

IT'S YOUR FAULT IF I AM, YOU KNOW.
I WAS *QUITE* CONTENT IN RETIREMENT, BEFORE YOU PULLED ME BACK INTO THE GAME.
DIDN'T TAKE *MUCH*, AS I RECALL.
AND I NEVER SAID YOU HAD TO GROW THAT MUSTACHE BACK.
WE JOKE, OF COURSE. BUT THERE ARE *DARK FORCES* GATHERING IN THIS WORLD, OLD FRIEND
AND FORCES WITHIN EUROPE THAT WOULD EXPLOIT ANCIENT POWERS FOR A PURPOSE TOO TERRIBLE TO IMAGINE.
THE WORLD SEEMED TO NEED ***THE STRANGER*** ONCE MORE.
AND SO, IT SEEMS, DO YOU.
OR AM I WRONG?

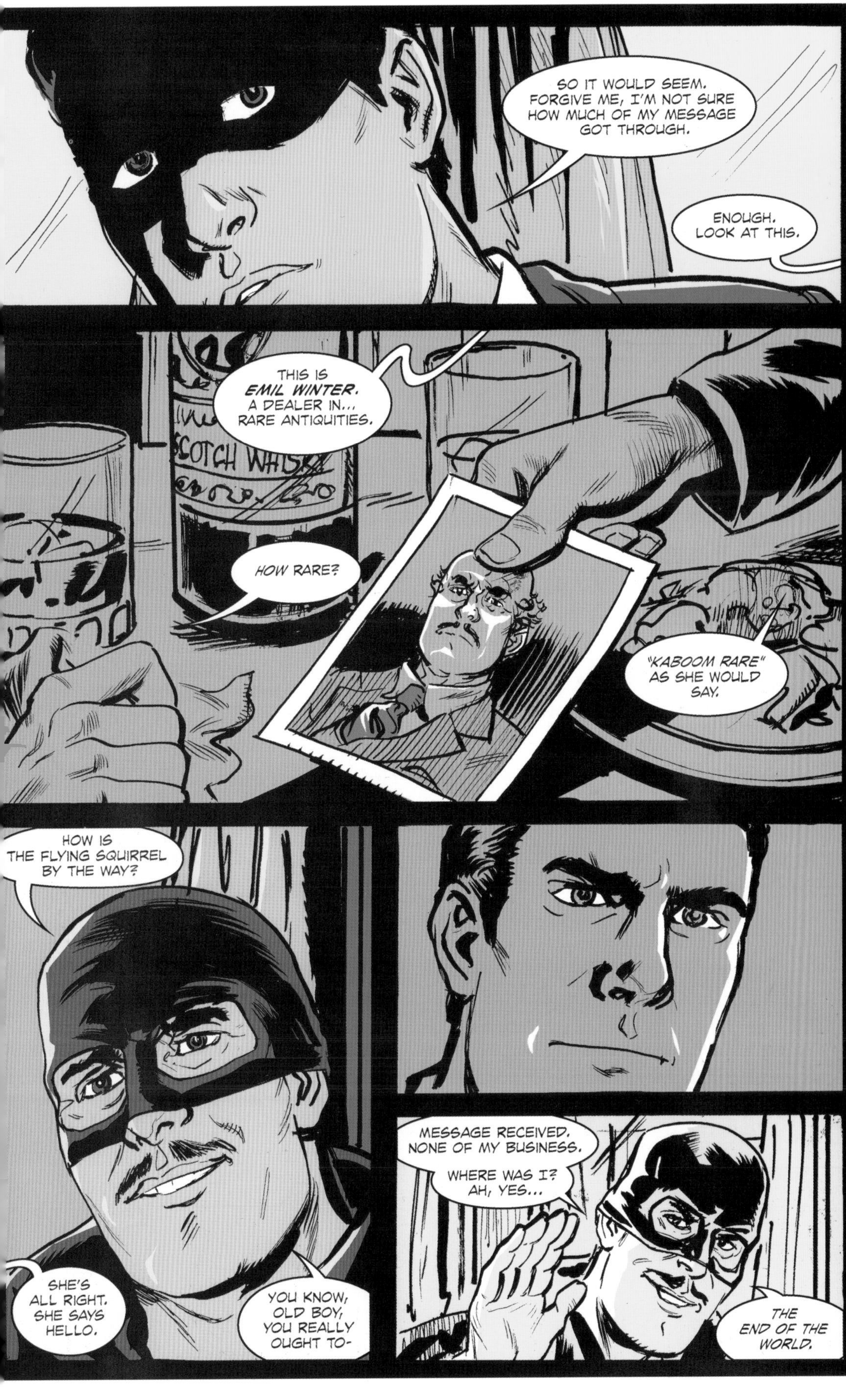
SO IT WOULD SEEM. FORGIVE ME, I'M NOT SURE HOW MUCH OF MY MESSAGE GOT THROUGH.
ENOUGH. LOOK AT THIS.
THIS IS *EMIL WINTER.* A DEALER IN... RARE ANTIQUITIES.
SCOTCH WHISKY
HOW RARE?
"KABOOM RARE" AS SHE WOULD SAY.
HOW IS THE FLYING SQUIRREL BY THE WAY?
SHE'S ALL RIGHT. SHE SAYS HELLO.
YOU KNOW, OLD BOY, YOU REALLY OUGHT TO-
MESSAGE RECEIVED. NONE OF MY BUSINESS.
WHERE WAS I? AH, YES...
THE END OF THE WORLD.

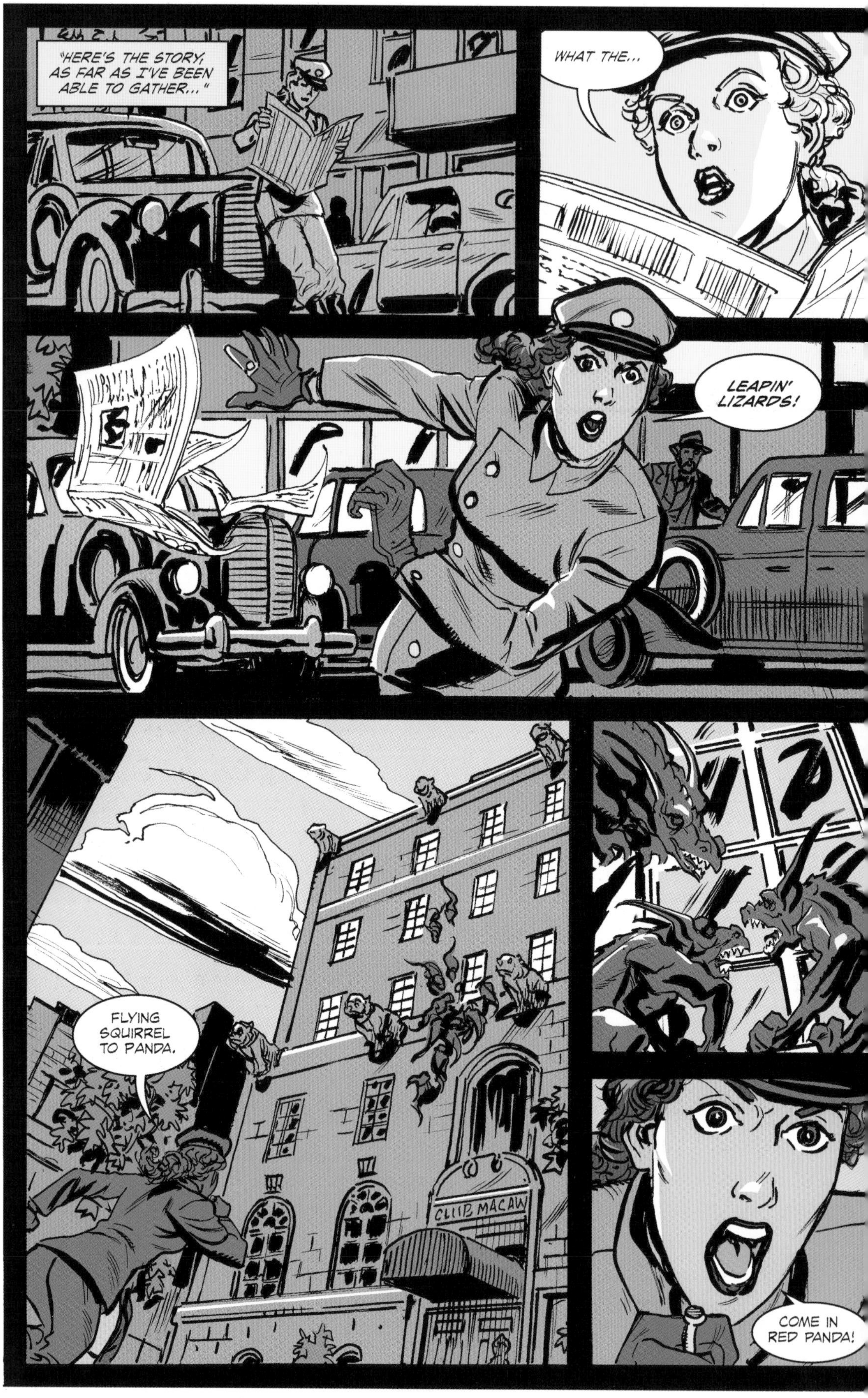
"HERE'S THE STORY, AS FAR AS I'VE BEEN ABLE TO GATHER..."
WHAT THE...
LEAPIN' LIZARDS!
FLYING SQUIRREL TO PANDA.
CLUB MACAW
COME IN RED PANDA!

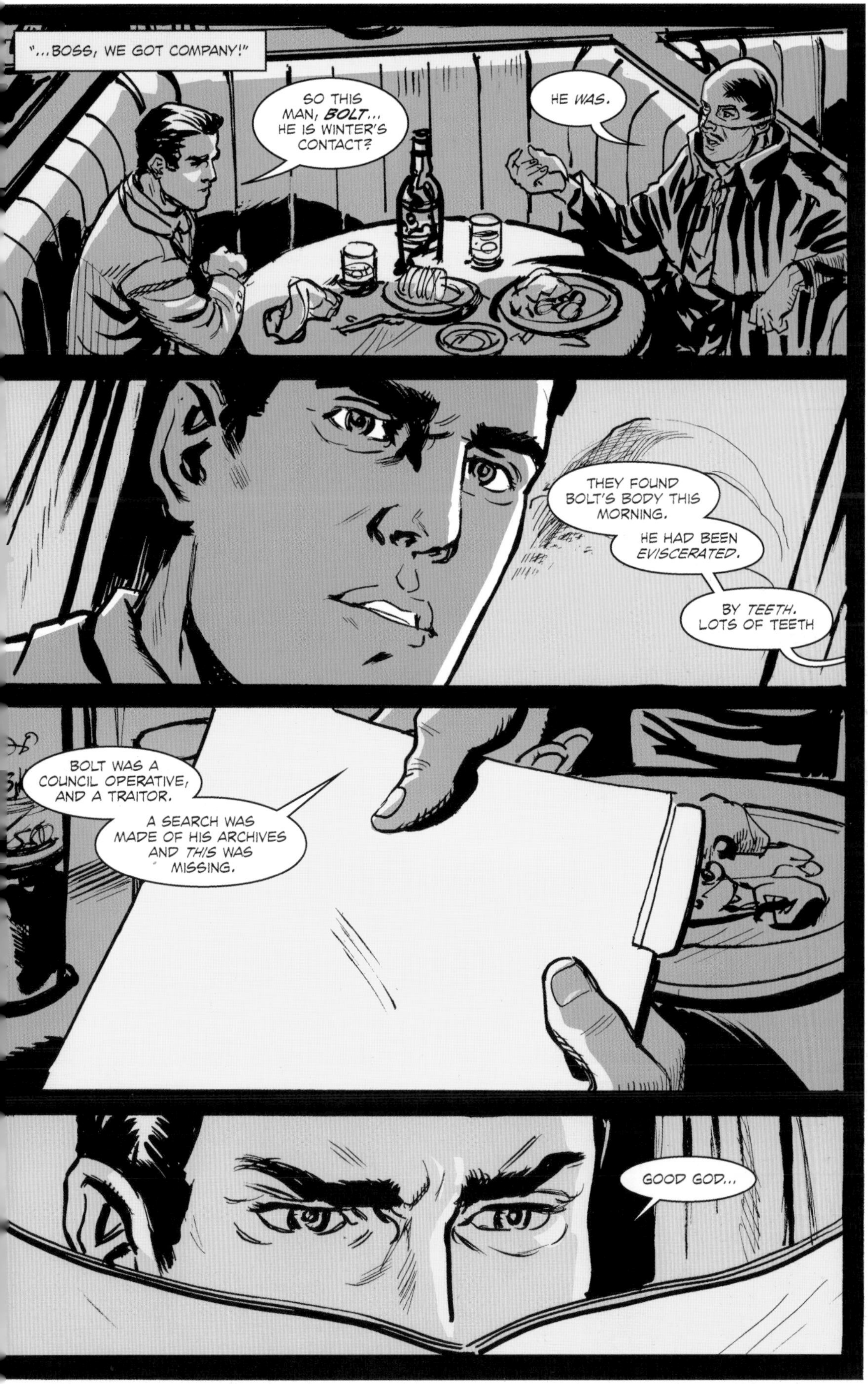
"...BOSS, WE GOT COMPANY!"
SO THIS MAN, *BOLT*... HE IS WINTER'S CONTACT?
HE *WAS*.
THEY FOUND BOLT'S BODY THIS MORNING.
HE HAD BEEN *EVISCERATED*.
BY *TEETH*. LOTS OF TEETH
BOLT WAS A COUNCIL OPERATIVE, AND A TRAITOR.
A SEARCH WAS MADE OF HIS ARCHIVES AND *THIS* WAS MISSING.
GOOD GOD...

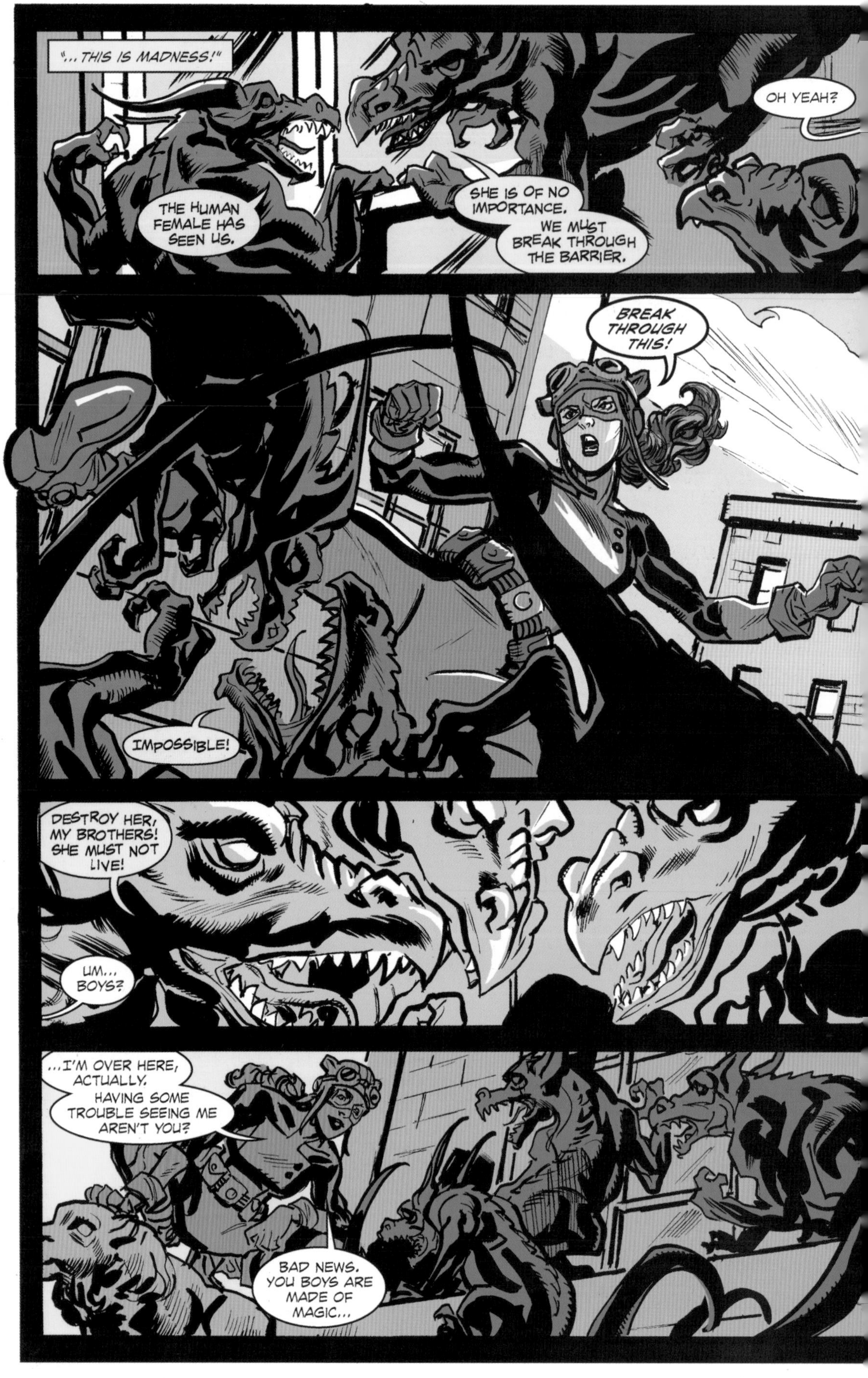
"...THIS IS MADNESS!"
THE HUMAN FEMALE HAS SEEN US.
SHE IS OF NO IMPORTANCE. WE MUST BREAK THROUGH THE BARRIER.
OH YEAH?
BREAK THROUGH THIS!
IMPOSSIBLE!
DESTROY HER, MY BROTHERS! SHE MUST NOT LIVE!
UM... BOYS?
...I'M OVER HERE, ACTUALLY. HAVING SOME TROUBLE SEEING ME AREN'T YOU?
BAD NEWS. YOU BOYS ARE MADE OF MAGIC...

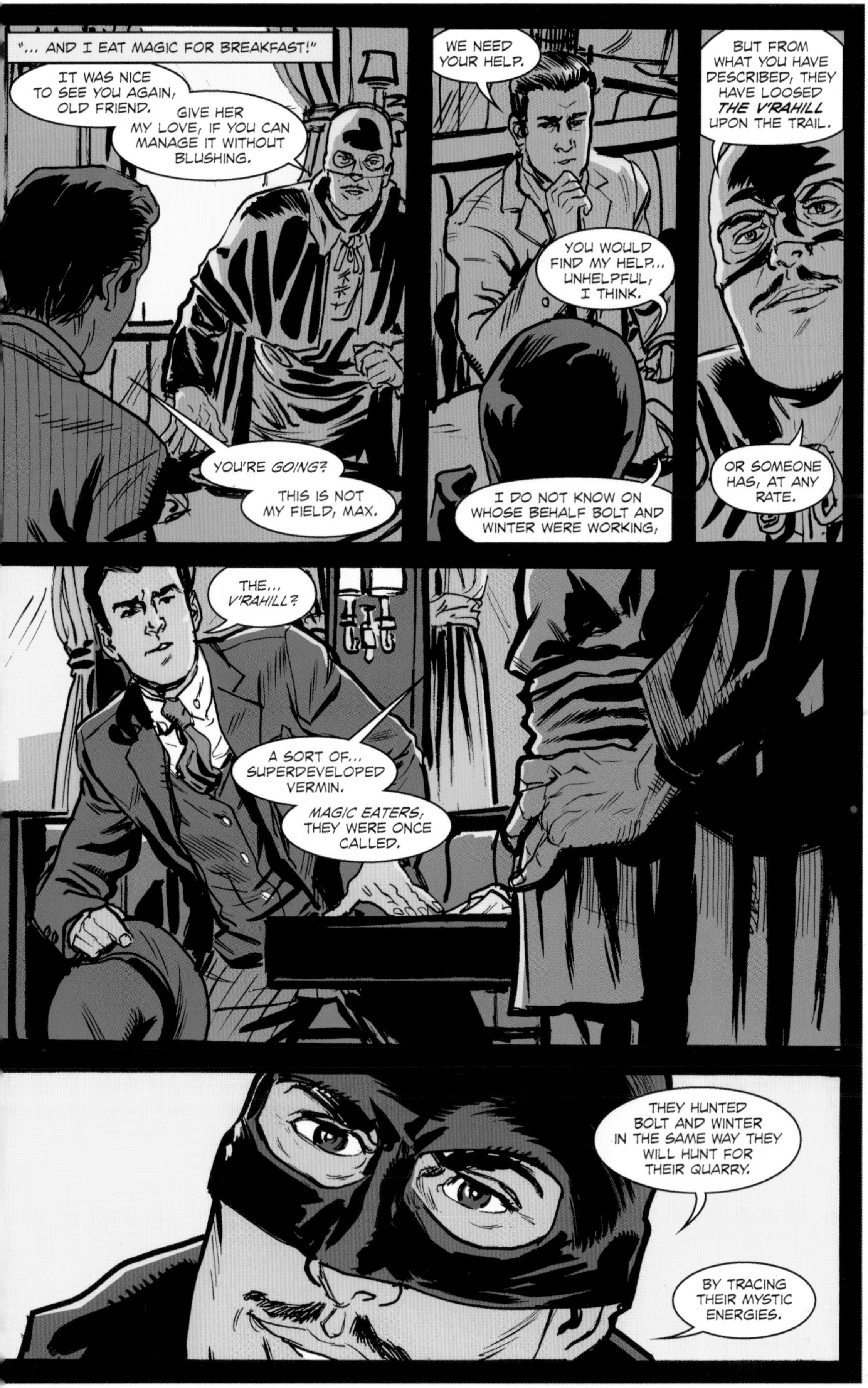
"... AND I EAT MAGIC FOR BREAKFAST!"
IT WAS NICE TO SEE YOU AGAIN, OLD FRIEND.
GIVE HER MY LOVE, IF YOU CAN MANAGE IT WITHOUT BLUSHING.
YOU'RE *GOING*?
THIS IS NOT MY FIELD, MAX.
WE NEED YOUR HELP.
YOU WOULD FIND MY HELP... UNHELPFUL, I THINK.
I DO NOT KNOW ON WHOSE BEHALF BOLT AND WINTER WERE WORKING,
BUT FROM WHAT YOU HAVE DESCRIBED, THEY HAVE LOOSED ***THE V'RAHILL*** UPON THE TRAIL.
OR SOMEONE HAS, AT ANY RATE.
THE... *V'RAHILL*?
A SORT OF... SUPERDEVELOPED VERMIN.
MAGIC EATERS, THEY WERE ONCE CALLED.
THEY HUNTED BOLT AND WINTER IN THE SAME WAY THEY WILL HUNT FOR THEIR QUARRY.
BY TRACING THEIR MYSTIC ENERGIES.

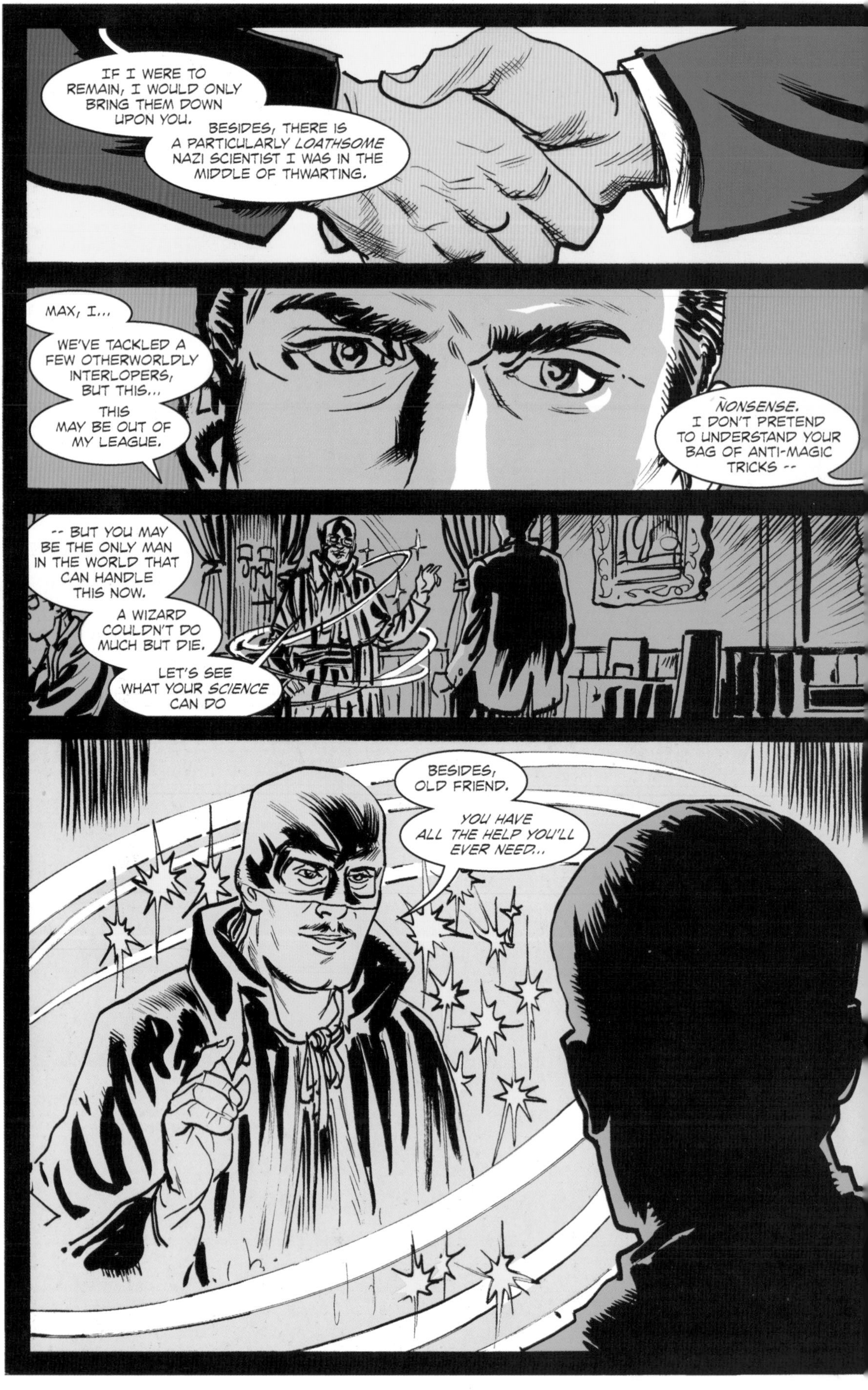
IF I WERE TO REMAIN, I WOULD ONLY BRING THEM DOWN UPON YOU.
BESIDES, THERE IS A PARTICULARLY *LOATHSOME* NAZI SCIENTIST I WAS IN THE MIDDLE OF THWARTING.
MAX, I...
WE'VE TACKLED A FEW OTHERWORLDLY INTERLOPERS, BUT THIS...
THIS MAY BE OUT OF MY LEAGUE.
NONSENSE. I DON'T PRETEND TO UNDERSTAND YOUR BAG OF ANTI-MAGIC TRICKS --
-- BUT YOU MAY BE THE ONLY MAN IN THE WORLD THAT CAN HANDLE THIS NOW.
A WIZARD COULDN'T DO MUCH BUT DIE.
LET'S SEE WHAT YOUR *SCIENCE* CAN DO
BESIDES, OLD FRIEND.
YOU HAVE ALL THE HELP YOU'LL EVER NEED...

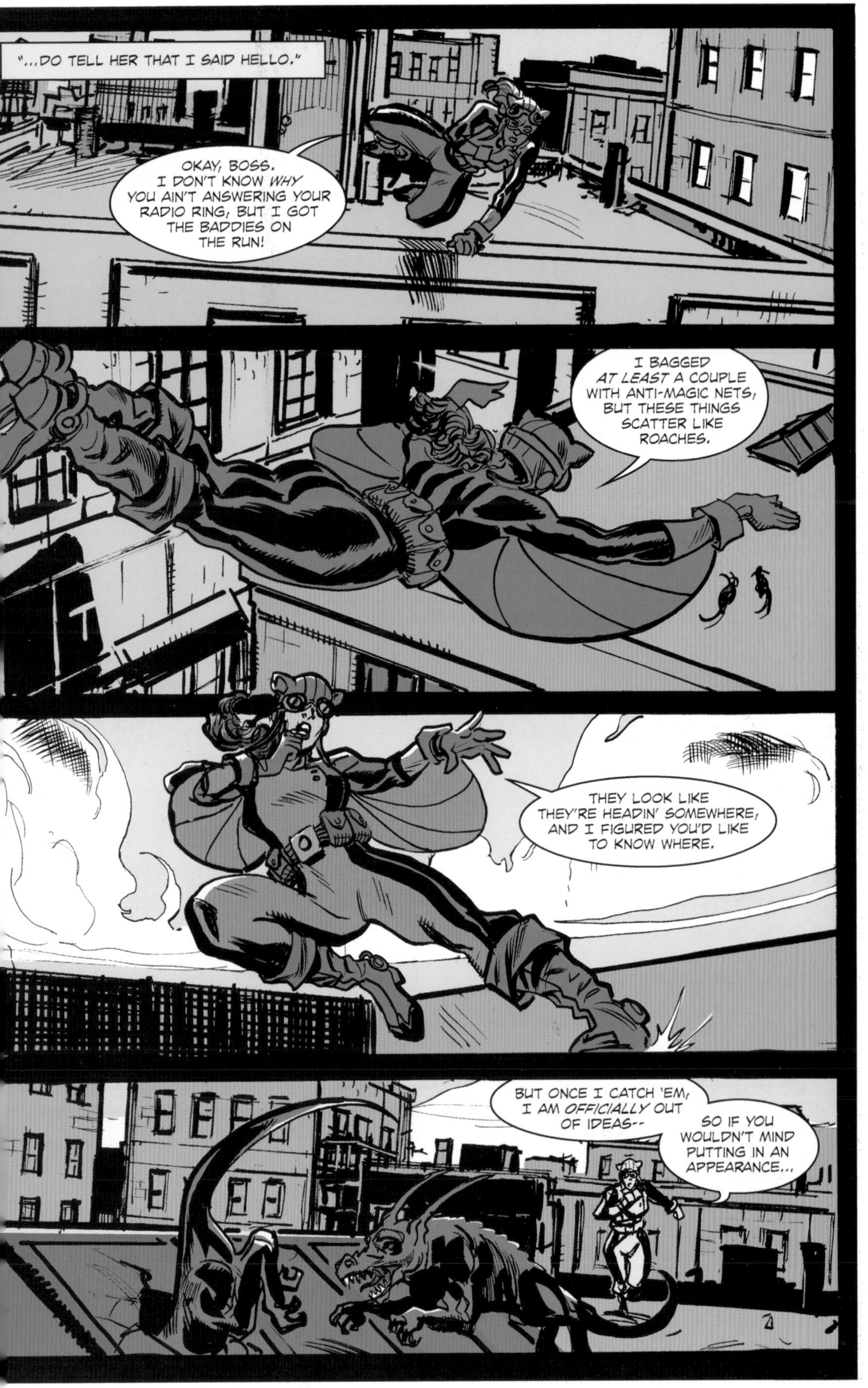
"...DO TELL HER THAT I SAID HELLO."
OKAY, BOSS. I DON'T KNOW *WHY* YOU AIN'T ANSWERING YOUR RADIO RING, BUT I GOT THE BADDIES ON THE RUN!
I BAGGED *AT LEAST* A COUPLE WITH ANTI-MAGIC NETS, BUT THESE THINGS SCATTER LIKE ROACHES.
THEY LOOK LIKE THEY'RE HEADIN' SOMEWHERE, AND I FIGURED YOU'D LIKE TO KNOW WHERE.
BUT ONCE I CATCH 'EM, I AM *OFFICIALLY* OUT OF IDEAS--
SO IF YOU WOULDN'T MIND PUTTING IN AN APPEARANCE...

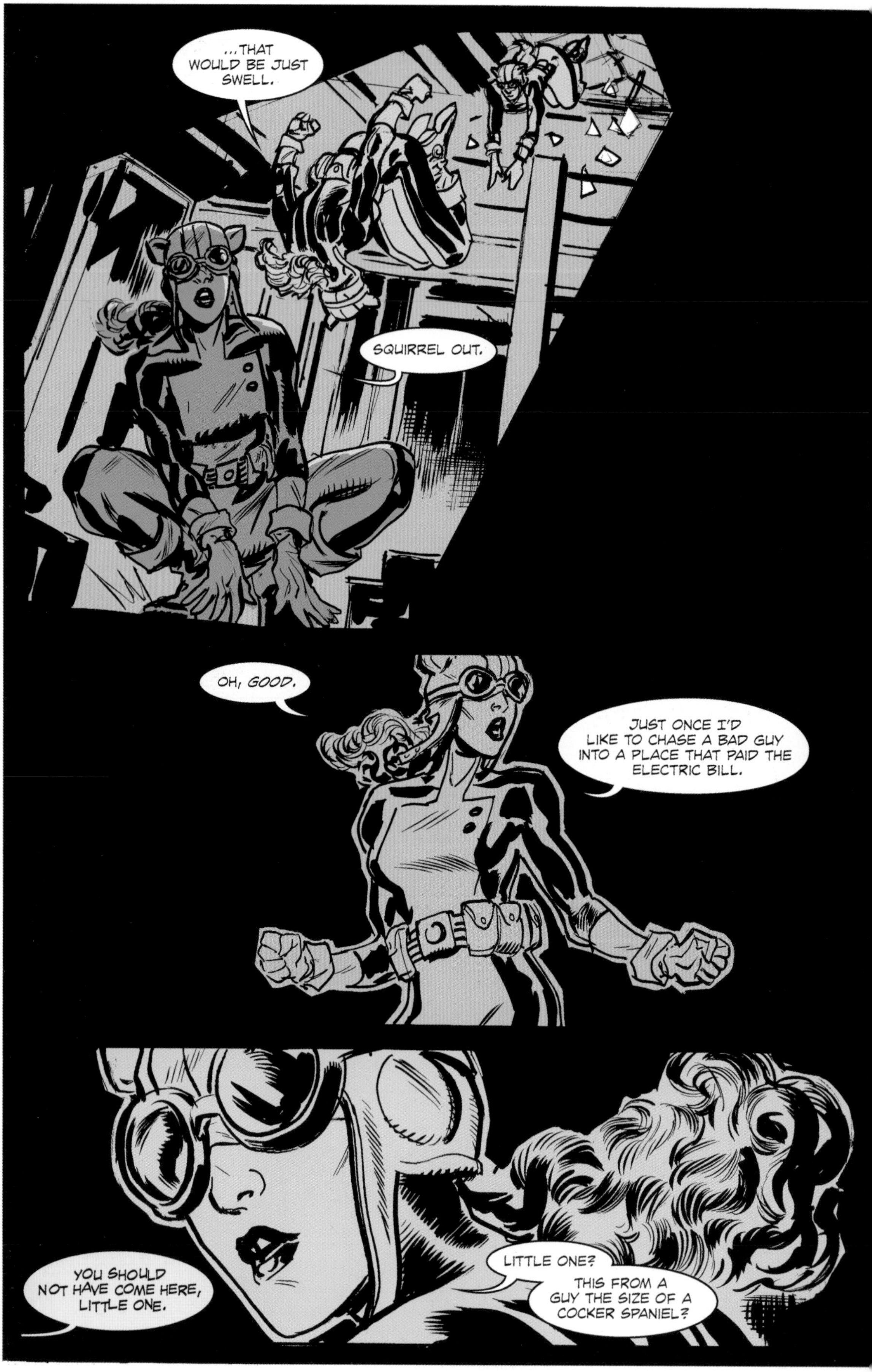

...THAT WOULD BE JUST SWELL.
SQUIRREL OUT.
OH, GOOD.
JUST ONCE I'D LIKE TO CHASE A BAD GUY INTO A PLACE THAT PAID THE ELECTRIC BILL.
YOU SHOULD NOT HAVE COME HERE, LITTLE ONE.
LITTLE ONE?
THIS FROM A GUY THE SIZE OF A COCKER SPANIEL?

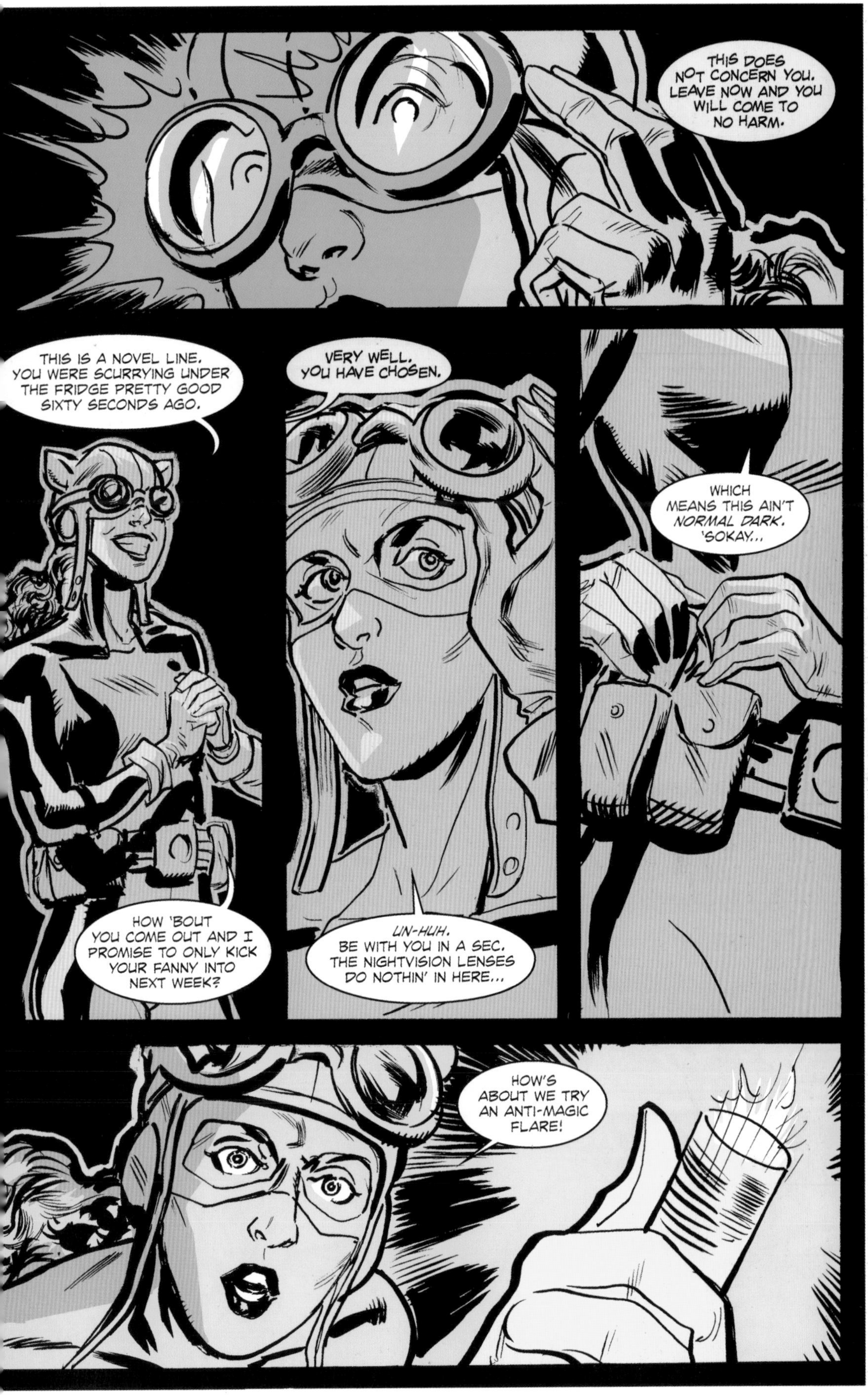
THIS DOES NOT CONCERN YOU. LEAVE NOW AND YOU WILL COME TO NO HARM.
THIS IS A NOVEL LINE. YOU WERE SCURRYING UNDER THE FRIDGE PRETTY GOOD SIXTY SECONDS AGO.
HOW 'BOUT YOU COME OUT AND I PROMISE TO ONLY KICK YOUR FANNY INTO NEXT WEEK?
VERY WELL. YOU HAVE CHOSEN.
UN-HUH. BE WITH YOU IN A SEC. THE NIGHTVISION LENSES DO NOTHIN' IN HERE...
WHICH MEANS THIS AIN'T NORMAL DARK. 'SOKAY...
HOW'S ABOUT WE TRY AN ANTI-MAGIC FLARE!

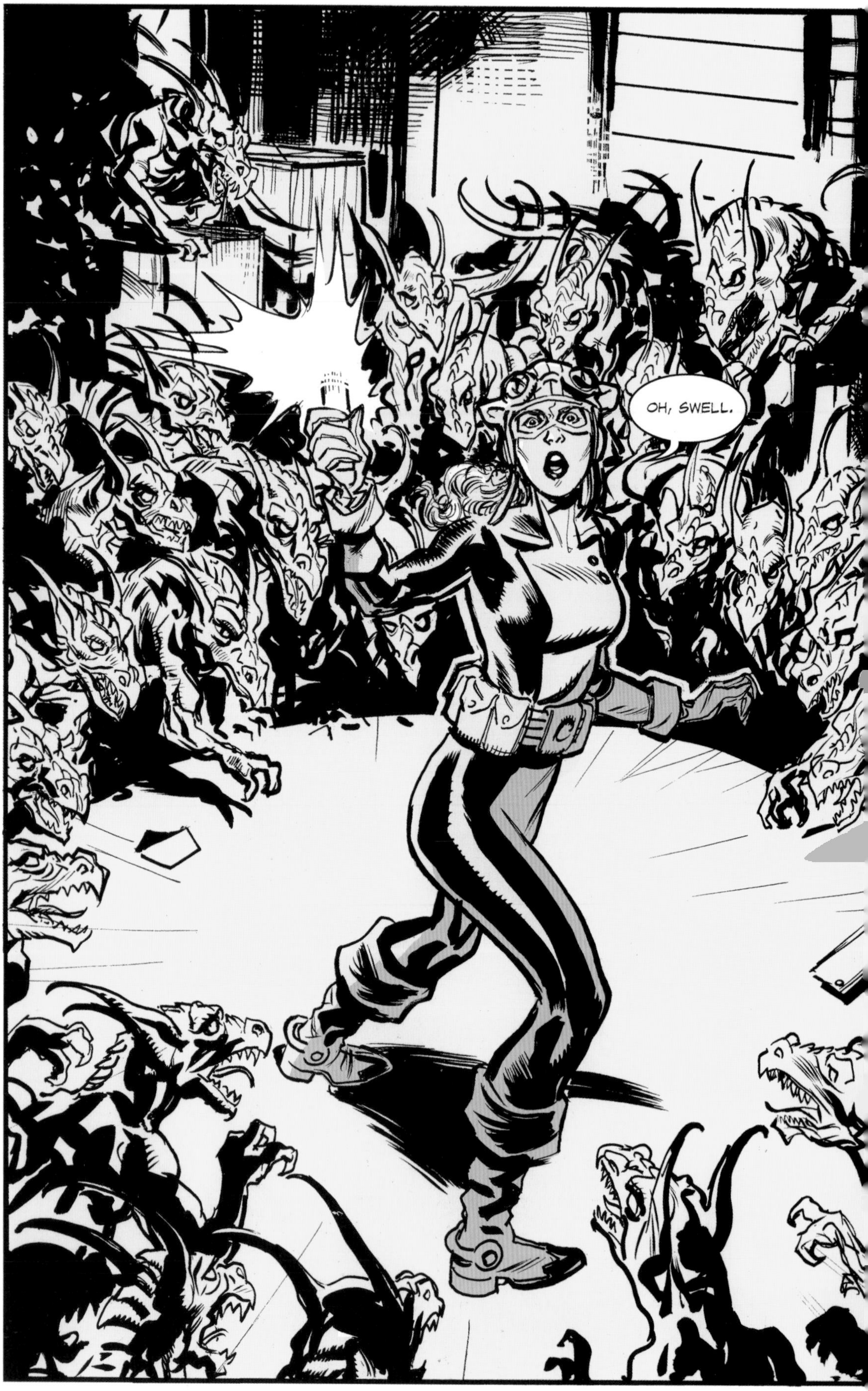
OH, SWELL.

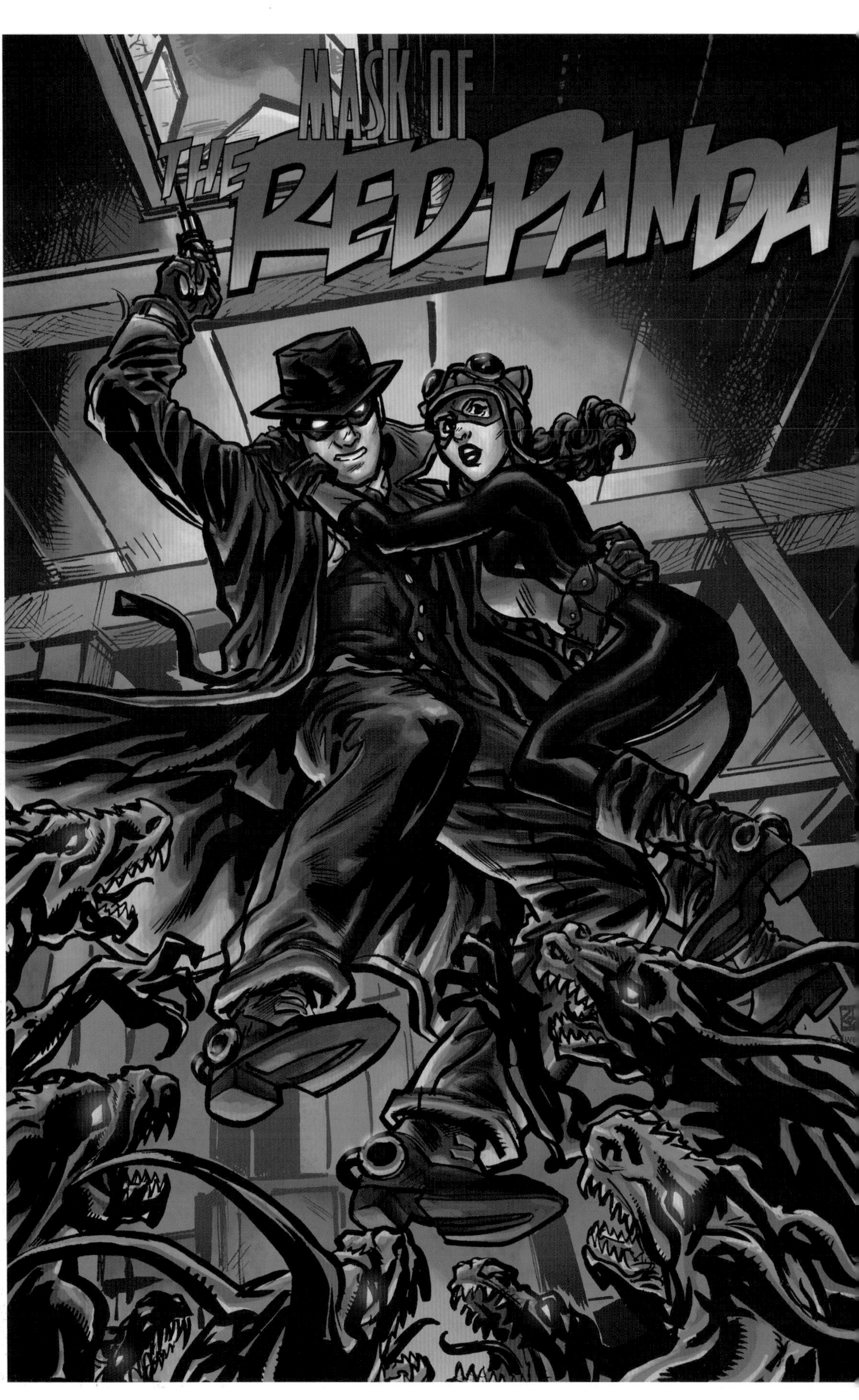
MASK OF
THE RED PANDA

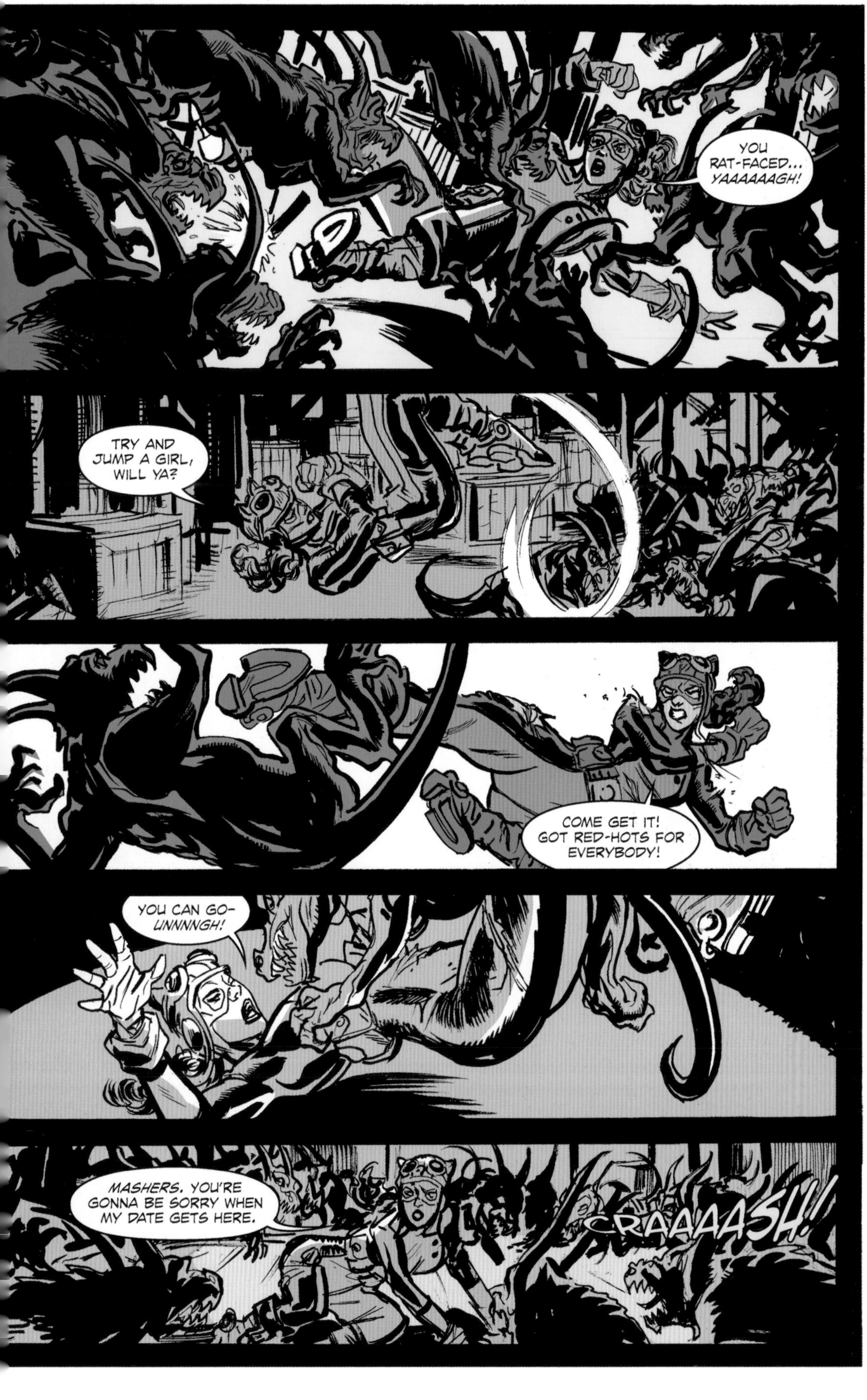
YOU RAT-FACED... YAAAAAAGH!
TRY AND JUMP A GIRL, WILL YA?
COME GET IT! GOT RED-HOTS FOR EVERYBODY!
YOU CAN GO-UNNNNGH!
MASHERS. YOU'RE GONNA BE SORRY WHEN MY DATE GETS HERE.
CRAAAASH!!

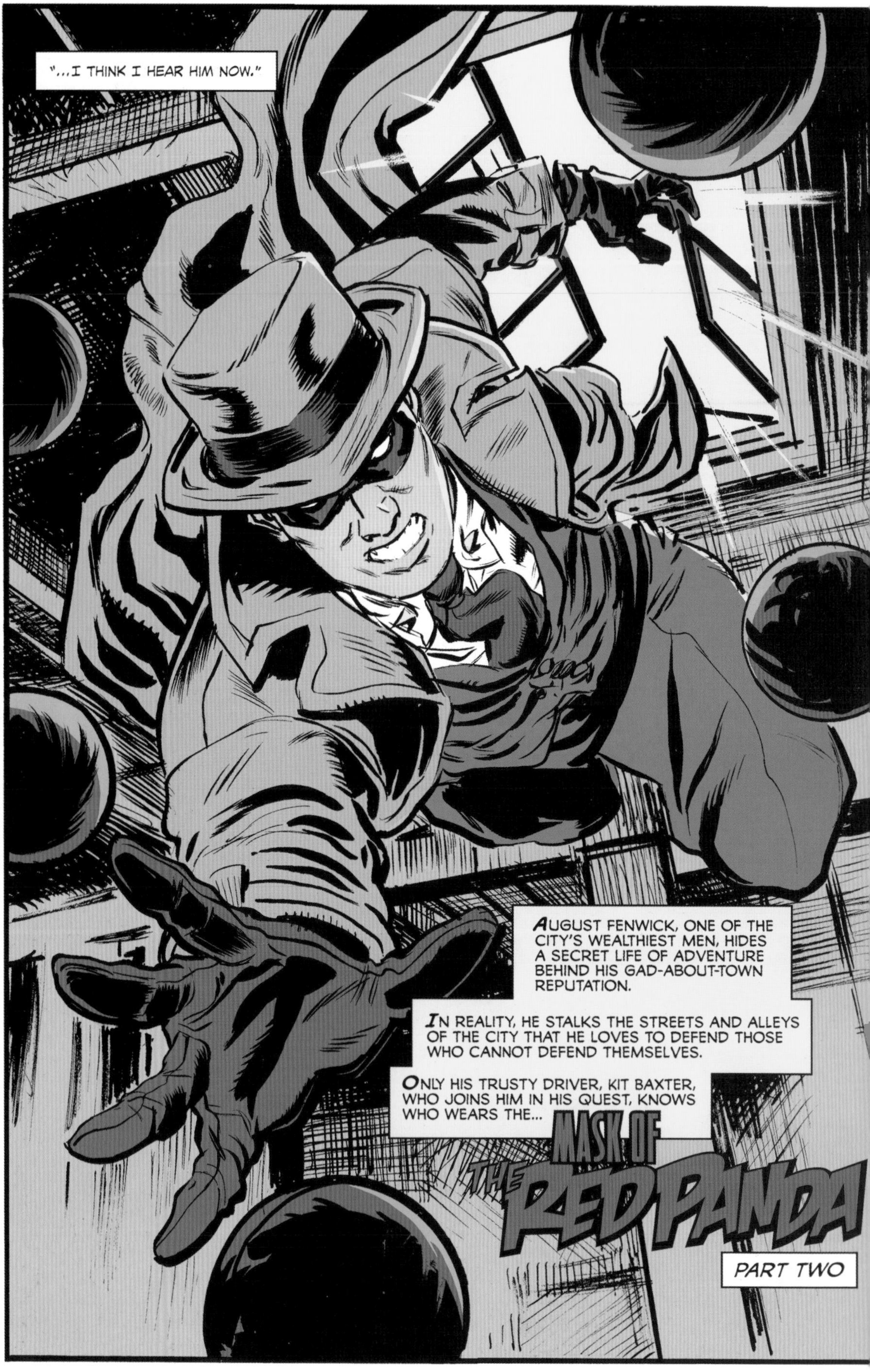
"...I THINK I HEAR HIM NOW."
AUGUST FENWICK, ONE OF THE CITY'S WEALTHIEST MEN, HIDES A SECRET LIFE OF ADVENTURE BEHIND HIS GAD-ABOUT-TOWN REPUTATION.
IN REALITY, HE STALKS THE STREETS AND ALLEYS OF THE CITY THAT HE LOVES TO DEFEND THOSE WHO CANNOT DEFEND THEMSELVES.
ONLY HIS TRUSTY DRIVER, KIT BAXTER, WHO JOINS HIM IN HIS QUEST, KNOWS WHO WEARS THE...
MASK OF THE RED PANDA
PART TWO

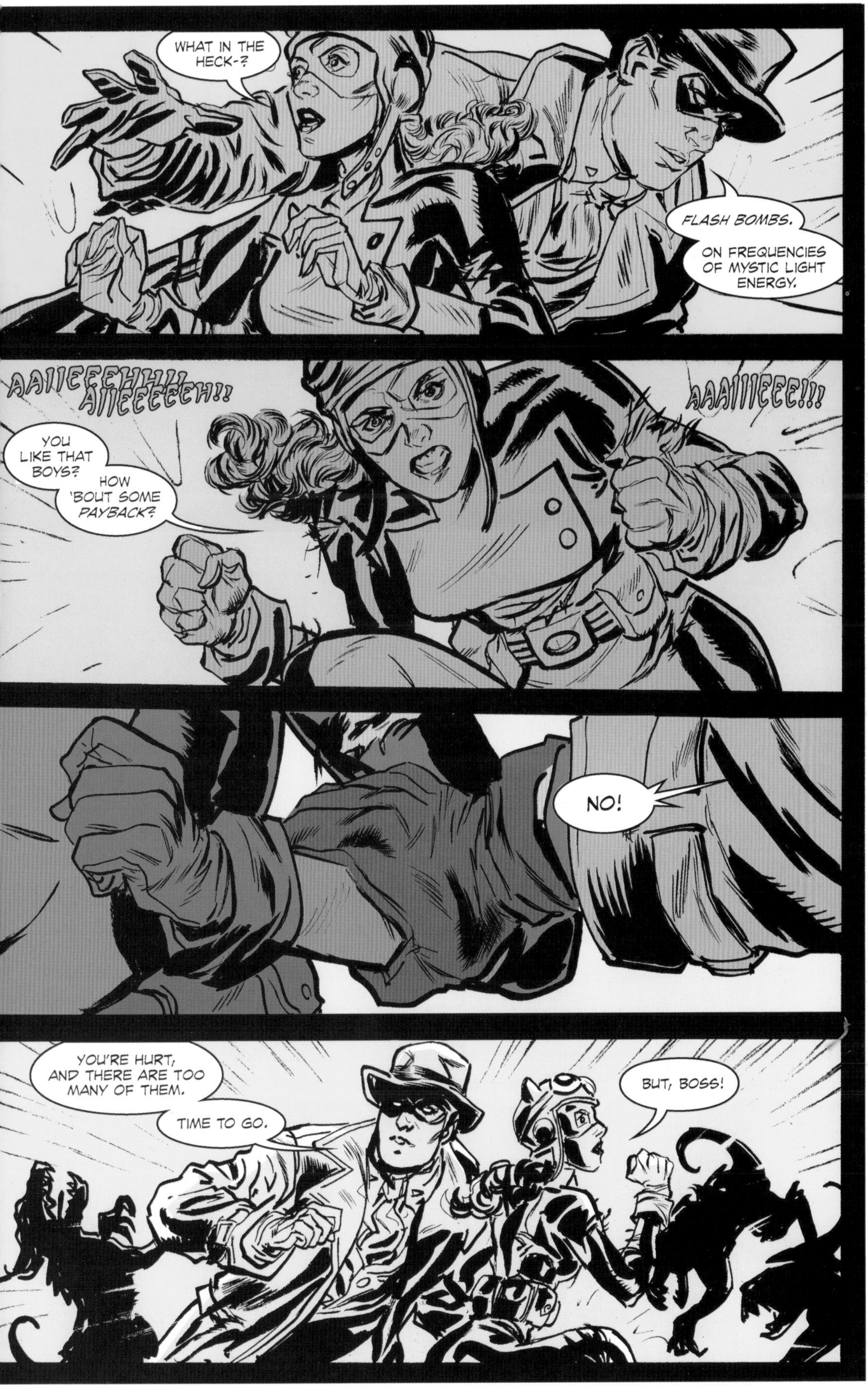
WHAT IN THE HECK-?
FLASH BOMBS.
ON FREQUENCIES OF MYSTIC LIGHT ENERGY.
AAIIEEEHH!! AIIEEEEEH!!
AAAIIIEEE!!!
YOU LIKE THAT BOYS?
HOW 'BOUT SOME PAYBACK?
NO!
YOU'RE HURT, AND THERE ARE TOO MANY OF THEM.
TIME TO GO.
BUT, BOSS!

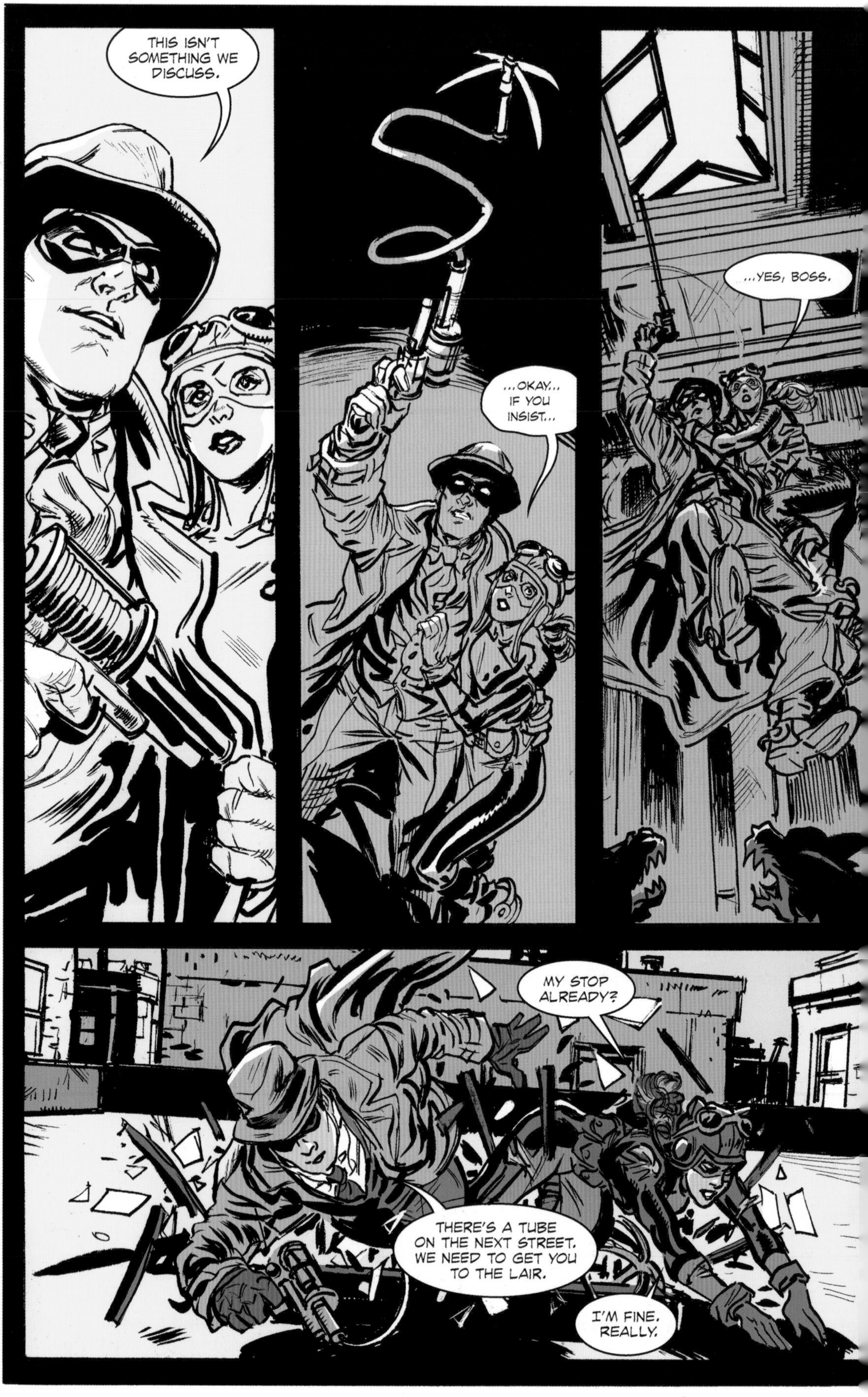
THIS ISN'T SOMETHING WE DISCUSS.
...OKAY... IF YOU INSIST...
...YES, BOSS.
MY STOP ALREADY?
THERE'S A TUBE ON THE NEXT STREET. WE NEED TO GET YOU TO THE LAIR.
I'M FINE. REALLY.

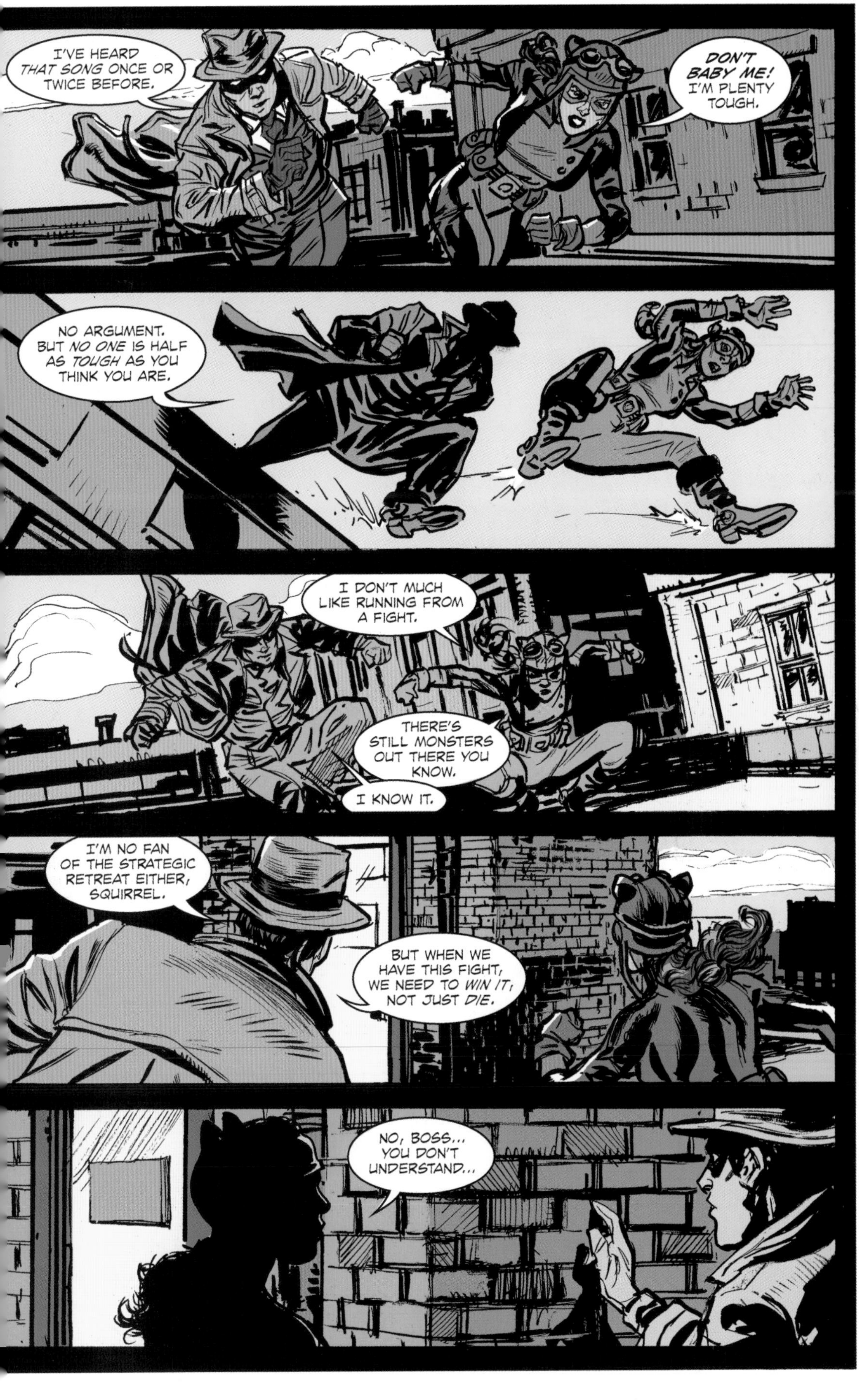
I'VE HEARD THAT SONG ONCE OR TWICE BEFORE.
DON'T BABY ME! I'M PLENTY TOUGH.
NO ARGUMENT. BUT NO ONE IS HALF AS TOUGH AS YOU THINK YOU ARE.
I DON'T MUCH LIKE RUNNING FROM A FIGHT.
THERE'S STILL MONSTERS OUT THERE YOU KNOW.
I KNOW IT.
I'M NO FAN OF THE STRATEGIC RETREAT EITHER, SQUIRREL.
BUT WHEN WE HAVE THIS FIGHT, WE NEED TO WIN IT, NOT JUST DIE.
NO, BOSS... YOU DON'T UNDERSTAND...

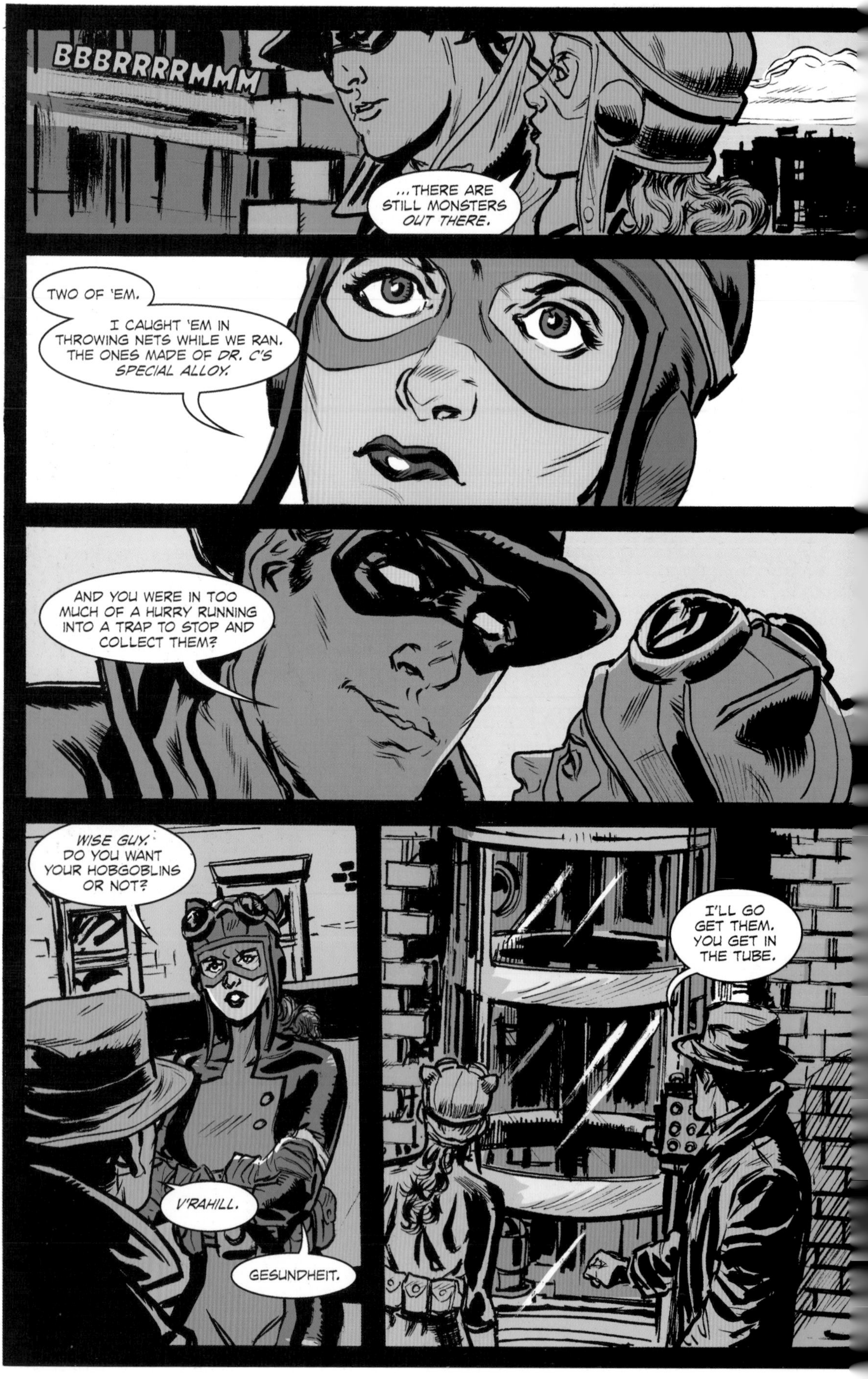
BBBRRRRRMMM
...THERE ARE STILL MONSTERS *OUT THERE.*
TWO OF 'EM.
I CAUGHT 'EM IN THROWING NETS WHILE WE RAN. THE ONES MADE OF *DR. C'S SPECIAL ALLOY.*
AND YOU WERE IN TOO MUCH OF A HURRY RUNNING INTO A TRAP TO STOP AND COLLECT THEM?
WISE GUY. DO YOU WANT YOUR HOBGOBLINS OR NOT?
V'RAHILL.
GESUNDHEIT.
I'LL GO GET THEM. YOU GET IN THE TUBE.

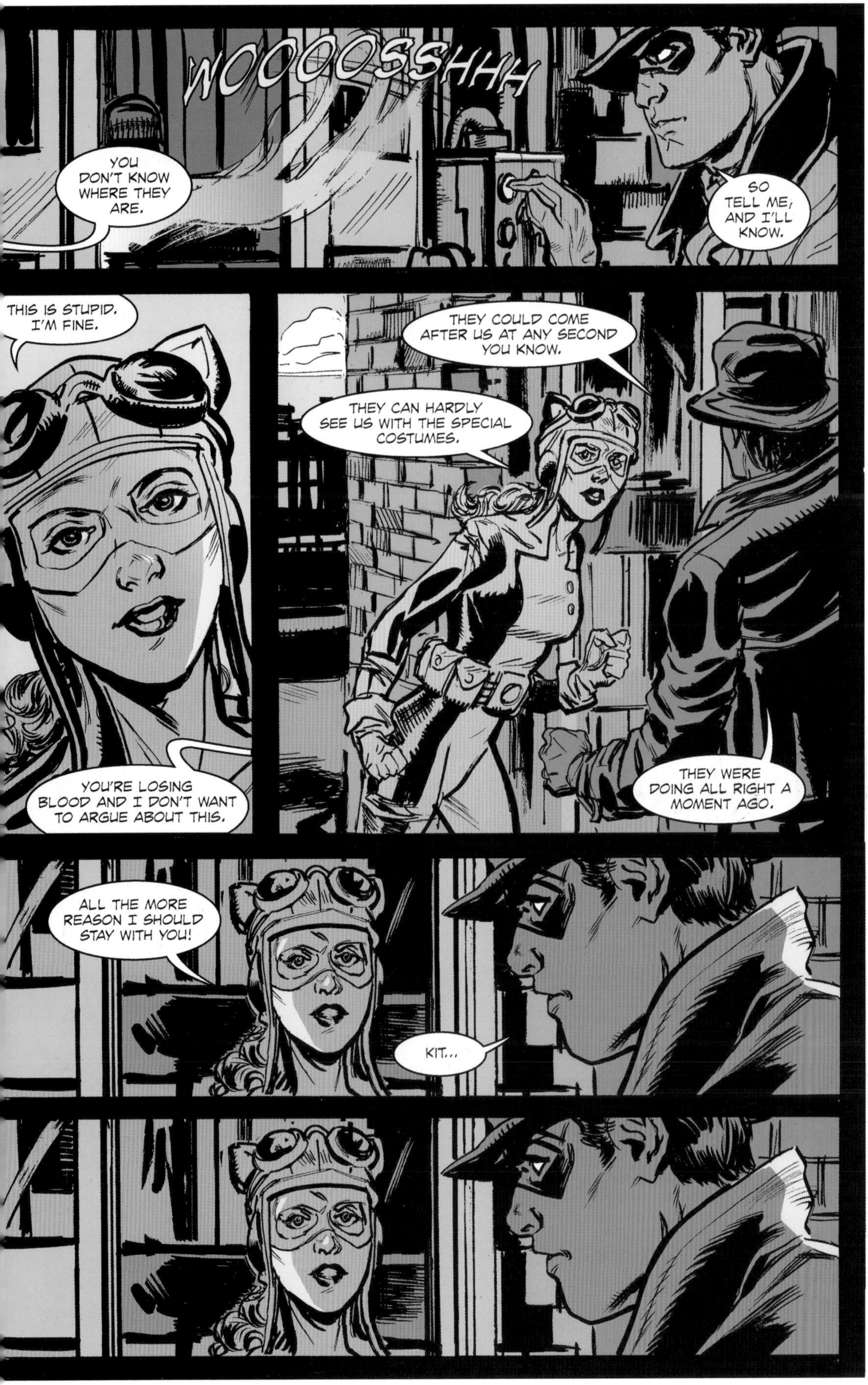
WOOOOSSHHH
YOU DON'T KNOW WHERE THEY ARE.
SO TELL ME, AND I'LL KNOW.
THIS IS STUPID. I'M FINE.
YOU'RE LOSING BLOOD AND I DON'T WANT TO ARGUE ABOUT THIS.
THEY COULD COME AFTER US AT ANY SECOND YOU KNOW.
THEY CAN HARDLY SEE US WITH THE SPECIAL COSTUMES.
THEY WERE DOING ALL RIGHT A MOMENT AGO.
ALL THE MORE REASON I SHOULD STAY WITH YOU!
KIT...

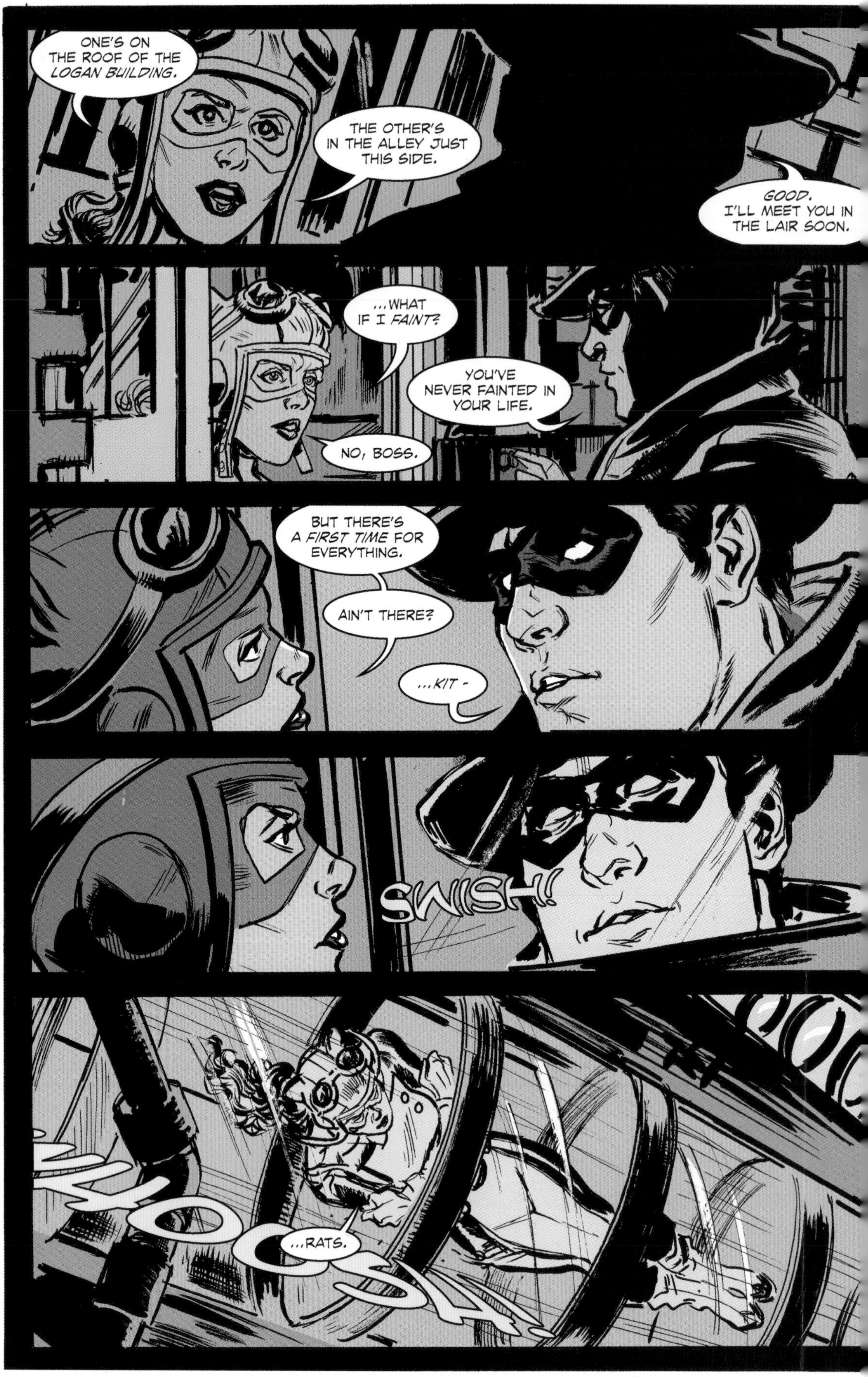
ONE'S ON THE ROOF OF THE *LOGAN BUILDING*.
THE OTHER'S IN THE ALLEY JUST THIS SIDE.
GOOD. I'LL MEET YOU IN THE LAIR SOON.
...WHAT IF I *FAINT?*
YOU'VE NEVER FAINTED IN YOUR LIFE.
NO, BOSS.
BUT THERE'S A *FIRST TIME* FOR EVERYTHING.
AIN'T THERE?
...KIT -
SWISH!
...RATS.

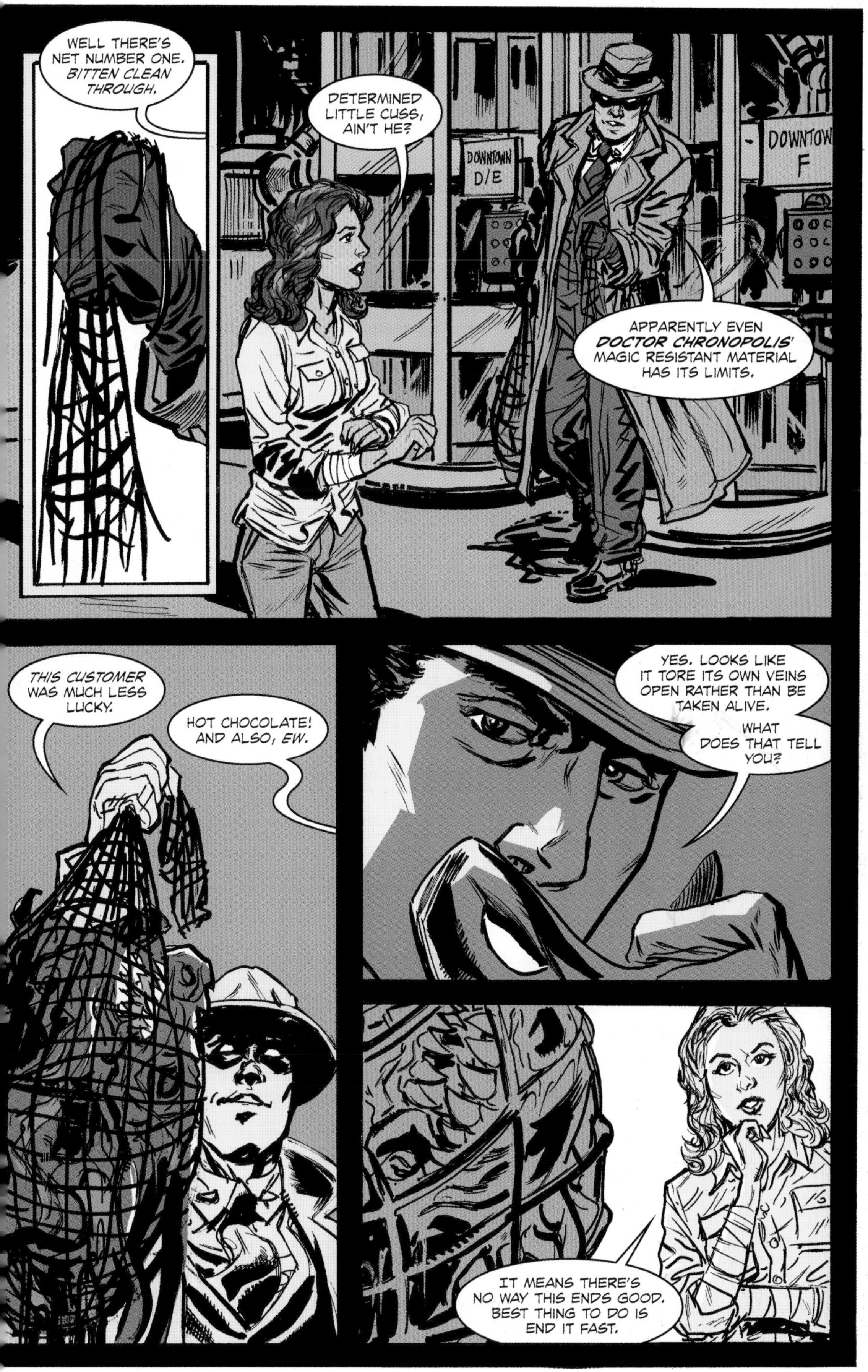
WELL THERE'S NET NUMBER ONE. *BITTEN CLEAN THROUGH.*
DETERMINED LITTLE CUSS, AIN'T HE?
DOWNTOWN D/E
DOWNTOWN F
APPARENTLY EVEN ***DOCTOR CHRONOPOLIS'*** MAGIC RESISTANT MATERIAL HAS ITS LIMITS.
THIS CUSTOMER WAS MUCH LESS LUCKY.
HOT CHOCOLATE! AND ALSO, *EW.*
YES. LOOKS LIKE IT TORE ITS OWN VEINS OPEN RATHER THAN BE TAKEN ALIVE.
WHAT DOES THAT TELL YOU?
IT MEANS THERE'S NO WAY THIS ENDS GOOD. BEST THING TO DO IS END IT FAST.

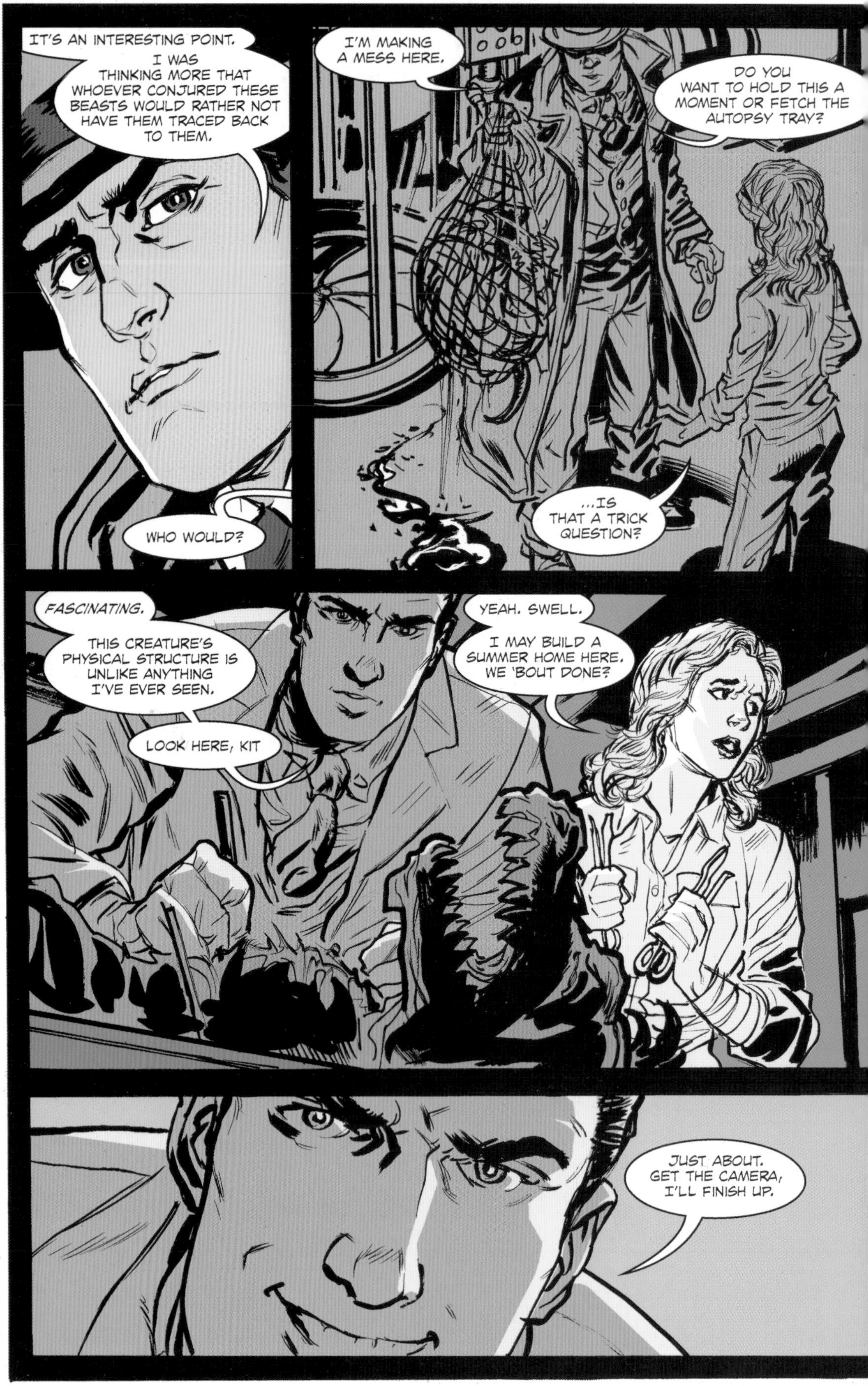
IT'S AN INTERESTING POINT.
I WAS THINKING MORE THAT WHOEVER CONJURED THESE BEASTS WOULD RATHER NOT HAVE THEM TRACED BACK TO THEM.
WHO WOULD?
I'M MAKING A MESS HERE.
DO YOU WANT TO HOLD THIS A MOMENT OR FETCH THE AUTOPSY TRAY?
...IS THAT A TRICK QUESTION?
FASCINATING.
THIS CREATURE'S PHYSICAL STRUCTURE IS UNLIKE ANYTHING I'VE EVER SEEN.
LOOK HERE, KIT
YEAH. SWELL.
I MAY BUILD A SUMMER HOME HERE. WE 'BOUT DONE?
JUST ABOUT. GET THE CAMERA, I'LL FINISH UP.

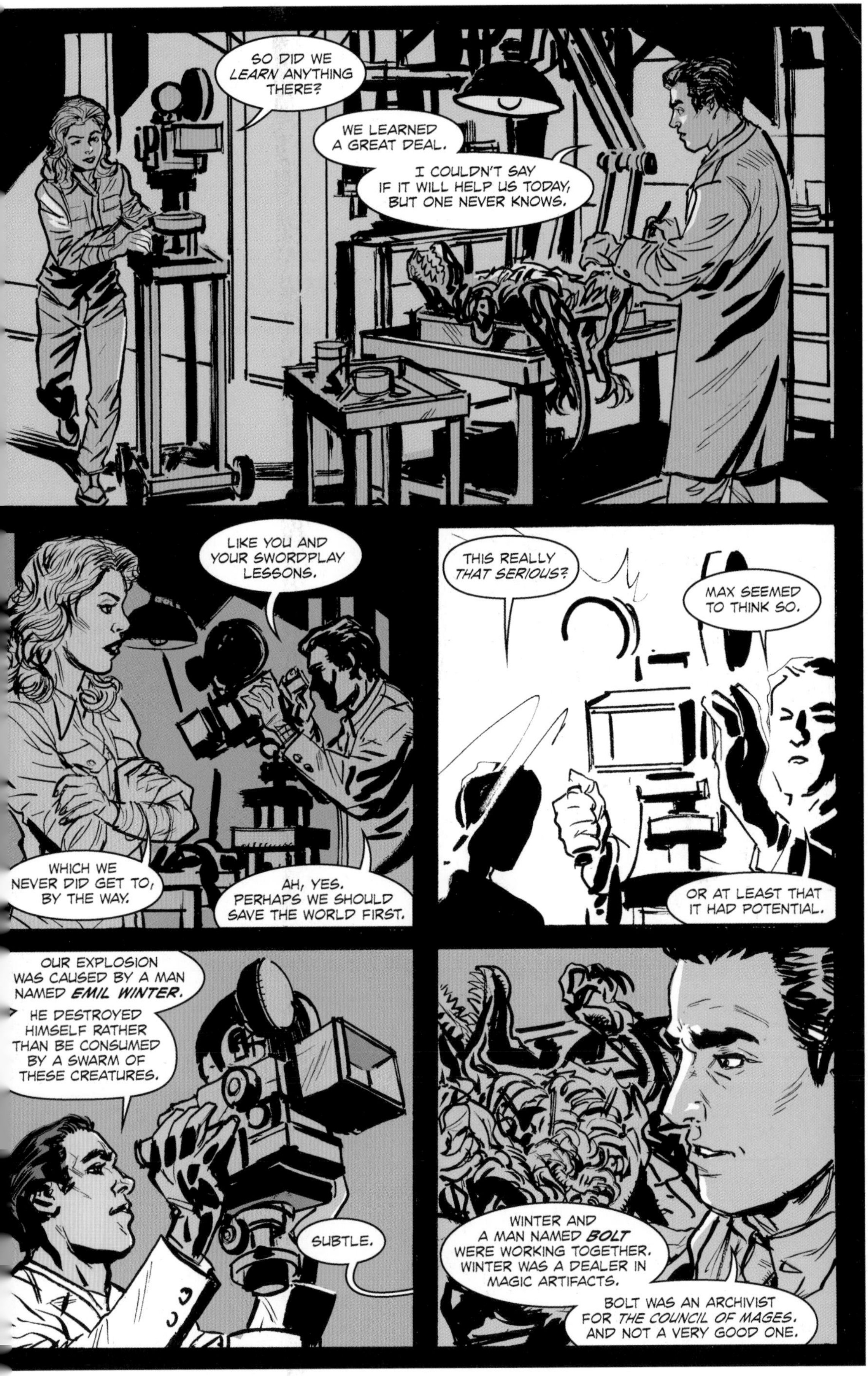
SO DID WE *LEARN* ANYTHING THERE?
WE LEARNED A GREAT DEAL.
I COULDN'T SAY IF IT WILL HELP US TODAY, BUT ONE NEVER KNOWS.
LIKE YOU AND YOUR SWORDPLAY LESSONS.
WHICH WE NEVER DID GET TO, BY THE WAY.
AH, YES. PERHAPS WE SHOULD SAVE THE WORLD FIRST.
THIS REALLY *THAT SERIOUS?*
MAX SEEMED TO THINK SO.
OR AT LEAST THAT IT HAD POTENTIAL.
OUR EXPLOSION WAS CAUSED BY A MAN NAMED ***EMIL WINTER***.
HE DESTROYED HIMSELF RATHER THAN BE CONSUMED BY A SWARM OF THESE CREATURES.
SUBTLE.
WINTER AND A MAN NAMED ***BOLT*** WERE WORKING TOGETHER. WINTER WAS A DEALER IN MAGIC ARTIFACTS.
BOLT WAS AN ARCHIVIST FOR *THE COUNCIL OF MAGES*. AND NOT A VERY GOOD ONE.

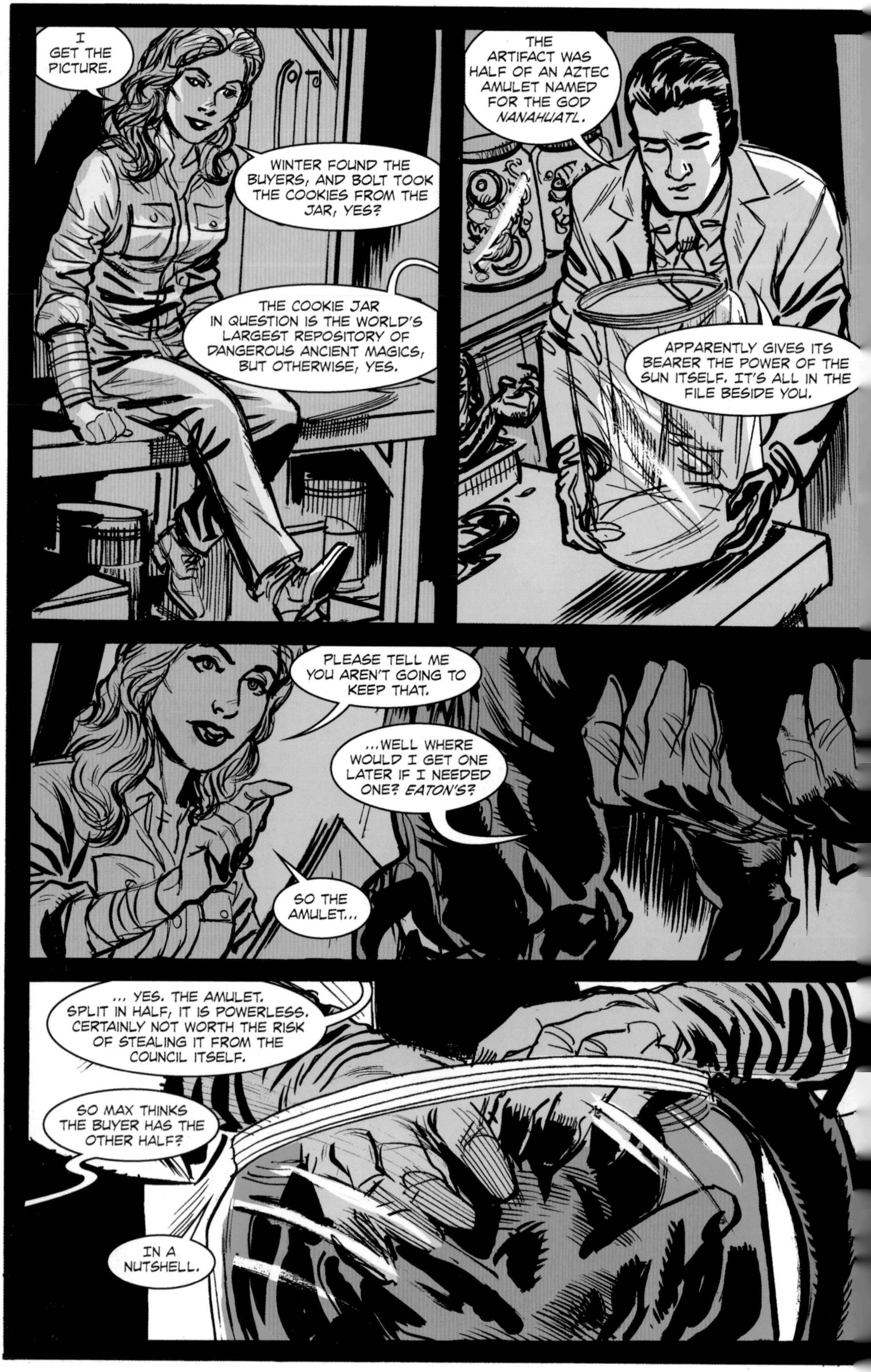
I GET THE PICTURE.
WINTER FOUND THE BUYERS, AND BOLT TOOK THE COOKIES FROM THE JAR, YES?
THE COOKIE JAR IN QUESTION IS THE WORLD'S LARGEST REPOSITORY OF DANGEROUS ANCIENT MAGICS, BUT OTHERWISE, YES.
THE ARTIFACT WAS HALF OF AN AZTEC AMULET NAMED FOR THE GOD *NANAHUATL*.
APPARENTLY GIVES ITS BEARER THE POWER OF THE SUN ITSELF. IT'S ALL IN THE FILE BESIDE YOU.
PLEASE TELL ME YOU AREN'T GOING TO KEEP THAT.
...WELL WHERE WOULD I GET ONE LATER IF I NEEDED ONE? *EATON'S*?
SO THE AMULET...
... YES. THE AMULET. SPLIT IN HALF, IT IS POWERLESS. CERTAINLY NOT WORTH THE RISK OF STEALING IT FROM THE COUNCIL ITSELF.
SO MAX THINKS THE BUYER HAS THE OTHER HALF?
IN A NUTSHELL.

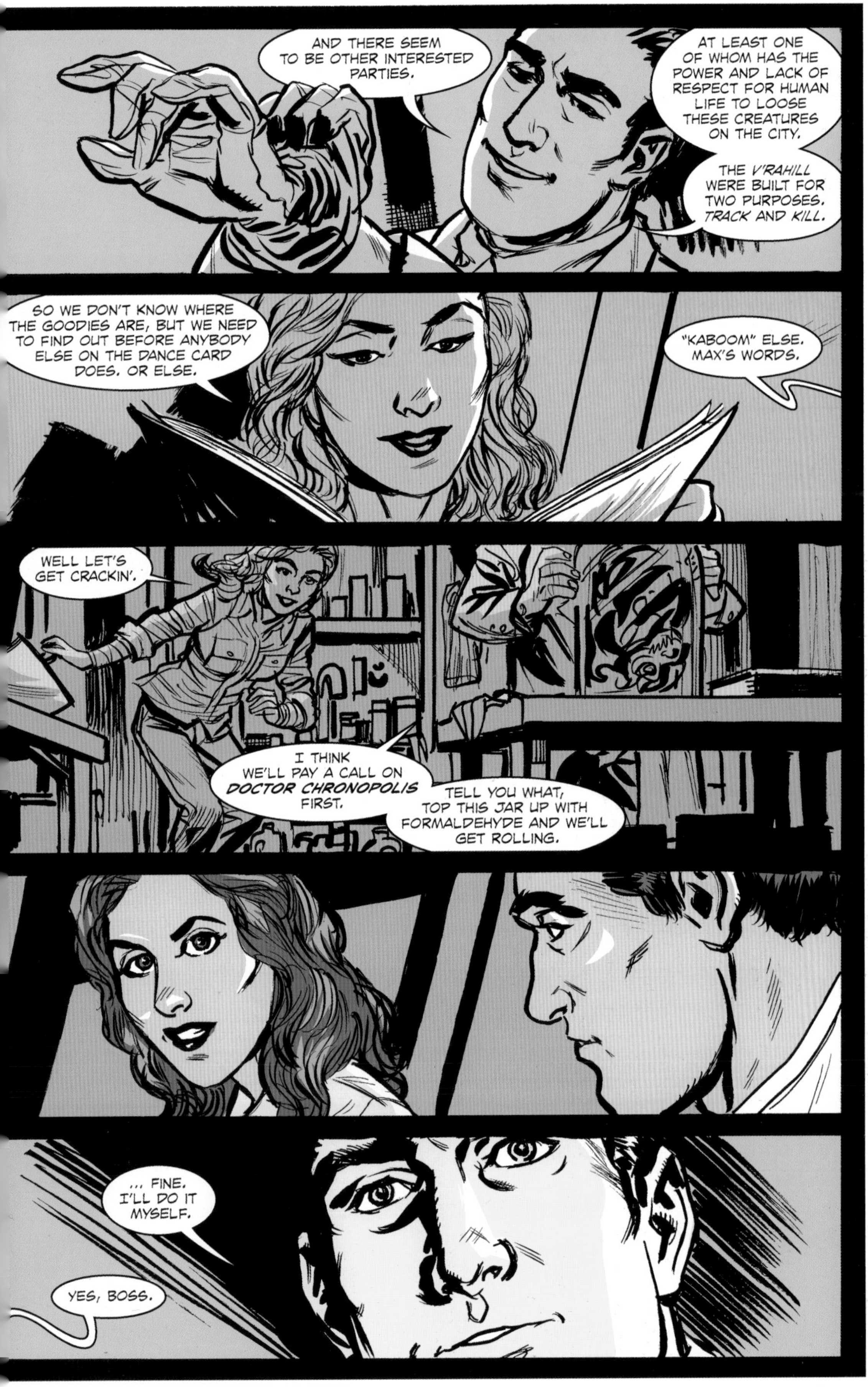
AND THERE SEEM TO BE OTHER INTERESTED PARTIES.
AT LEAST ONE OF WHOM HAS THE POWER AND LACK OF RESPECT FOR HUMAN LIFE TO LOOSE THESE CREATURES ON THE CITY.
THE *V'RAHILL* WERE BUILT FOR TWO PURPOSES. *TRACK* AND *KILL*.
SO WE DON'T KNOW WHERE THE GOODIES ARE, BUT WE NEED TO FIND OUT BEFORE ANYBODY ELSE ON THE DANCE CARD DOES. OR ELSE.
"KABOOM" ELSE. MAX'S WORDS.
WELL LET'S GET CRACKIN'.
I THINK WE'LL PAY A CALL ON **DOCTOR CHRONOPOLIS** FIRST.
TELL YOU WHAT, TOP THIS JAR UP WITH FORMALDEHYDE AND WE'LL GET ROLLING.
... FINE. I'LL DO IT MYSELF.
YES, BOSS.

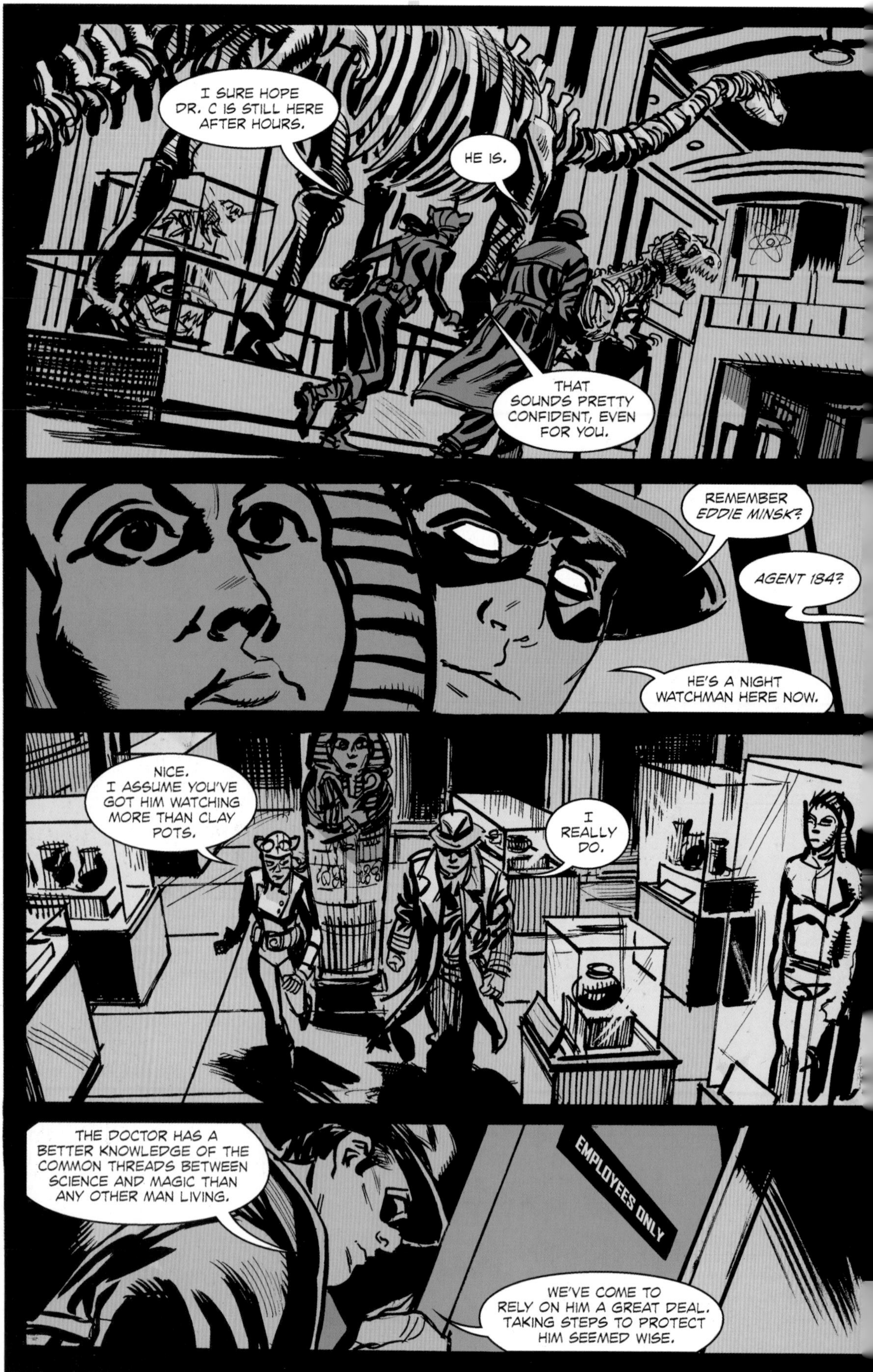

I SURE HOPE DR. C IS STILL HERE AFTER HOURS.
HE IS.
THAT SOUNDS PRETTY CONFIDENT, EVEN FOR YOU.
REMEMBER *EDDIE MINSK?*
AGENT 184?
HE'S A NIGHT WATCHMAN HERE NOW.
NICE. I ASSUME YOU'VE GOT HIM WATCHING MORE THAN CLAY POTS.
I REALLY DO.
THE DOCTOR HAS A BETTER KNOWLEDGE OF THE COMMON THREADS BETWEEN SCIENCE AND MAGIC THAN ANY OTHER MAN LIVING.
EMPLOYEES ONLY
WE'VE COME TO RELY ON HIM A GREAT DEAL. TAKING STEPS TO PROTECT HIM SEEMED WISE.

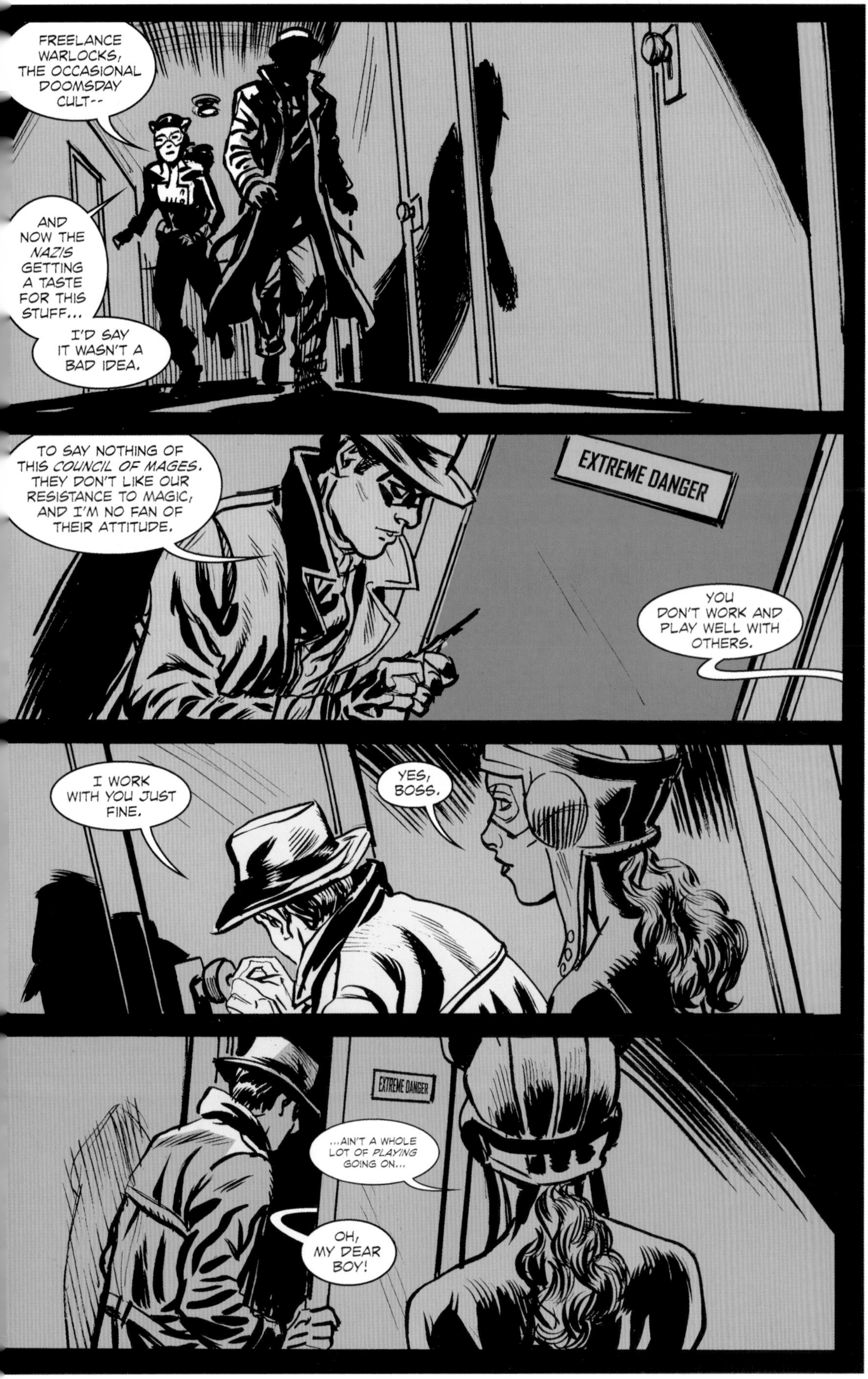
FREELANCE WARLOCKS, THE OCCASIONAL DOOMSDAY CULT--
AND NOW THE *NAZIS* GETTING A TASTE FOR THIS STUFF...
I'D SAY IT WASN'T A BAD IDEA.
TO SAY NOTHING OF THIS *COUNCIL OF MAGES*. THEY DON'T LIKE OUR RESISTANCE TO MAGIC, AND I'M NO FAN OF THEIR ATTITUDE.
EXTREME DANGER
YOU DON'T WORK AND PLAY WELL WITH OTHERS.
I WORK WITH YOU JUST FINE.
YES, BOSS.
EXTREME DANGER
...AIN'T A WHOLE LOT OF *PLAYING* GOING ON...
OH, MY DEAR BOY!

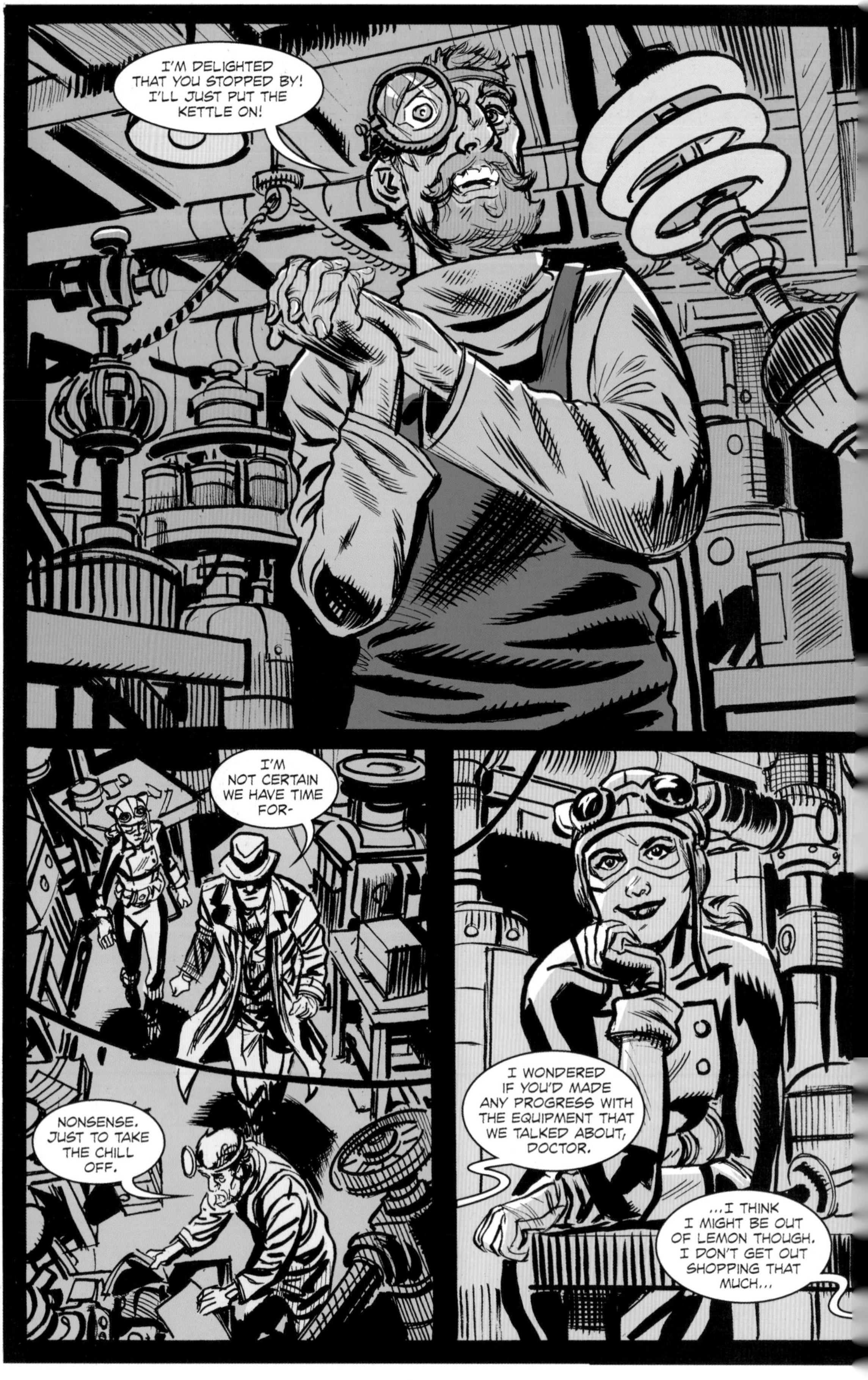
I'M DELIGHTED THAT YOU STOPPED BY! I'LL JUST PUT THE KETTLE ON!
I'M NOT CERTAIN WE HAVE TIME FOR-
NONSENSE. JUST TO TAKE THE CHILL OFF.
I WONDERED IF YOU'D MADE ANY PROGRESS WITH THE EQUIPMENT THAT WE TALKED ABOUT, DOCTOR.
...I THINK I MIGHT BE OUT OF LEMON THOUGH. I DON'T GET OUT SHOPPING THAT MUCH...

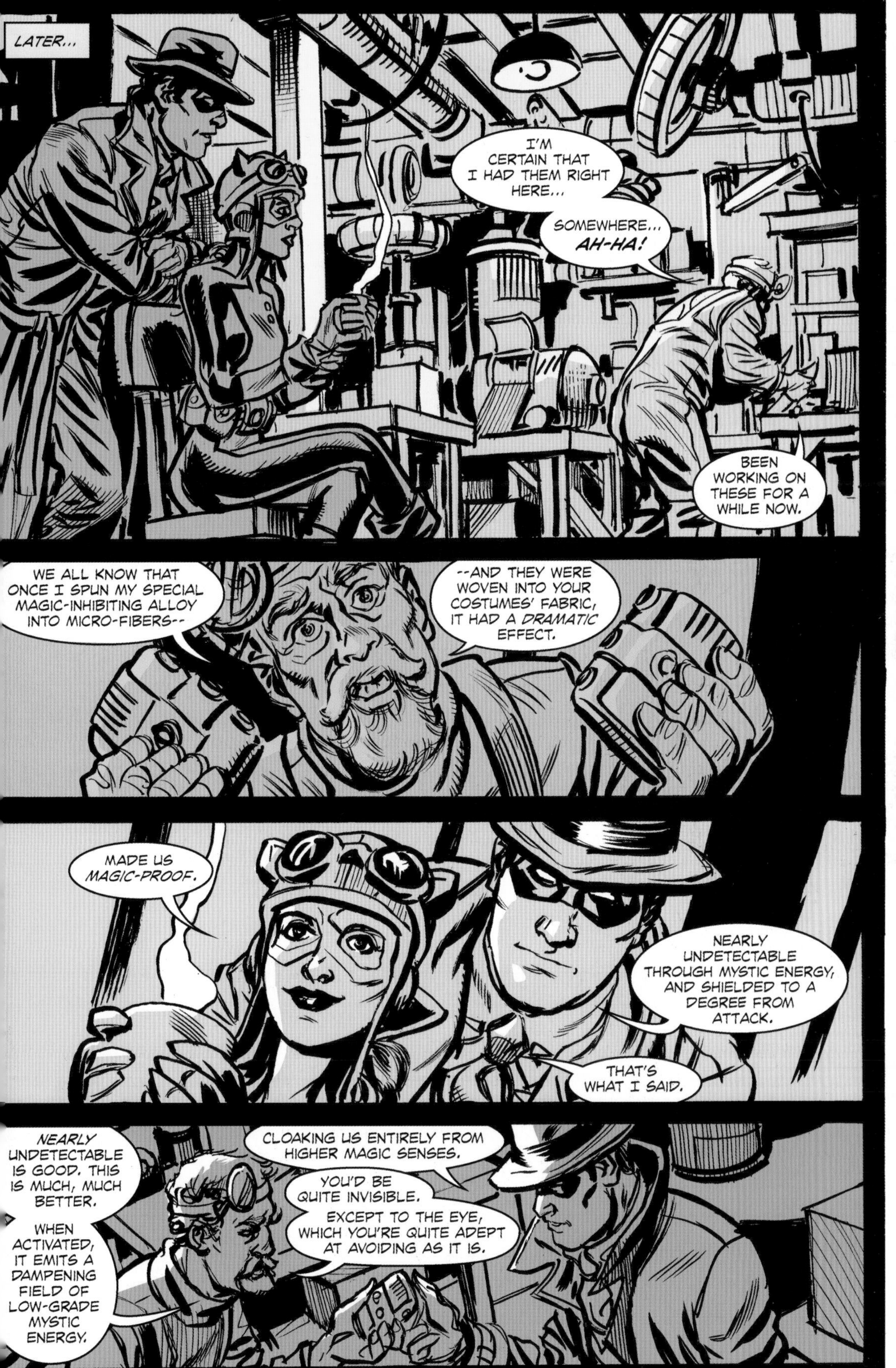
LATER...
I'M CERTAIN THAT I HAD THEM RIGHT HERE...
SOMEWHERE... *AH-HA!*
BEEN WORKING ON THESE FOR A WHILE NOW.
WE ALL KNOW THAT ONCE I SPUN MY SPECIAL MAGIC-INHIBITING ALLOY INTO MICRO-FIBERS--
--AND THEY WERE WOVEN INTO YOUR COSTUMES' FABRIC, IT HAD A *DRAMATIC* EFFECT.
MADE US *MAGIC-PROOF.*
NEARLY UNDETECTABLE THROUGH MYSTIC ENERGY, AND SHIELDED TO A DEGREE FROM ATTACK.
THAT'S WHAT I SAID.
NEARLY UNDETECTABLE IS GOOD. THIS IS MUCH, MUCH BETTER.
WHEN ACTIVATED, IT EMITS A DAMPENING FIELD OF LOW-GRADE MYSTIC ENERGY.
CLOAKING US ENTIRELY FROM HIGHER MAGIC SENSES.
YOU'D BE QUITE INVISIBLE.
EXCEPT TO THE EYE, WHICH YOU'RE QUITE ADEPT AT AVOIDING AS IT IS.

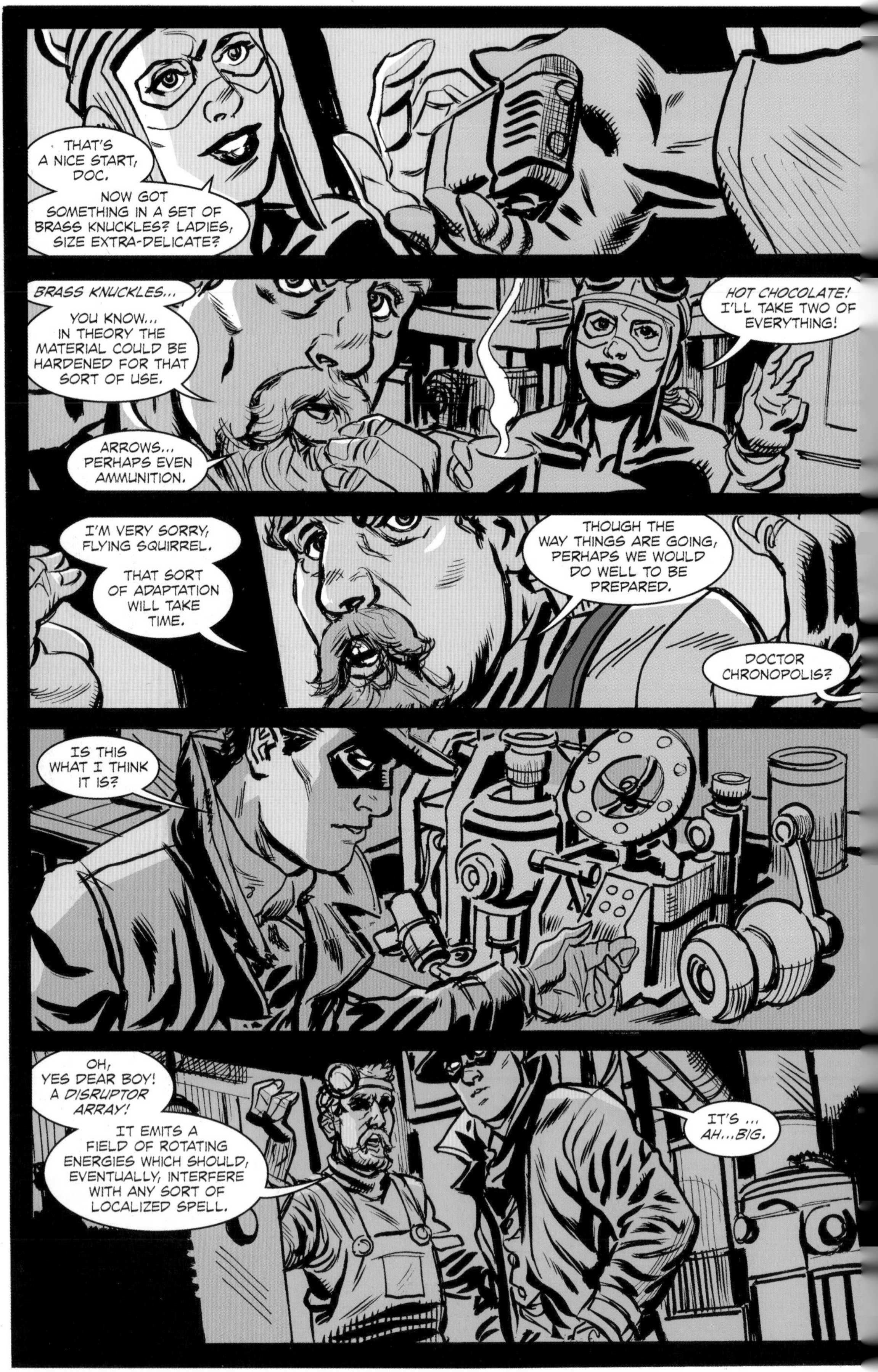
THAT'S A NICE START, DOC.
NOW GOT SOMETHING IN A SET OF BRASS KNUCKLES? LADIES, SIZE EXTRA-DELICATE?
BRASS KNUCKLES...
YOU KNOW... IN THEORY THE MATERIAL COULD BE HARDENED FOR THAT SORT OF USE.
HOT CHOCOLATE! I'LL TAKE TWO OF EVERYTHING!
ARROWS... PERHAPS EVEN AMMUNITION.
I'M VERY SORRY, FLYING SQUIRREL.
THAT SORT OF ADAPTATION WILL TAKE TIME.
THOUGH THE WAY THINGS ARE GOING, PERHAPS WE WOULD DO WELL TO BE PREPARED.
DOCTOR CHRONOPOLIS?
IS THIS WHAT I THINK IT IS?
OH, YES DEAR BOY! A DISRUPTOR ARRAY!
IT EMITS A FIELD OF ROTATING ENERGIES WHICH SHOULD, EVENTUALLY, INTERFERE WITH ANY SORT OF LOCALIZED SPELL.
IT'S ... AH...BIG.

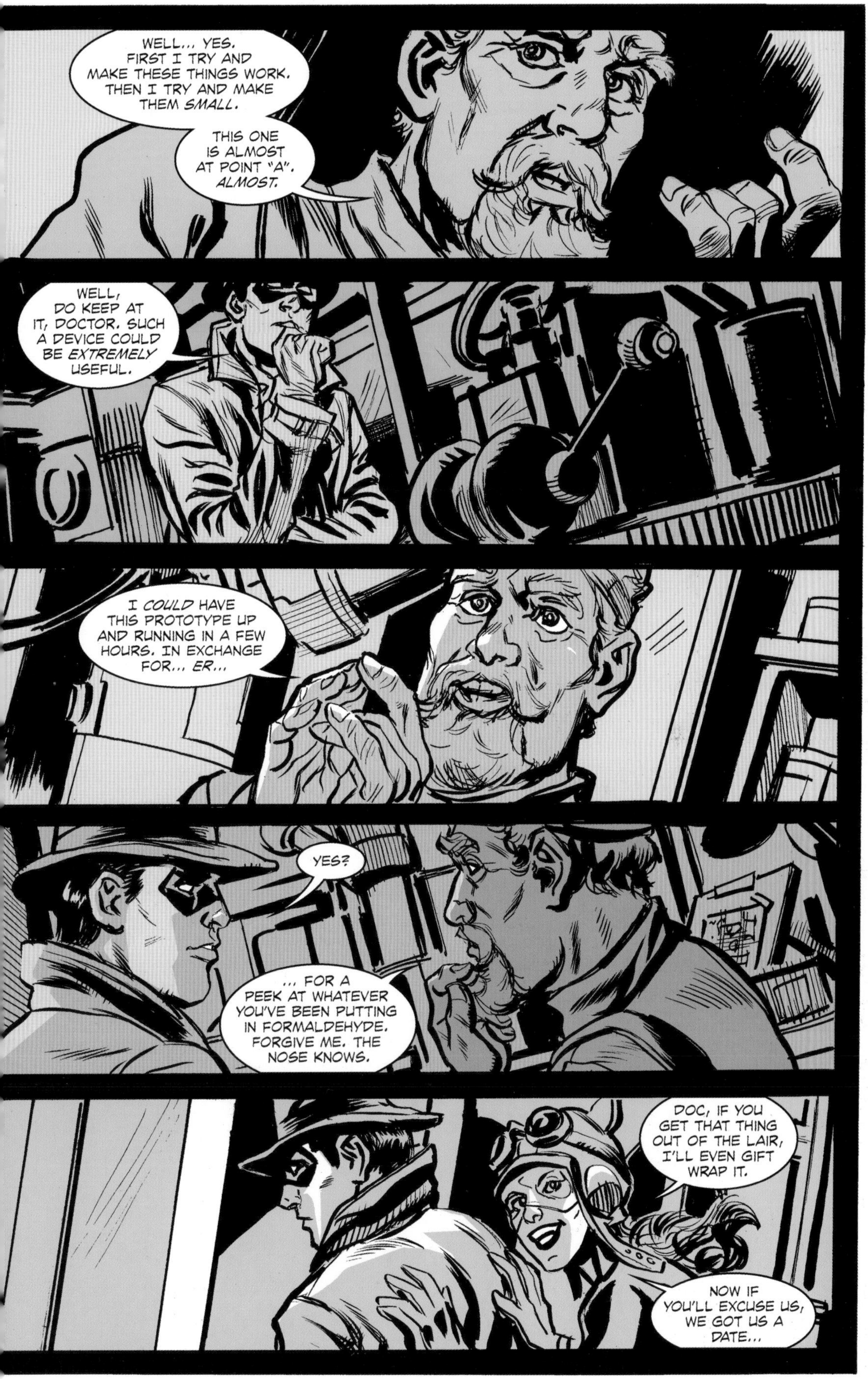
WELL... YES. FIRST I TRY AND MAKE THESE THINGS WORK. THEN I TRY AND MAKE THEM *SMALL*.
THIS ONE IS ALMOST AT POINT "A". *ALMOST.*
WELL, DO KEEP AT IT, DOCTOR. SUCH A DEVICE COULD BE *EXTREMELY* USEFUL.
I *COULD* HAVE THIS PROTOTYPE UP AND RUNNING IN A FEW HOURS. IN EXCHANGE FOR... *ER*...
YES?
... FOR A PEEK AT WHATEVER YOU'VE BEEN PUTTING IN FORMALDEHYDE. FORGIVE ME. THE NOSE KNOWS.
DOC, IF YOU GET THAT THING OUT OF THE LAIR, I'LL EVEN GIFT WRAP IT.
NOW IF YOU'LL EXCUSE US, WE GOT US A DATE...

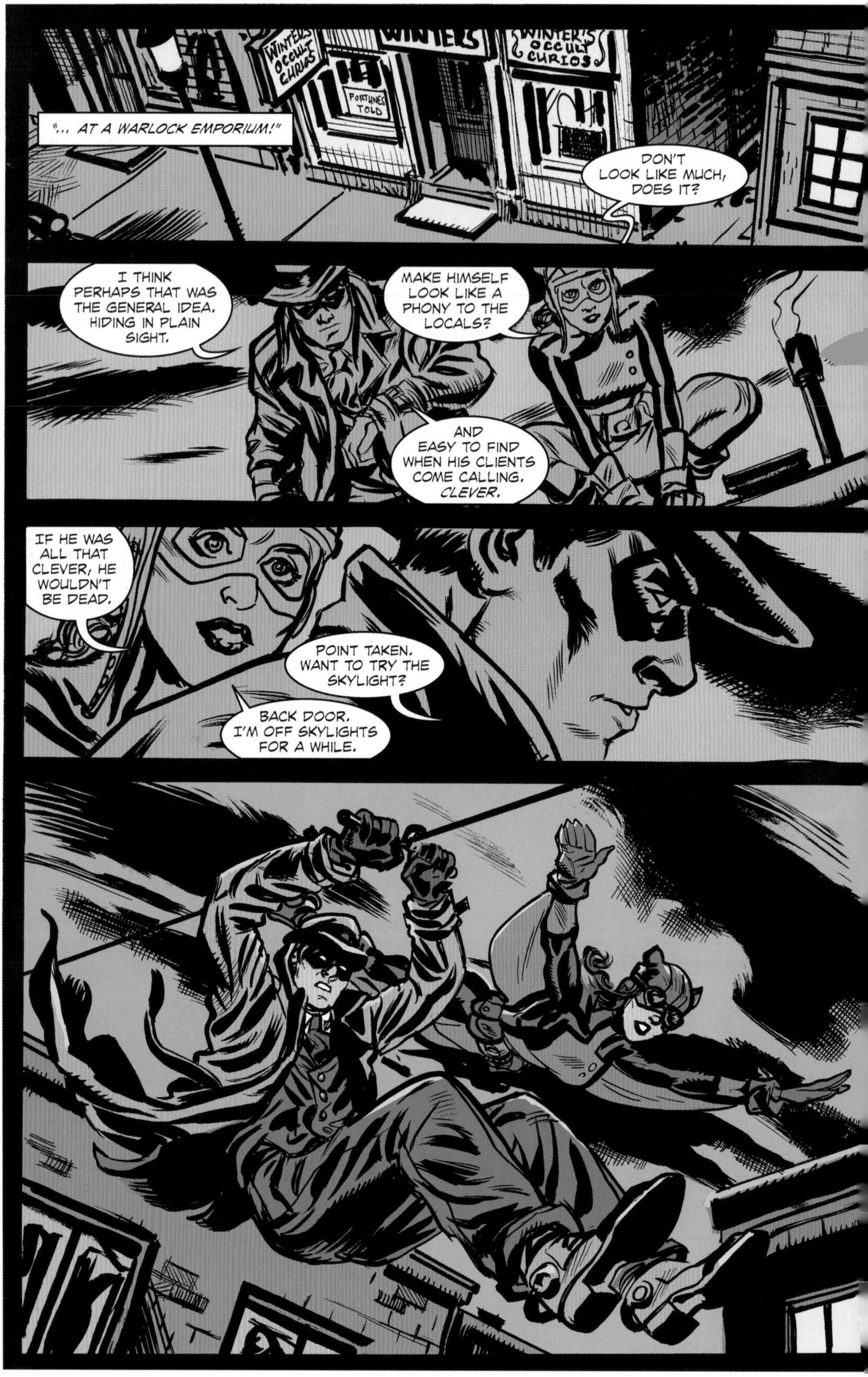
WINTER'S OCCULT CURIOS
WINTERS
WINTER'S OCCULT CURIOS
FORTUNES TOLD
"... AT A WARLOCK EMPORIUM!"
DON'T LOOK LIKE MUCH, DOES IT?
I THINK PERHAPS THAT WAS THE GENERAL IDEA. HIDING IN PLAIN SIGHT.
MAKE HIMSELF LOOK LIKE A PHONY TO THE LOCALS?
AND EASY TO FIND WHEN HIS CLIENTS COME CALLING. *CLEVER.*
IF HE WAS ALL THAT CLEVER, HE WOULDN'T BE DEAD.
POINT TAKEN. WANT TO TRY THE SKYLIGHT?
BACK DOOR. I'M OFF SKYLIGHTS FOR A WHILE.

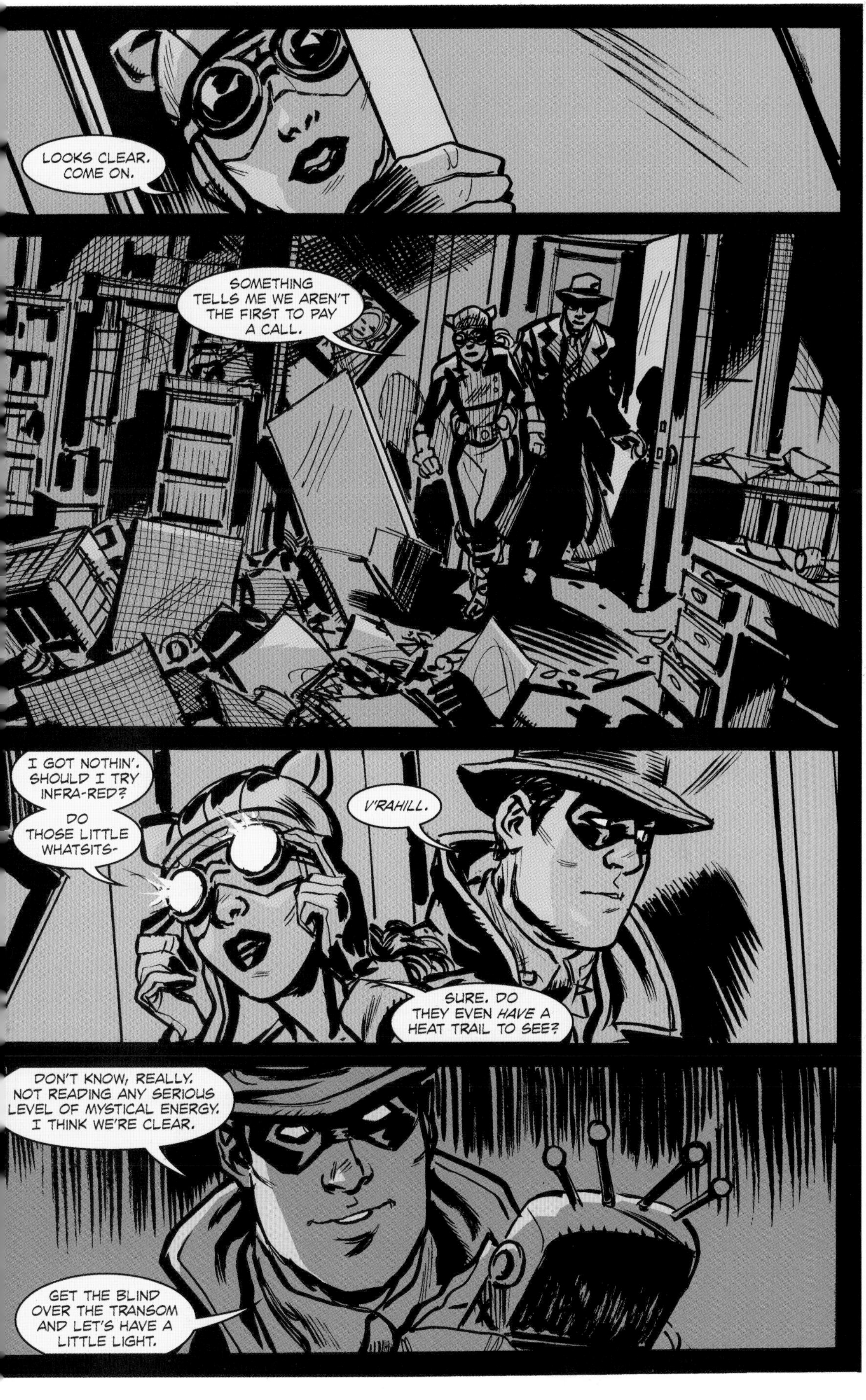

LOOKS CLEAR. COME ON.
SOMETHING TELLS ME WE AREN'T THE FIRST TO PAY A CALL.
I GOT NOTHIN'. SHOULD I TRY INFRA-RED?
V'RAHILL.
DO THOSE LITTLE WHATSITS-
SURE. DO THEY EVEN *HAVE* A HEAT TRAIL TO SEE?
DON'T KNOW, REALLY. NOT READING ANY SERIOUS LEVEL OF MYSTICAL ENERGY. I THINK WE'RE CLEAR.
GET THE BLIND OVER THE TRANSOM AND LET'S HAVE A LITTLE LIGHT.

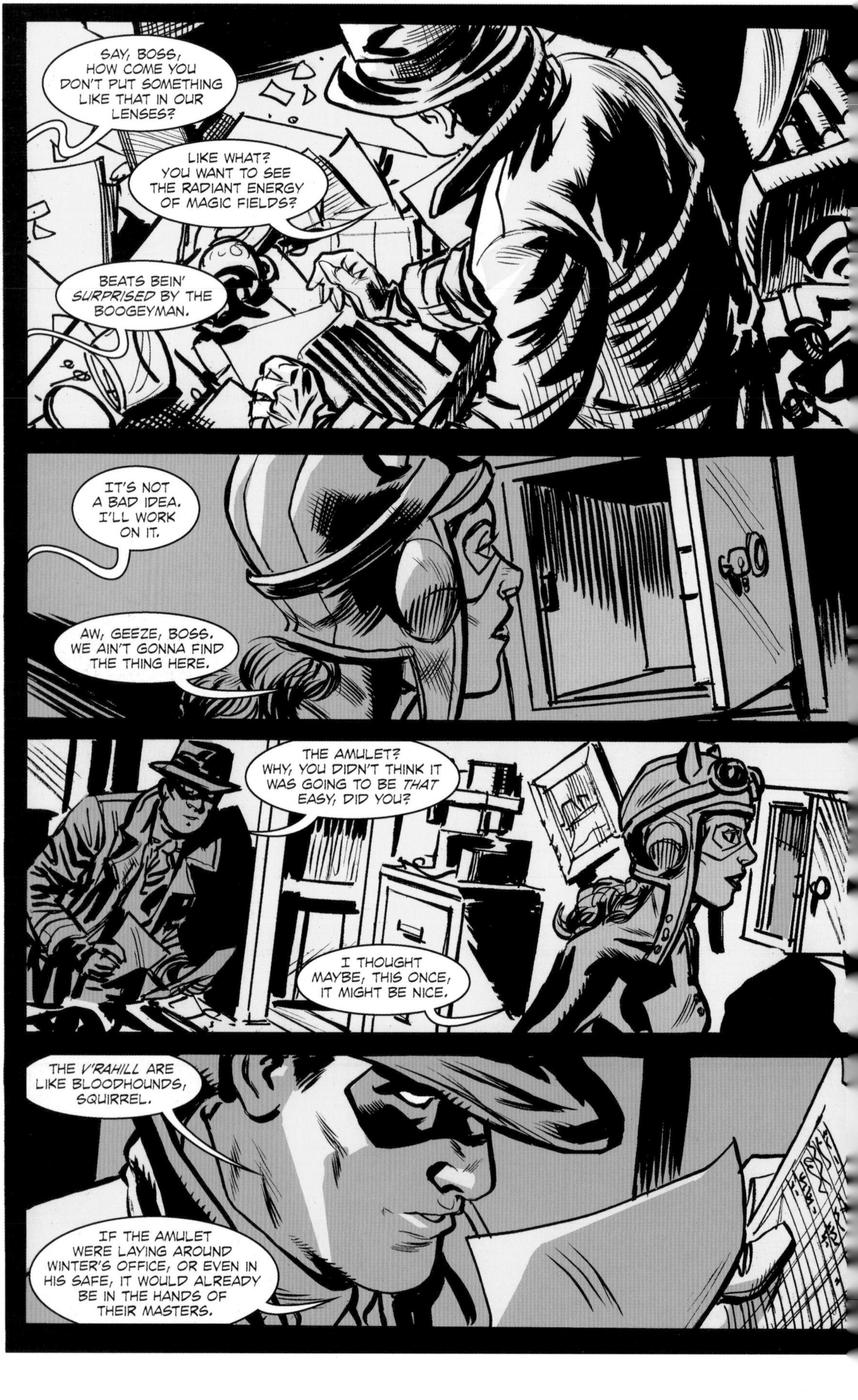
SAY, BOSS, HOW COME YOU DON'T PUT SOMETHING LIKE THAT IN OUR LENSES?
LIKE WHAT? YOU WANT TO SEE THE RADIANT ENERGY OF MAGIC FIELDS?
BEATS BEIN' *SURPRISED* BY THE BOOGEYMAN.
IT'S NOT A BAD IDEA. I'LL WORK ON IT.
AW, GEEZE, BOSS. WE AIN'T GONNA FIND THE THING HERE.
THE AMULET? WHY, YOU DIDN'T THINK IT WAS GOING TO BE *THAT* EASY, DID YOU?
I THOUGHT MAYBE, THIS ONCE, IT MIGHT BE NICE.
THE *V'RAHILL* ARE LIKE BLOODHOUNDS, SQUIRREL.
IF THE AMULET WERE LAYING AROUND WINTER'S OFFICE, OR EVEN IN HIS SAFE, IT WOULD ALREADY BE IN THE HANDS OF THEIR MASTERS.

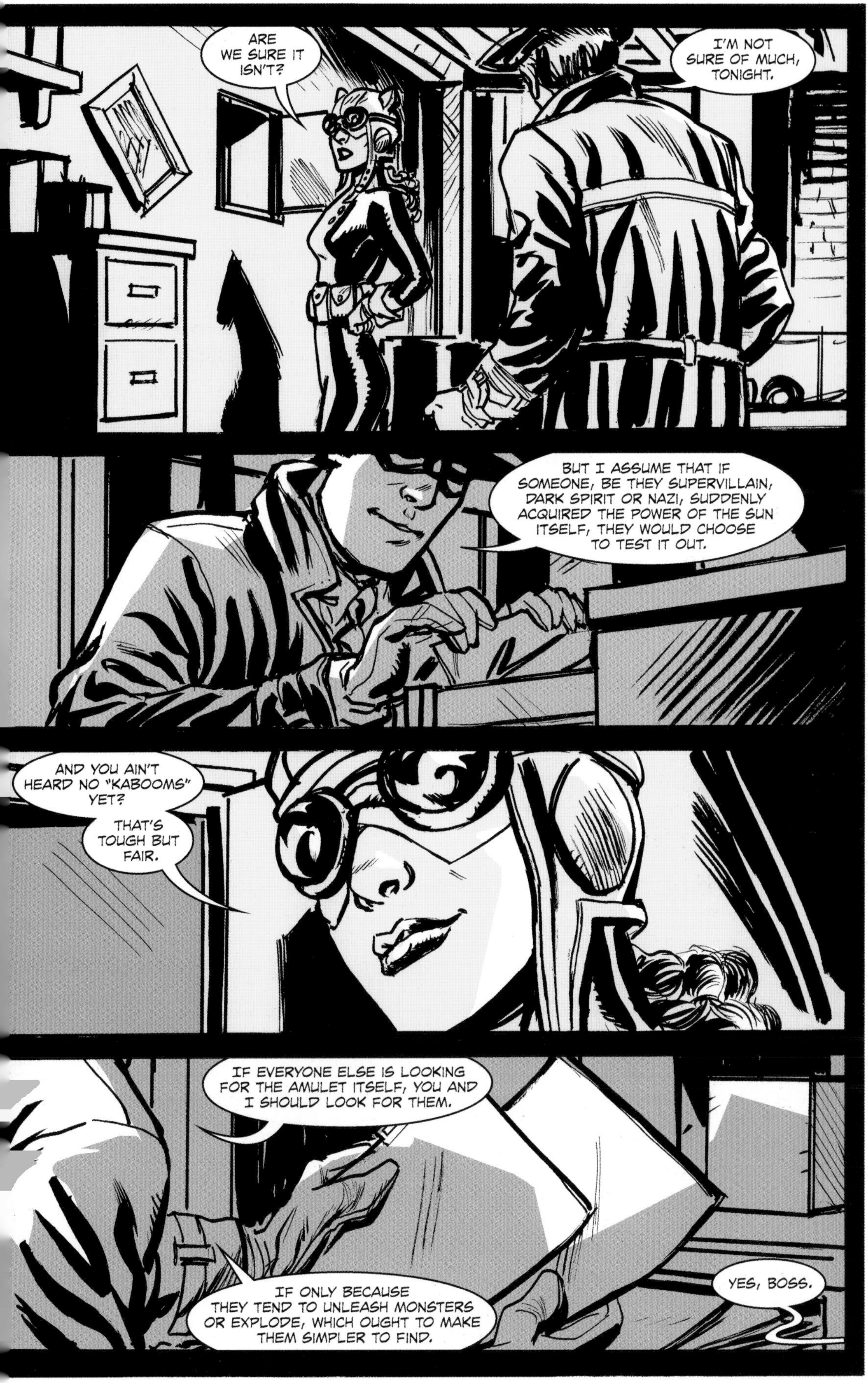
ARE WE SURE IT ISN'T?
I'M NOT SURE OF MUCH, TONIGHT.
BUT I ASSUME THAT IF SOMEONE, BE THEY SUPERVILLAIN, DARK SPIRIT OR NAZI, SUDDENLY ACQUIRED THE POWER OF THE SUN ITSELF, THEY WOULD CHOOSE TO TEST IT OUT.
AND YOU AIN'T HEARD NO "KABOOMS" YET?
THAT'S TOUGH BUT FAIR.
IF EVERYONE ELSE IS LOOKING FOR THE AMULET ITSELF, YOU AND I SHOULD LOOK FOR THEM.
IF ONLY BECAUSE THEY TEND TO UNLEASH MONSTERS OR EXPLODE, WHICH OUGHT TO MAKE THEM SIMPLER TO FIND.
YES, BOSS.

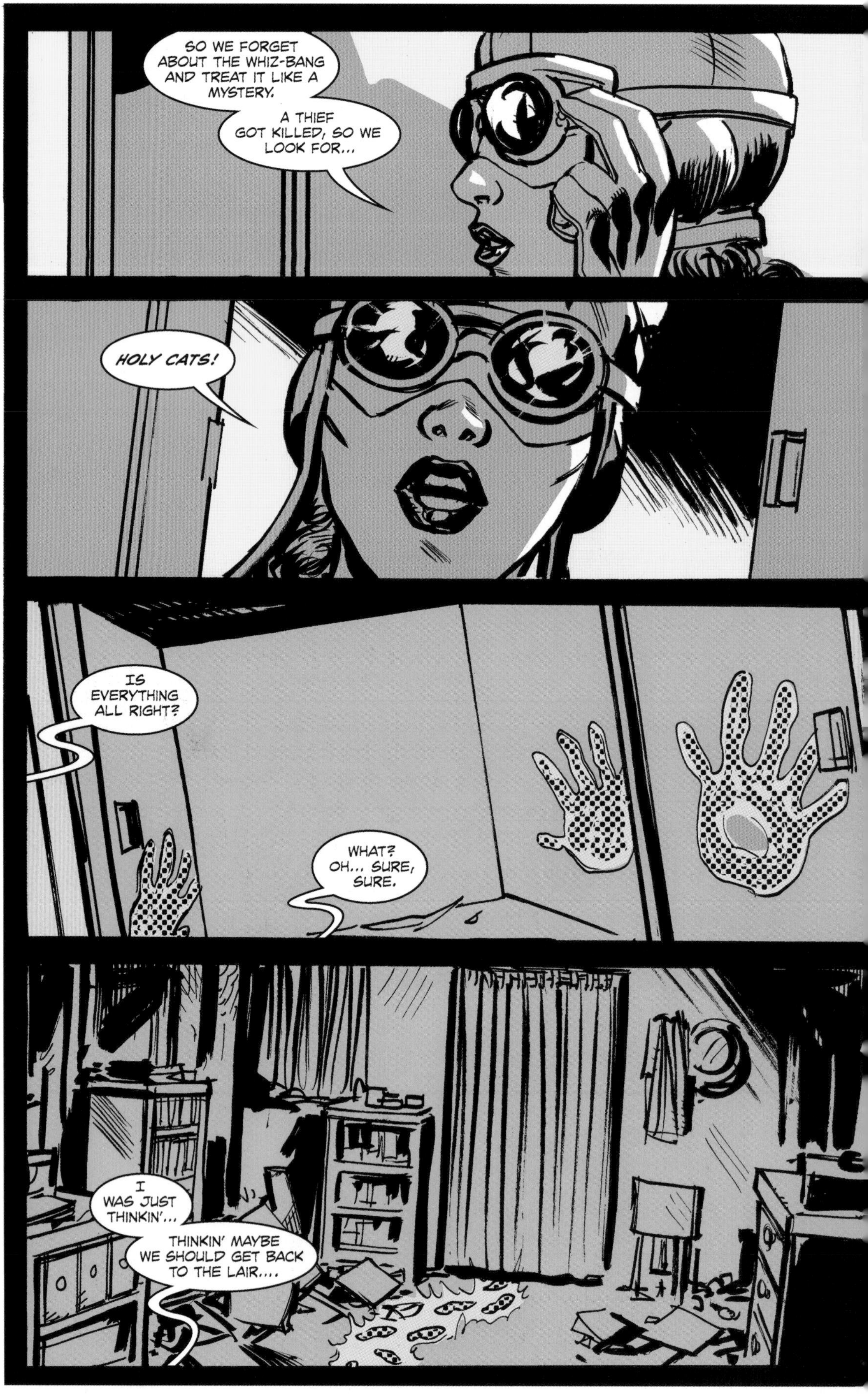
SO WE FORGET ABOUT THE WHIZ-BANG AND TREAT IT LIKE A MYSTERY.
A THIEF GOT KILLED, SO WE LOOK FOR...
HOLY CATS!
IS EVERYTHING ALL RIGHT?
WHAT? OH... SURE, SURE.
I WAS JUST THINKIN'...
THINKIN' MAYBE WE SHOULD GET BACK TO THE LAIR....

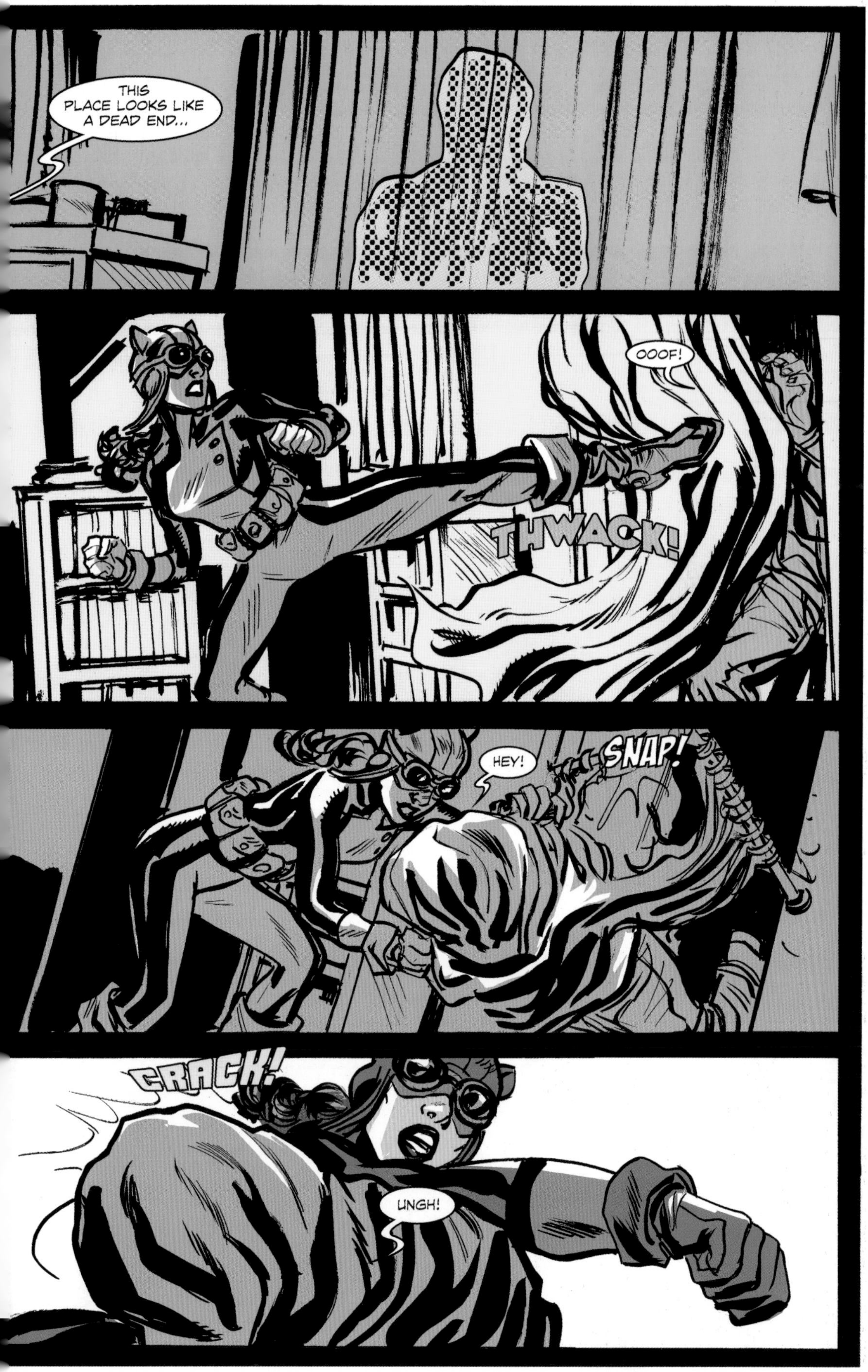
THIS PLACE LOOKS LIKE A DEAD END...
OOOF!
THWACK!
HEY!
SNAP!
CRACK!
UNGH!

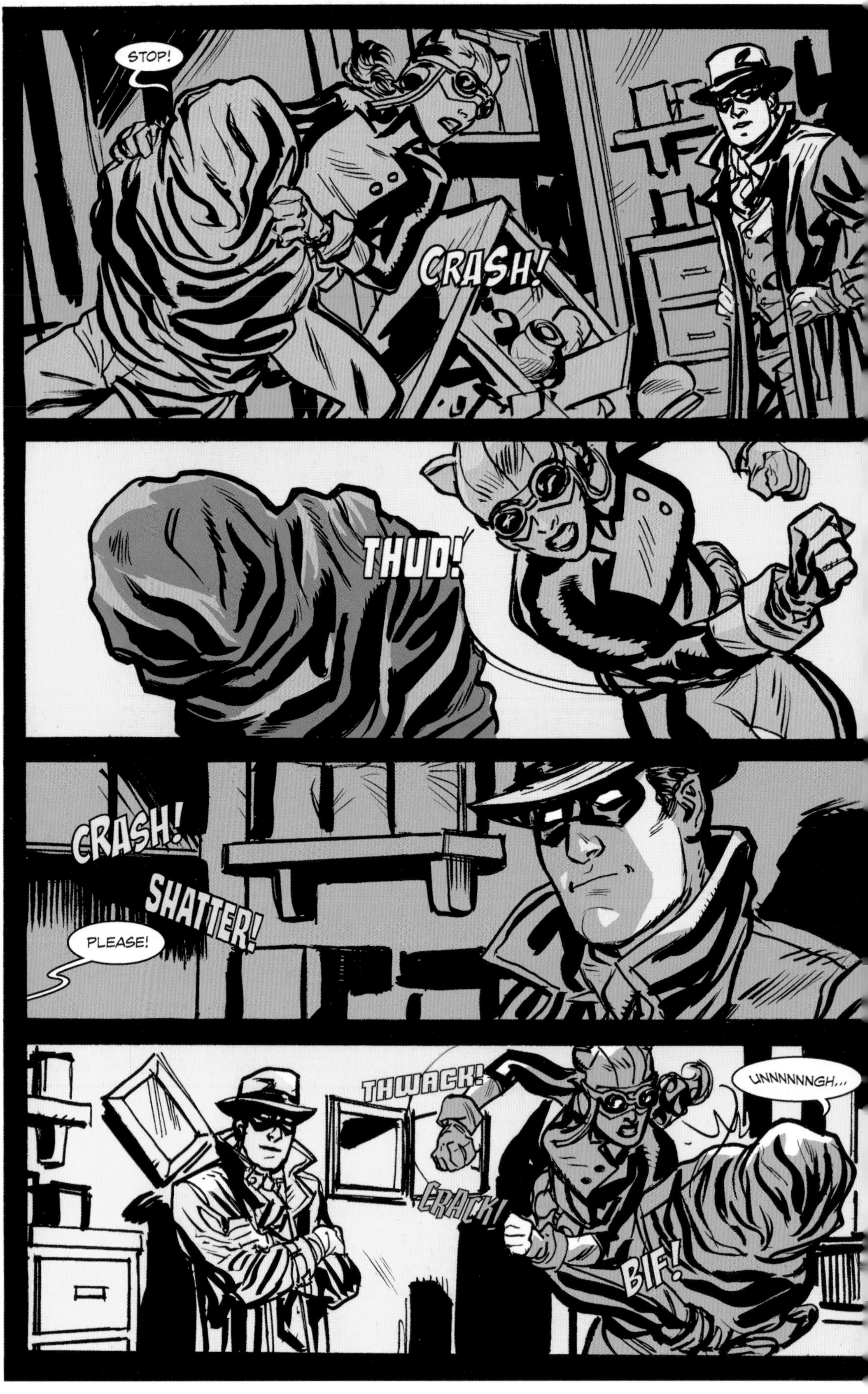
STOP!
CRASH!
THUD!
CRASH!
SHATTER!
PLEASE!
THWACK!
UNNNNNNGH...
CRACK!
BIF!

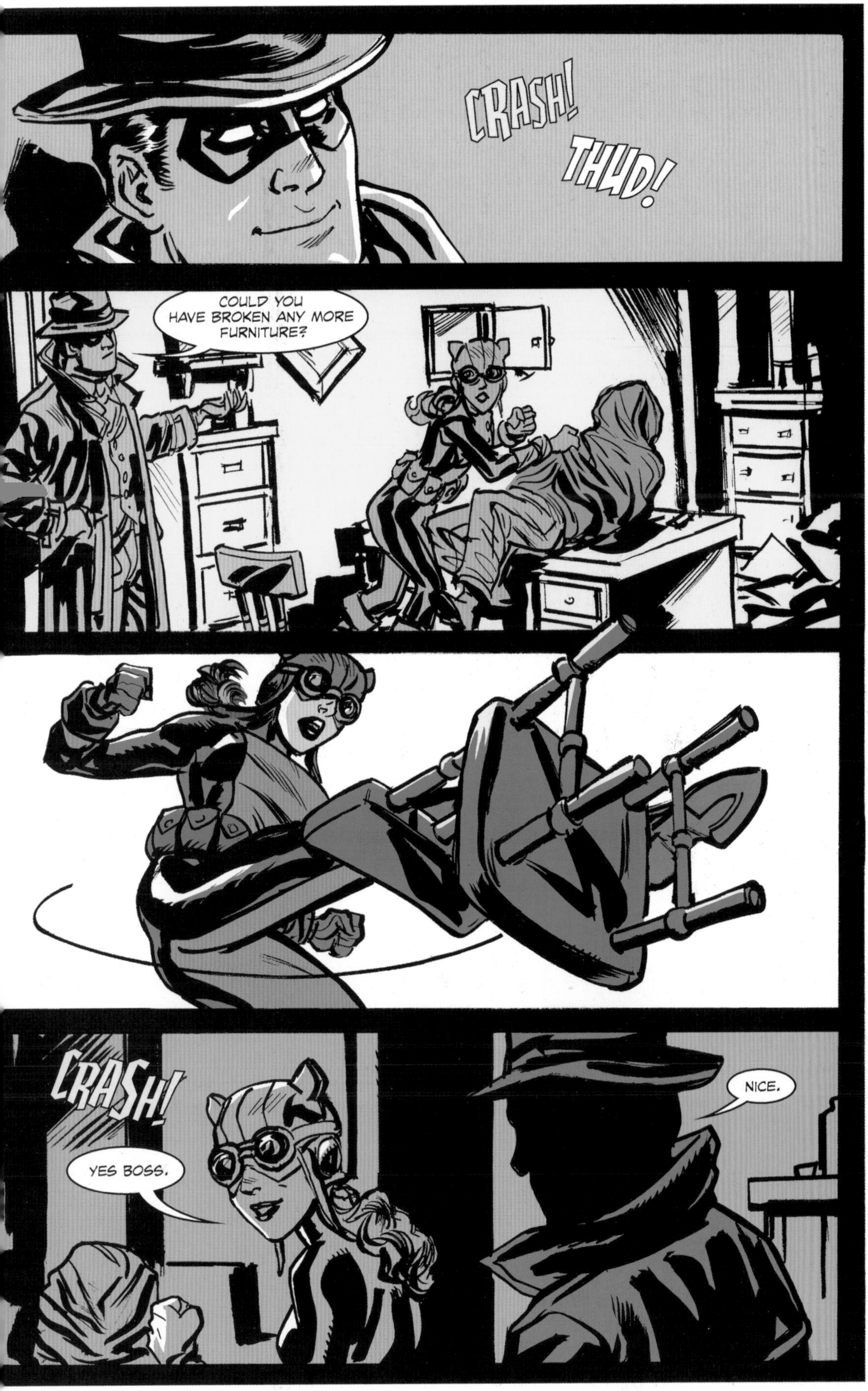
CRASH!
THUD!
COULD YOU HAVE BROKEN ANY MORE FURNITURE?
CRASH!
NICE.
YES BOSS.

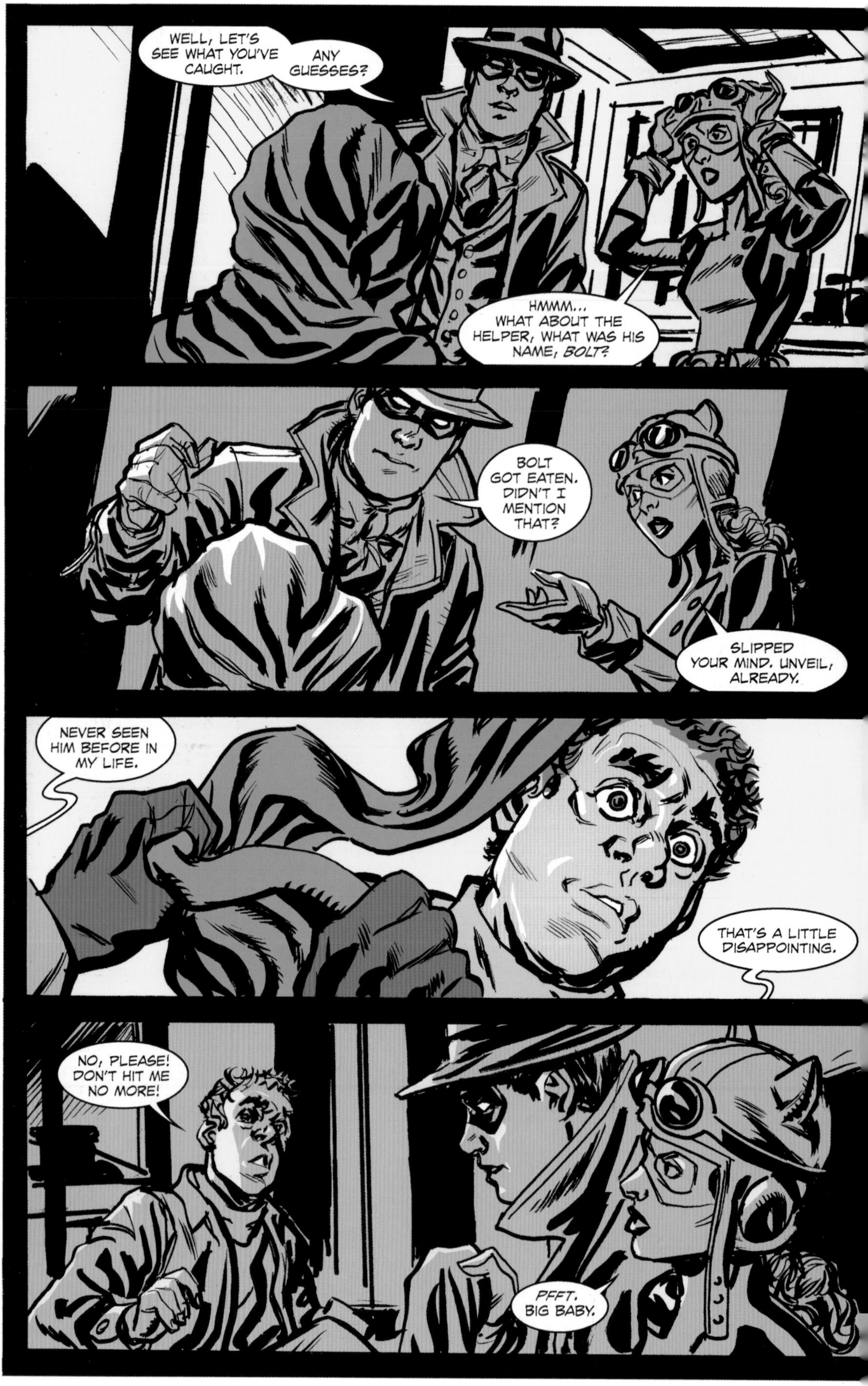
WELL, LET'S SEE WHAT YOU'VE CAUGHT.
ANY GUESSES?
HMMM... WHAT ABOUT THE HELPER, WHAT WAS HIS NAME, *BOLT*?
BOLT GOT EATEN. DIDN'T I MENTION THAT?
SLIPPED YOUR MIND. UNVEIL, ALREADY.
NEVER SEEN HIM BEFORE IN MY LIFE.
THAT'S A LITTLE DISAPPOINTING.
NO, PLEASE! DON'T HIT ME NO MORE!
PFFT. BIG BABY.

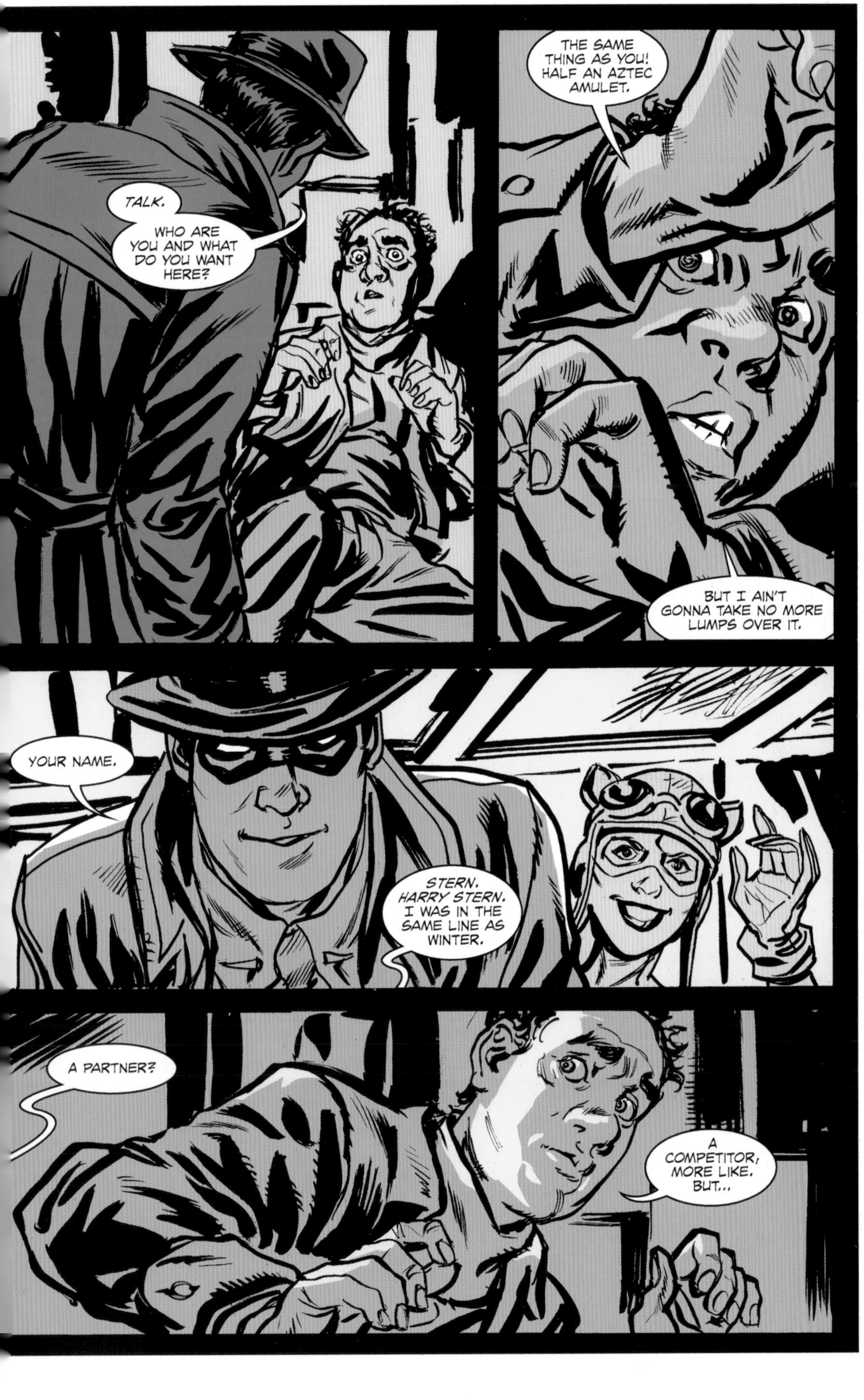

TALK.
WHO ARE YOU AND WHAT DO YOU WANT HERE?
THE SAME THING AS YOU! HALF AN AZTEC AMULET.
BUT I AIN'T GONNA TAKE NO MORE LUMPS OVER IT.
YOUR NAME.
STERN. HARRY STERN. I WAS IN THE SAME LINE AS WINTER.
A PARTNER?
A COMPETITOR, MORE LIKE. BUT...

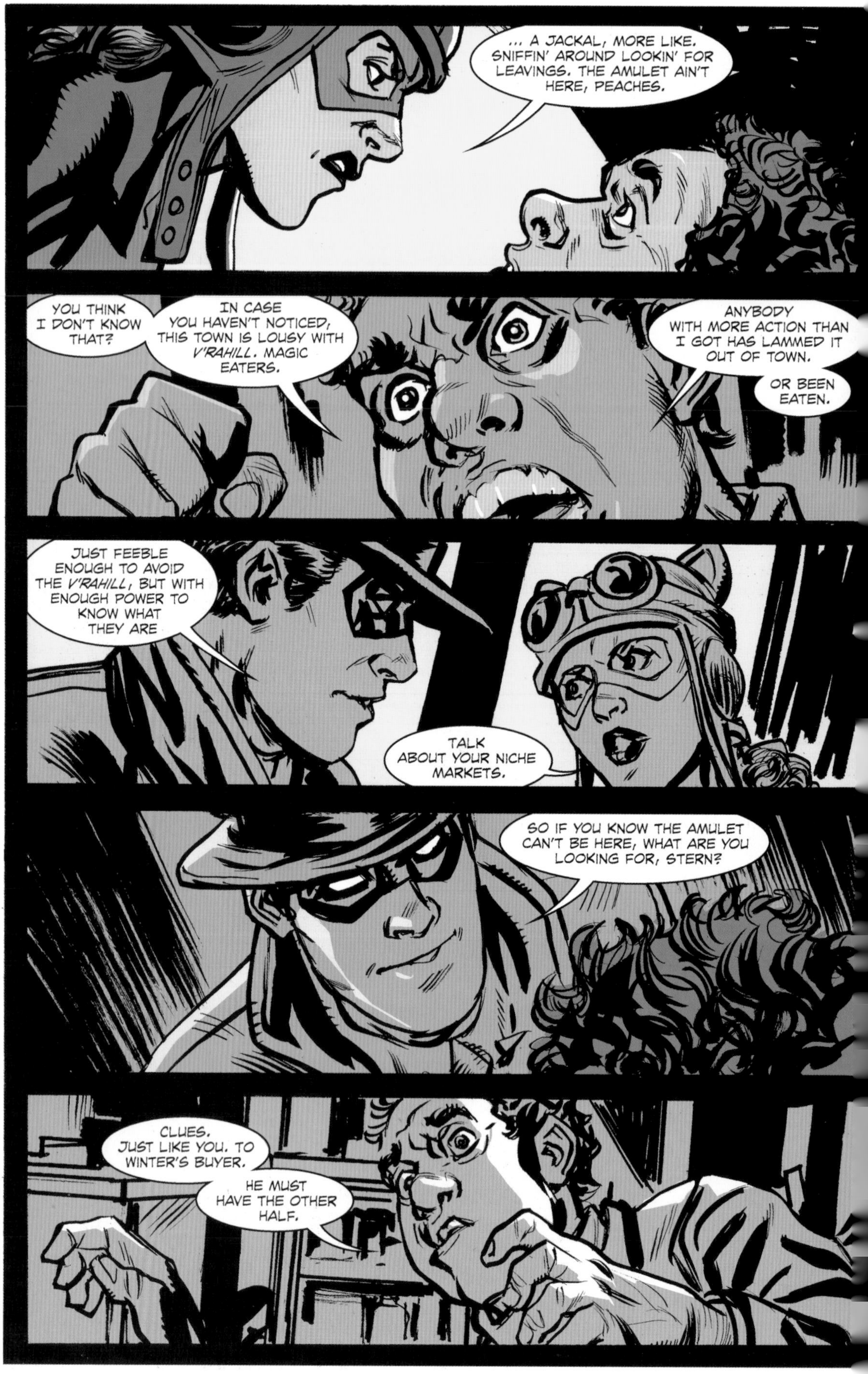
... A JACKAL, MORE LIKE. SNIFFIN' AROUND LOOKIN' FOR LEAVINGS. THE AMULET AIN'T HERE, PEACHES.
YOU THINK I DON'T KNOW THAT?
IN CASE YOU HAVEN'T NOTICED, THIS TOWN IS LOUSY WITH *V'RAHILL*. MAGIC EATERS.
ANYBODY WITH MORE ACTION THAN I GOT HAS LAMMED IT OUT OF TOWN.
OR BEEN EATEN.
JUST FEEBLE ENOUGH TO AVOID THE *V'RAHILL*, BUT WITH ENOUGH POWER TO KNOW WHAT THEY ARE
TALK ABOUT YOUR NICHE MARKETS.
SO IF YOU KNOW THE AMULET CAN'T BE HERE, WHAT ARE YOU LOOKING FOR, STERN?
CLUES. JUST LIKE YOU. TO WINTER'S BUYER.
HE MUST HAVE THE OTHER HALF.

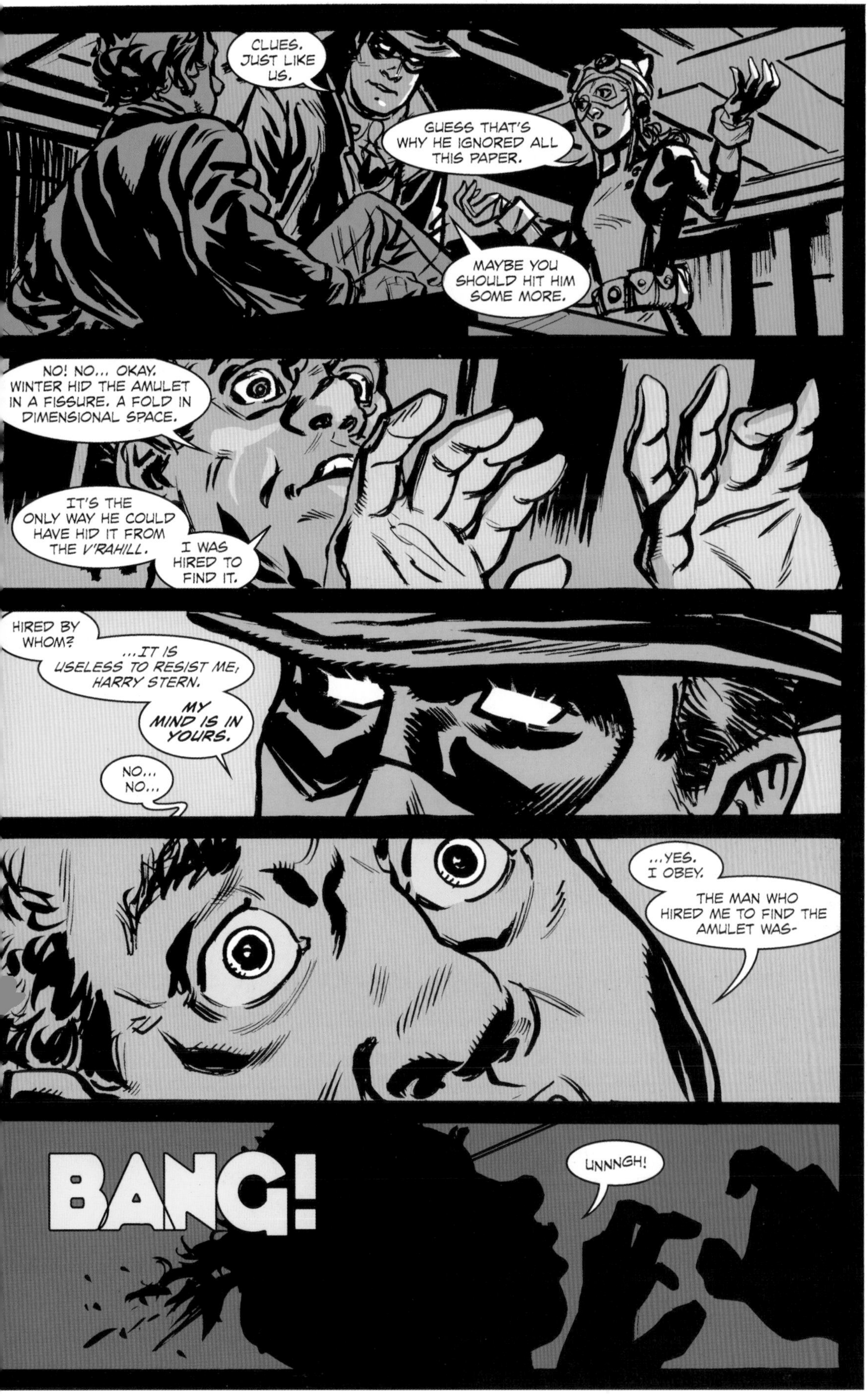
CLUES. JUST LIKE US.
GUESS THAT'S WHY HE IGNORED ALL THIS PAPER.
MAYBE YOU SHOULD HIT HIM SOME MORE.
NO! NO... OKAY. WINTER HID THE AMULET IN A FISSURE. A FOLD IN DIMENSIONAL SPACE.
IT'S THE ONLY WAY HE COULD HAVE HID IT FROM THE *V'RAHILL*.
I WAS HIRED TO FIND IT.
HIRED BY WHOM?
...IT IS USELESS TO RESIST ME, HARRY STERN.
MY MIND IS IN YOURS.
NO... NO...
...YES. I OBEY.
THE MAN WHO HIRED ME TO FIND THE AMULET WAS-
BANG!
UNNNGH!

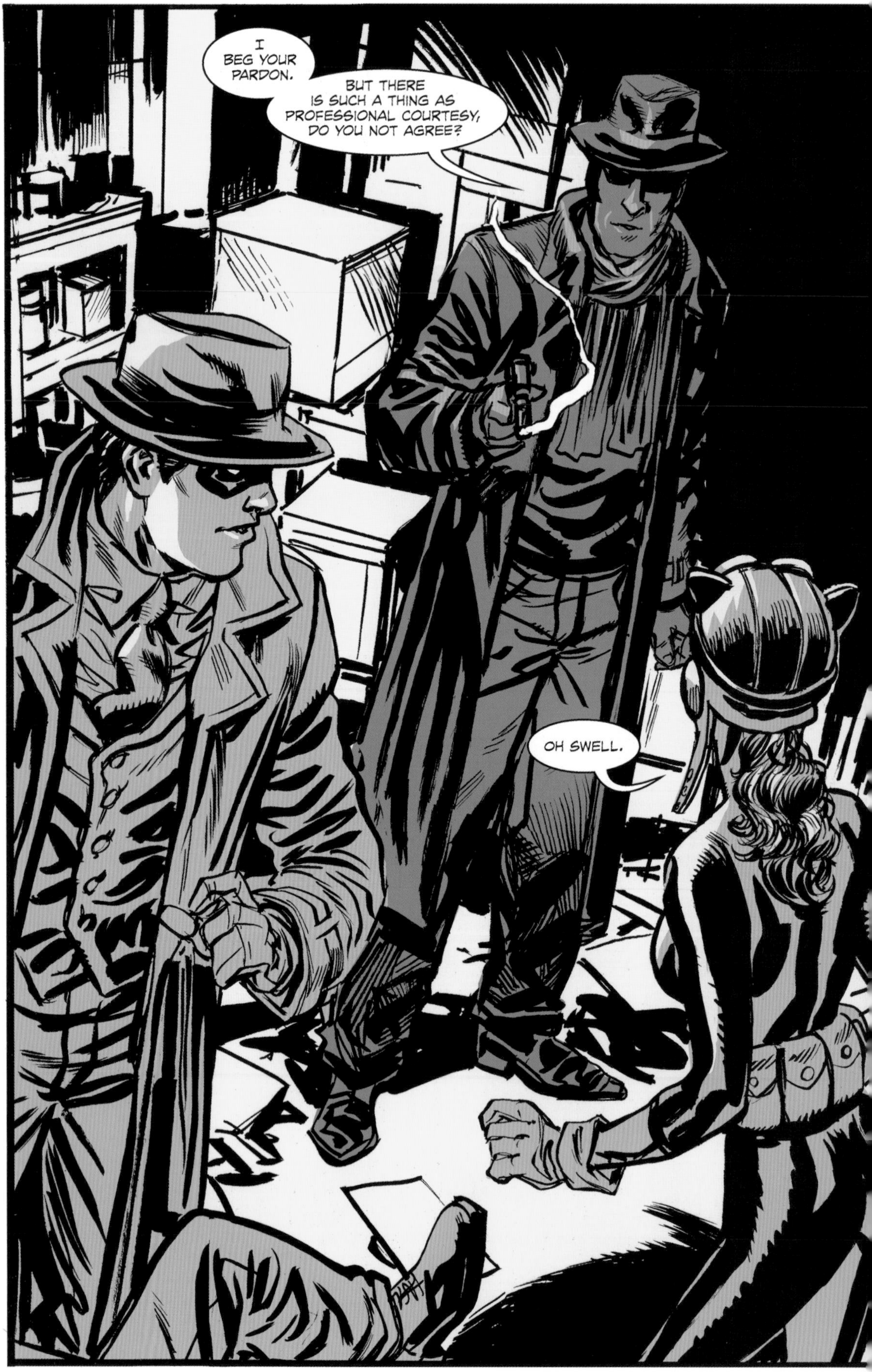
I BEG YOUR PARDON.
BUT THERE IS SUCH A THING AS PROFESSIONAL COURTESY, DO YOU NOT AGREE?
OH SWELL.

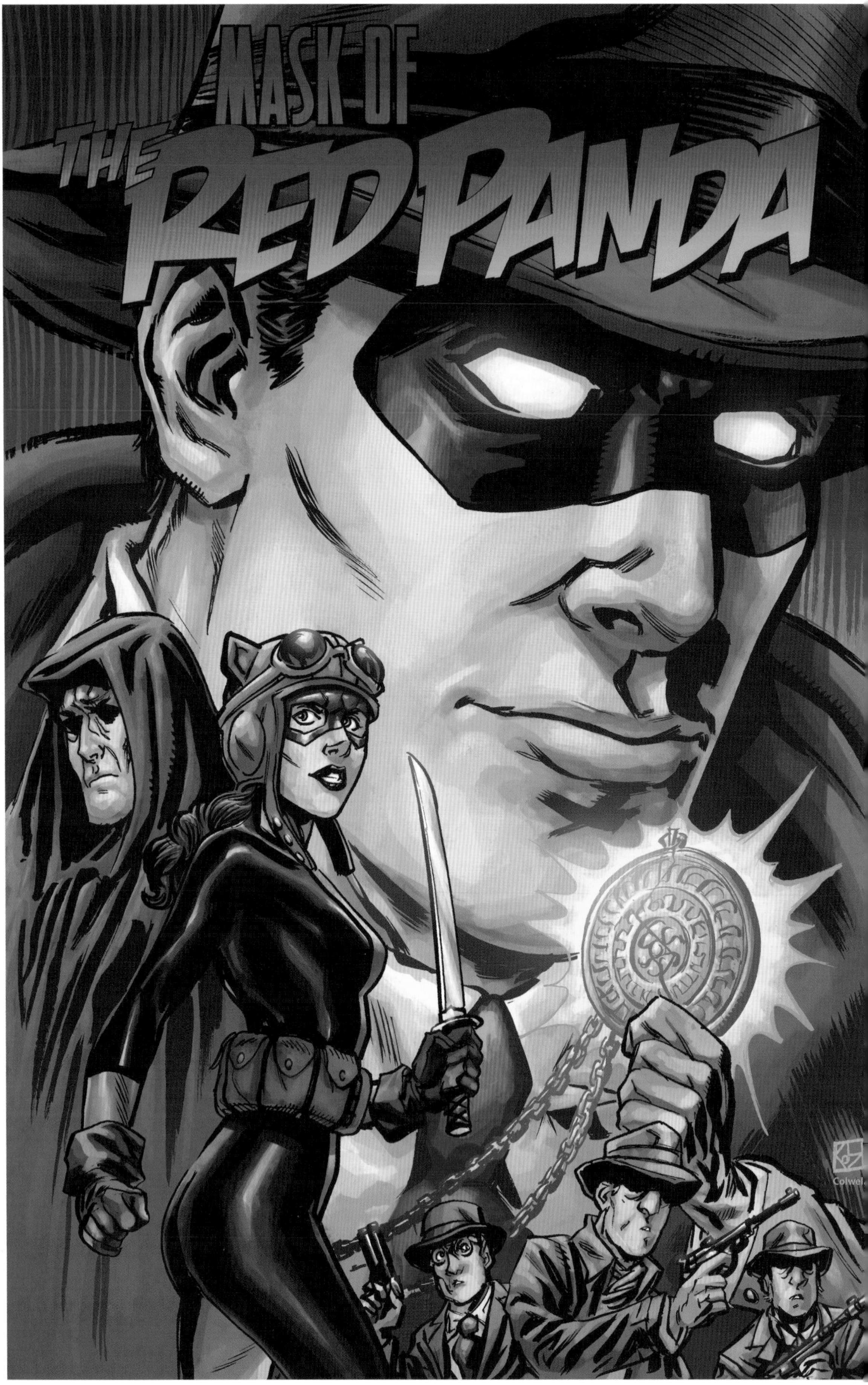
MASK OF
THE RED PANDA

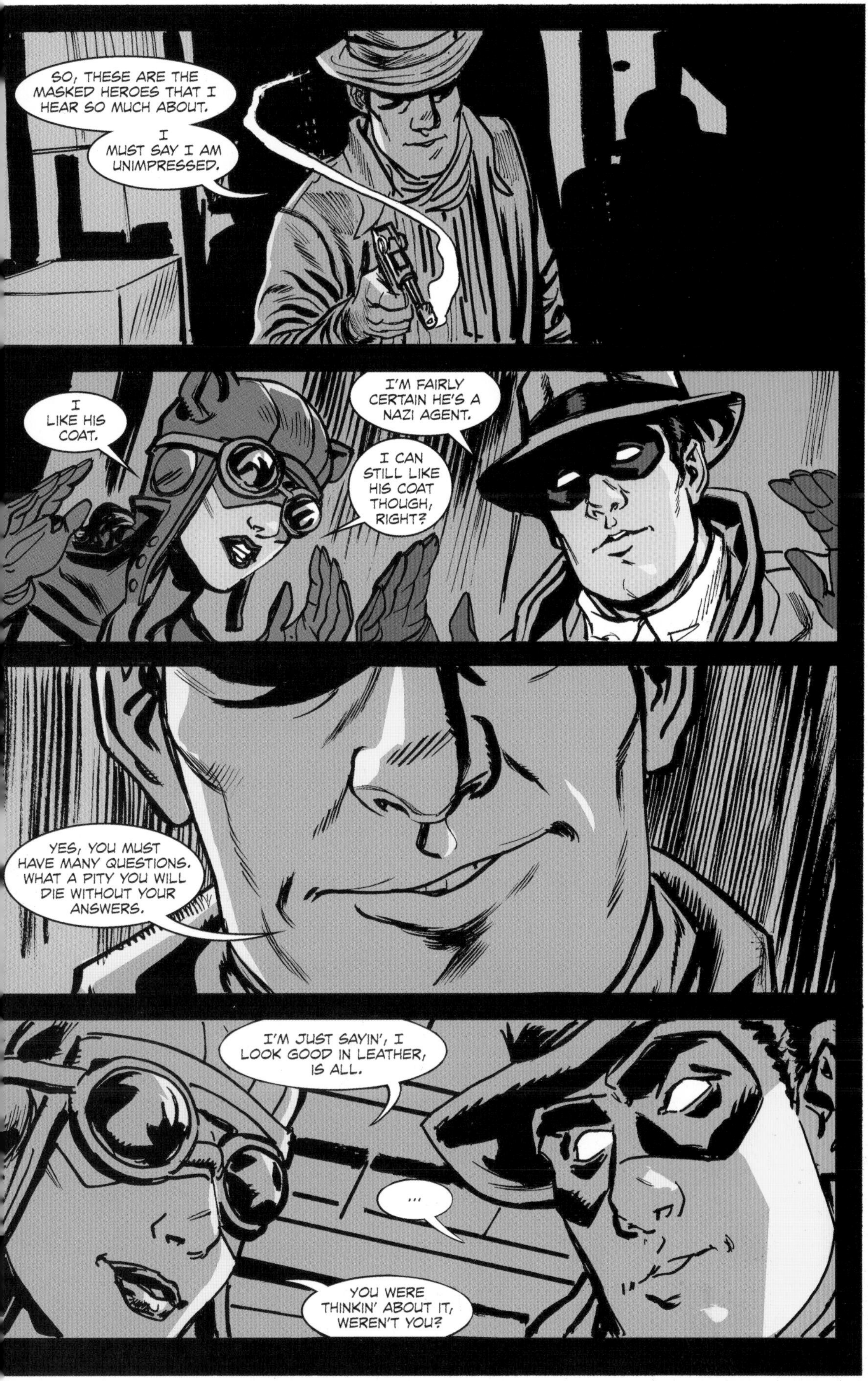

SO, THESE ARE THE MASKED HEROES THAT I HEAR SO MUCH ABOUT.
I MUST SAY I AM UNIMPRESSED.
I LIKE HIS COAT.
I'M FAIRLY CERTAIN HE'S A NAZI AGENT.
I CAN STILL LIKE HIS COAT THOUGH, RIGHT?
YES, YOU MUST HAVE MANY QUESTIONS. WHAT A PITY YOU WILL DIE WITHOUT YOUR ANSWERS.
I'M JUST SAYIN', I LOOK GOOD IN LEATHER, IS ALL.
...
YOU WERE THINKIN' ABOUT IT, WEREN'T YOU?

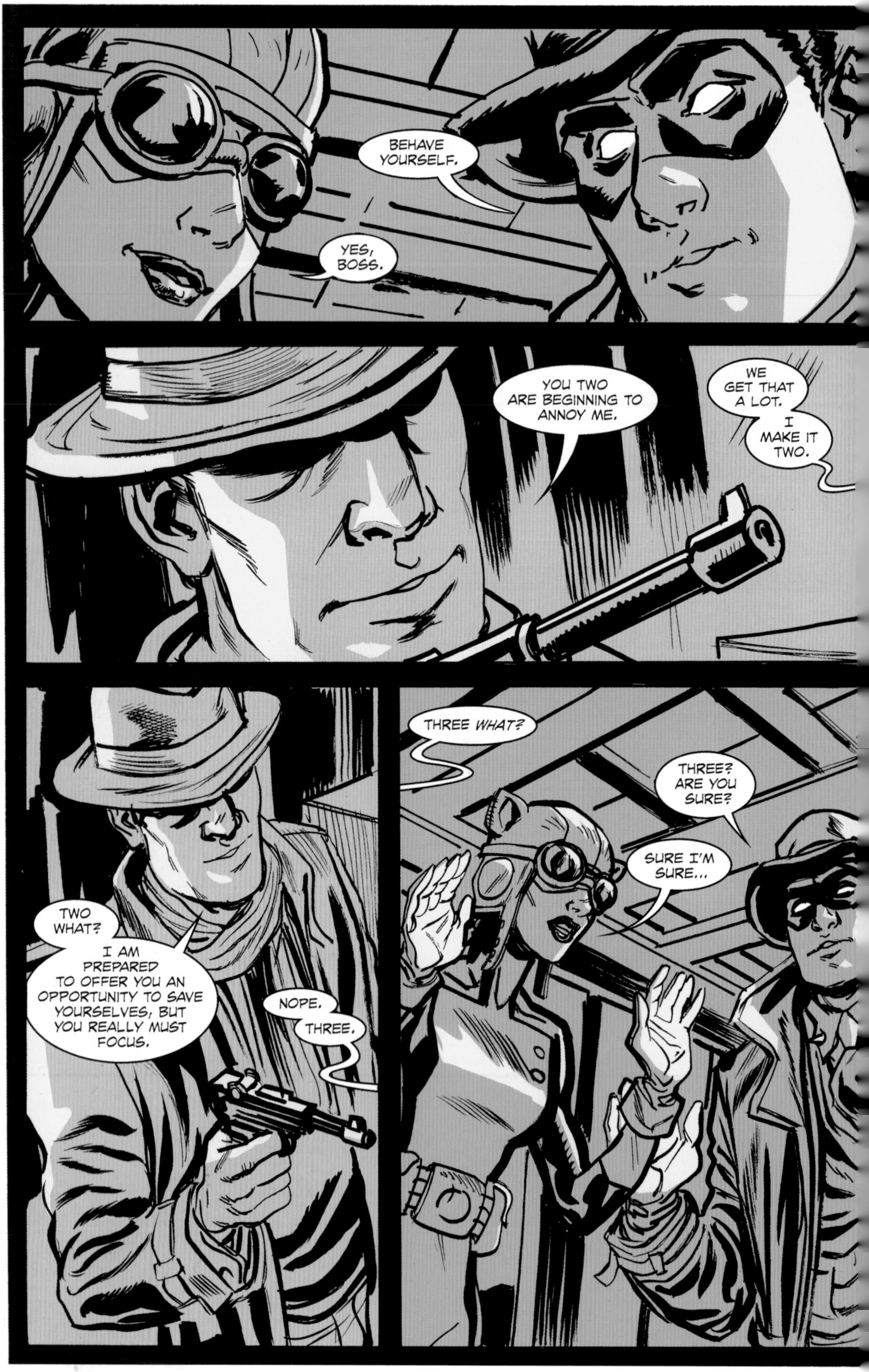

BEHAVE YOURSELF.
YES, BOSS.
YOU TWO ARE BEGINNING TO ANNOY ME.
WE GET THAT A LOT.
I MAKE IT TWO.
TWO WHAT?
I AM PREPARED TO OFFER YOU AN OPPORTUNITY TO SAVE YOURSELVES, BUT YOU REALLY MUST FOCUS.
NOPE.
THREE.
THREE *WHAT?*
THREE? ARE YOU SURE?
SURE I'M SURE...

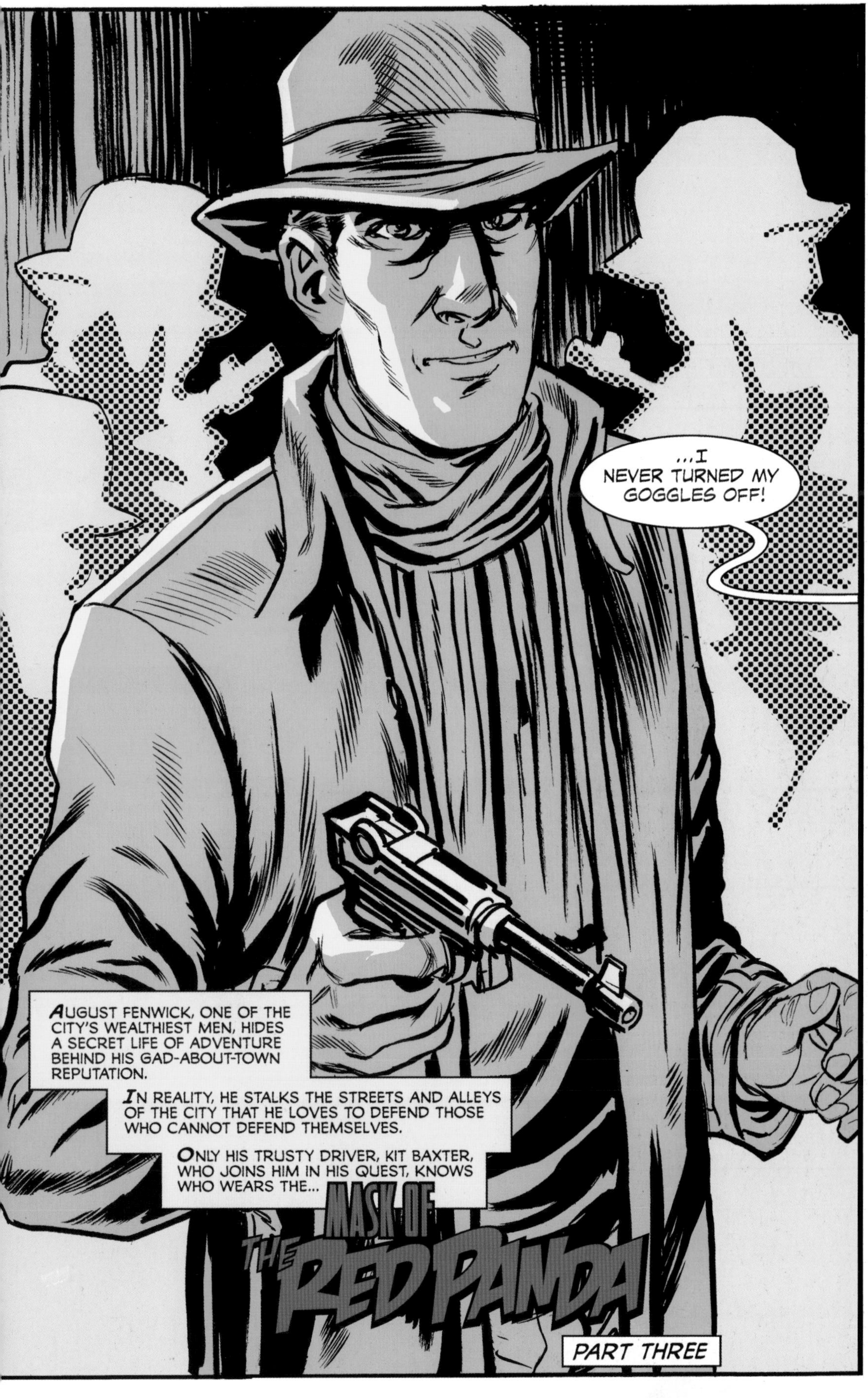

...I NEVER TURNED MY GOGGLES OFF!
AUGUST FENWICK, ONE OF THE CITY'S WEALTHIEST MEN, HIDES A SECRET LIFE OF ADVENTURE BEHIND HIS GAD-ABOUT-TOWN REPUTATION.
IN REALITY, HE STALKS THE STREETS AND ALLEYS OF THE CITY THAT HE LOVES TO DEFEND THOSE WHO CANNOT DEFEND THEMSELVES.
ONLY HIS TRUSTY DRIVER, KIT BAXTER, WHO JOINS HIM IN HIS QUEST, KNOWS WHO WEARS THE...
MASK OF THE RED PANDA
PART THREE

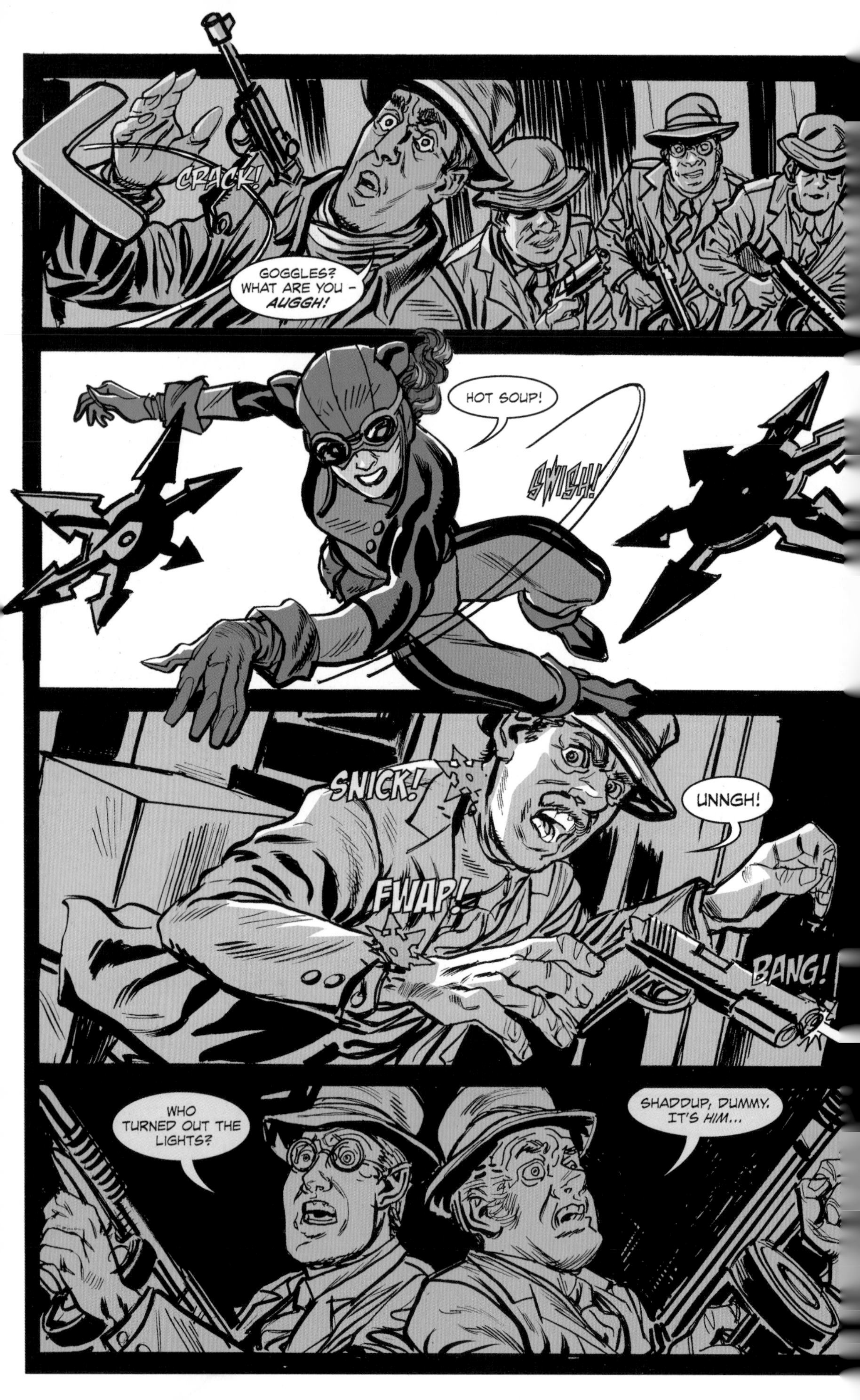
CRACK!
GOGGLES? WHAT ARE YOU - AUGGH!
HOT SOUP!
SWISH!
SNICK!
UNNGH!
FWAP!
BANG!
WHO TURNED OUT THE LIGHTS?
SHADDUP, DUMMY. IT'S HIM...

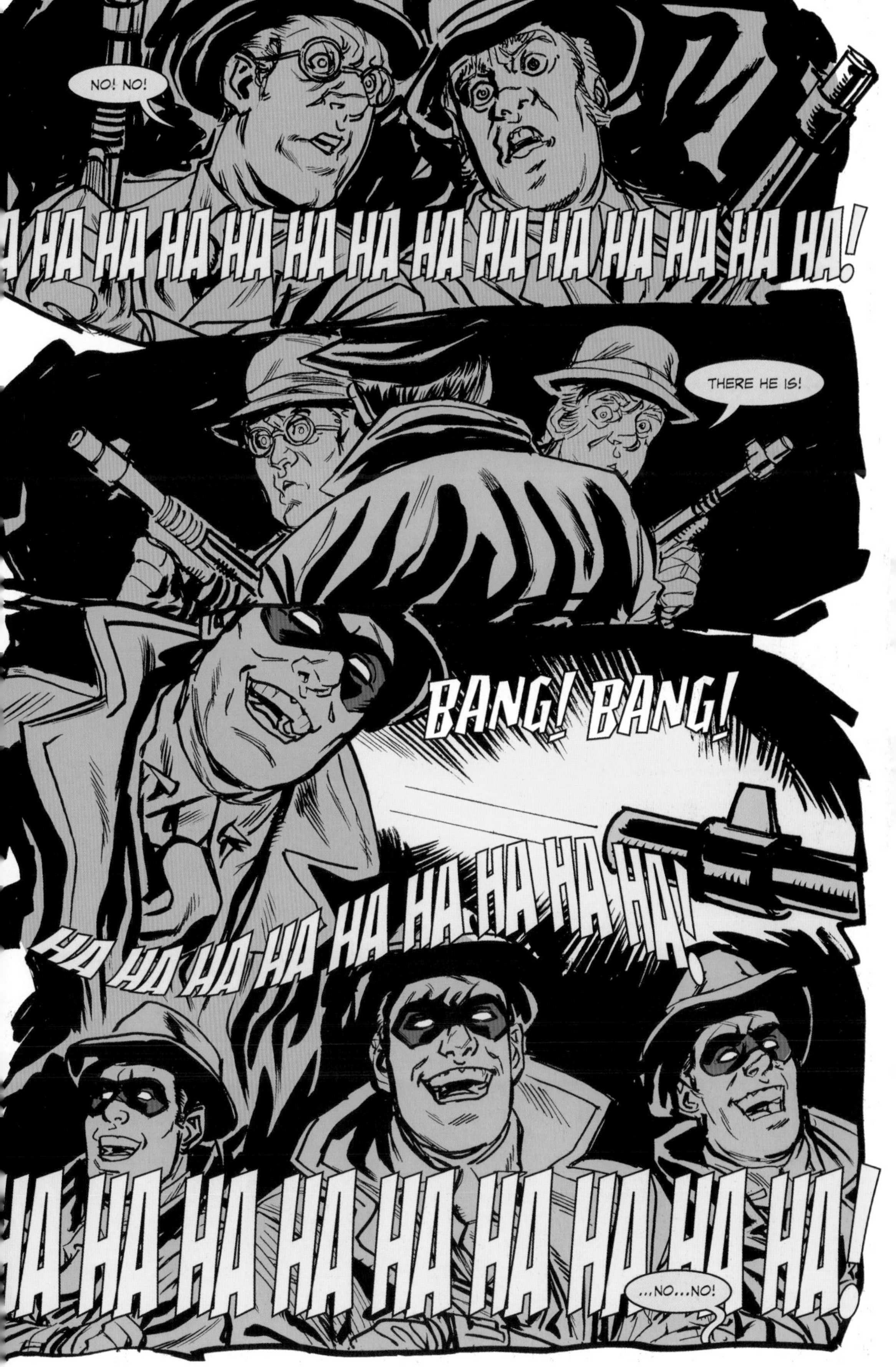
NO! NO!
HA HA HA HA HA HA HA HA HA HA HA HA HA!
THERE HE IS!
BANG! BANG!
HA HA HA HA HA HA HA HA HA HA!
HA HA HA HA HA HA HA HA HA HA HA HA!
...NO...NO!

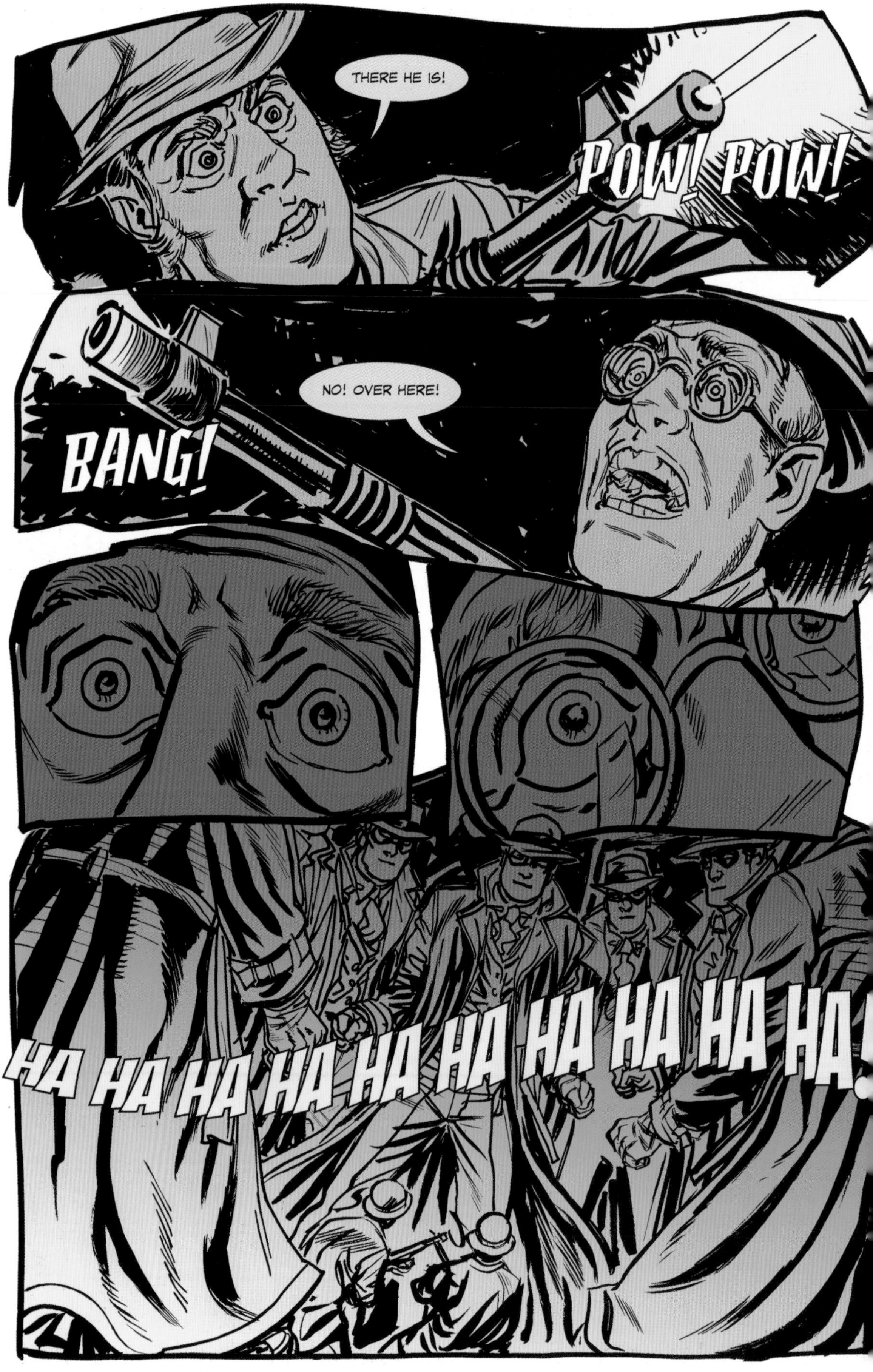
THERE HE IS!
POW! POW!
NO! OVER HERE!
BANG!
HA HA HA HA HA HA HA HA HA HA

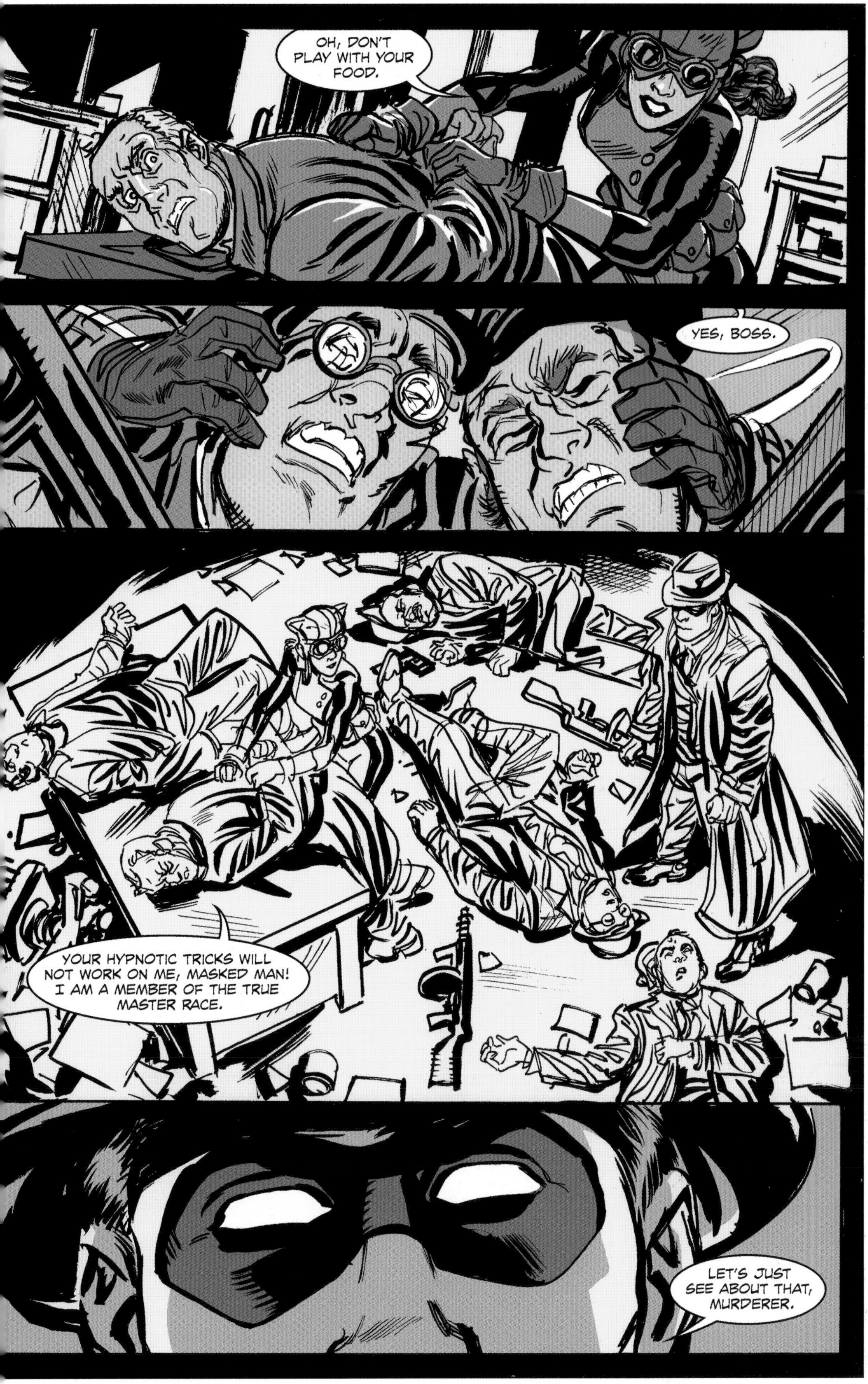
OH, DON'T PLAY WITH YOUR FOOD.
YES, BOSS.
YOUR HYPNOTIC TRICKS WILL NOT WORK ON ME, MASKED MAN! I AM A MEMBER OF THE TRUE MASTER RACE.
LET'S JUST SEE ABOUT THAT, MURDERER.

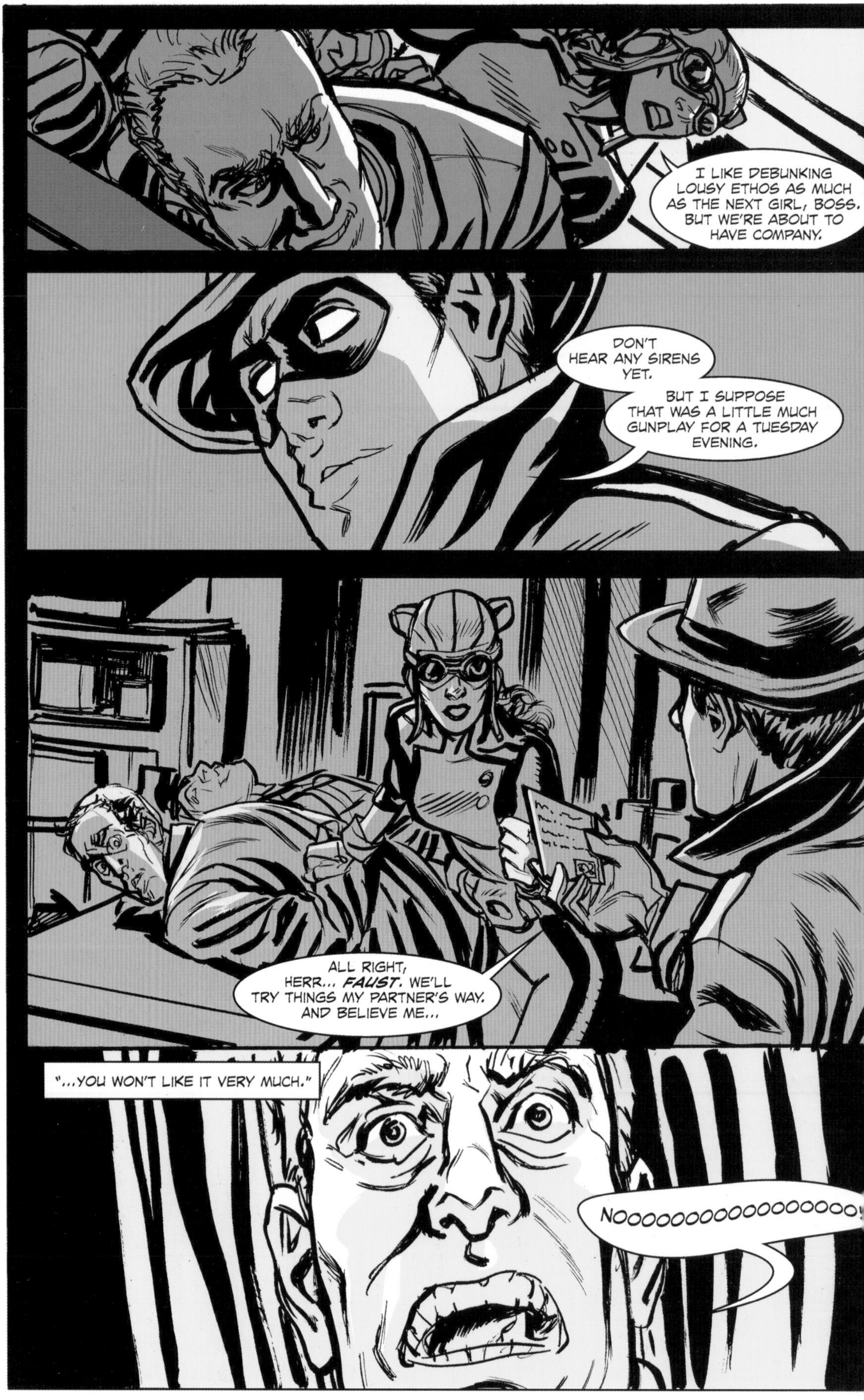
I LIKE DEBUNKING LOUSY ETHOS AS MUCH AS THE NEXT GIRL, BOSS. BUT WE'RE ABOUT TO HAVE COMPANY.
DON'T HEAR ANY SIRENS YET.
BUT I SUPPOSE THAT WAS A LITTLE MUCH GUNPLAY FOR A TUESDAY EVENING.
ALL RIGHT, HERR... FAUST. WE'LL TRY THINGS MY PARTNER'S WAY. AND BELIEVE ME...
"...YOU WON'T LIKE IT VERY MUCH."
NOOOOOOOOOOOOOOOOO!

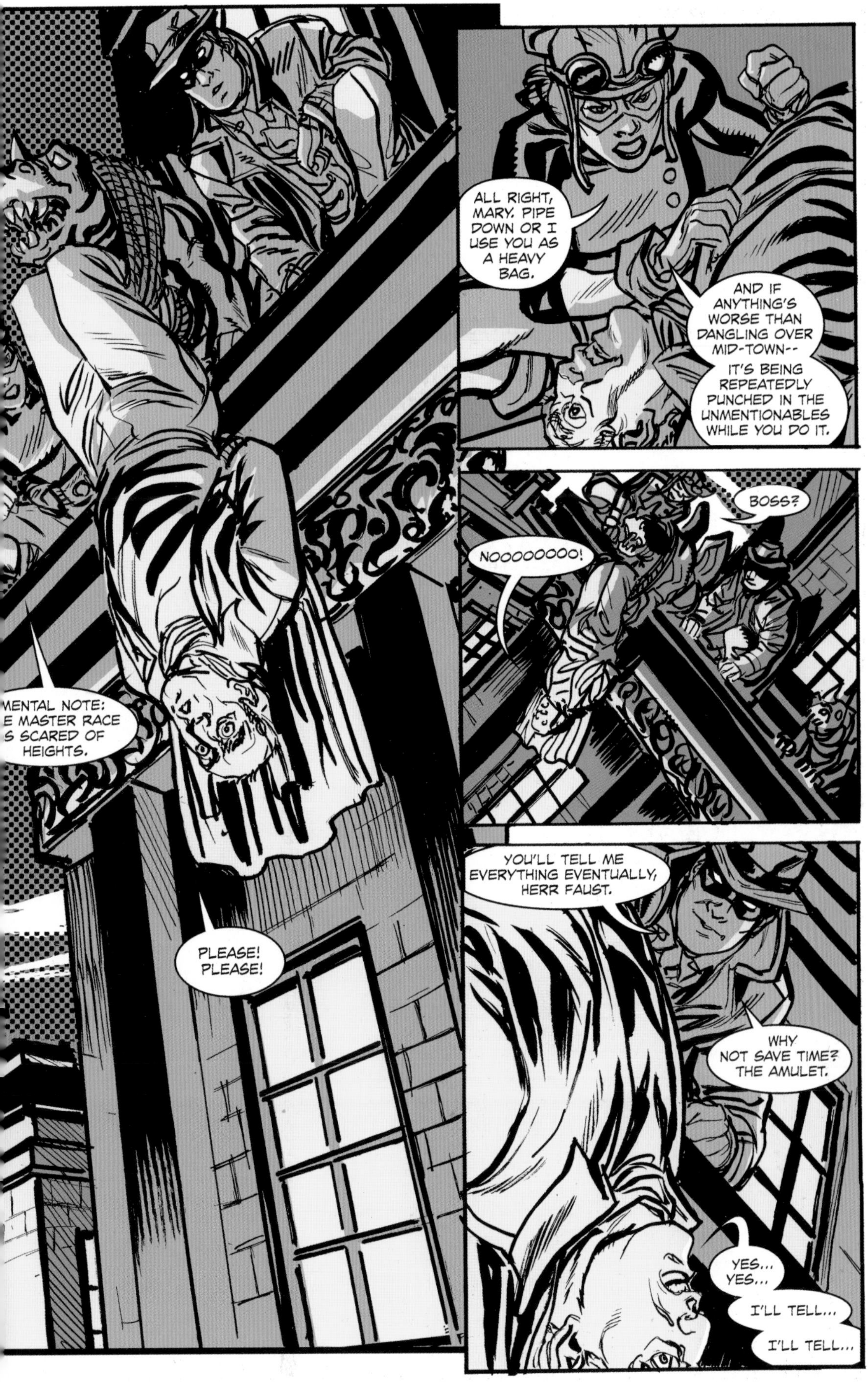
MENTAL NOTE: E MASTER RACE S SCARED OF HEIGHTS.
PLEASE! PLEASE!
ALL RIGHT, MARY. PIPE DOWN OR I USE YOU AS A HEAVY BAG.
AND IF ANYTHING'S WORSE THAN DANGLING OVER MID-TOWN--
IT'S BEING REPEATEDLY PUNCHED IN THE UNMENTIONABLES WHILE YOU DO IT.
BOSS?
NOOOOOOOO!
YOU'LL TELL ME EVERYTHING EVENTUALLY, HERR FAUST.
WHY NOT SAVE TIME? THE AMULET.
YES... YES...
I'LL TELL...
I'LL TELL...

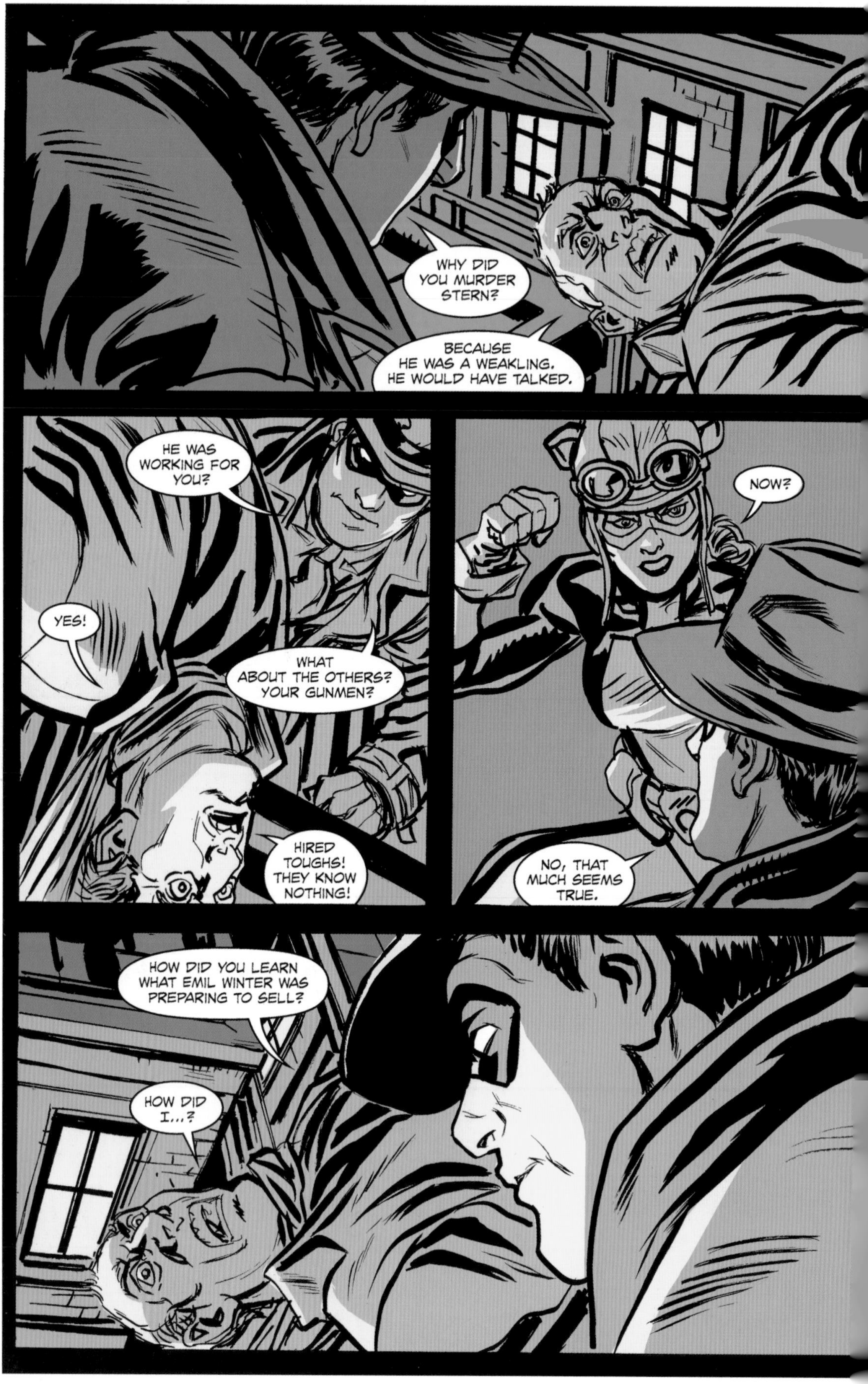
WHY DID YOU MURDER STERN?
BECAUSE HE WAS A WEAKLING. HE WOULD HAVE TALKED.
HE WAS WORKING FOR YOU?
YES!
WHAT ABOUT THE OTHERS? YOUR GUNMEN?
HIRED TOUGHS! THEY KNOW NOTHING!
NOW?
NO, THAT MUCH SEEMS TRUE.
HOW DID YOU LEARN WHAT EMIL WINTER WAS PREPARING TO SELL?
HOW DID I...?

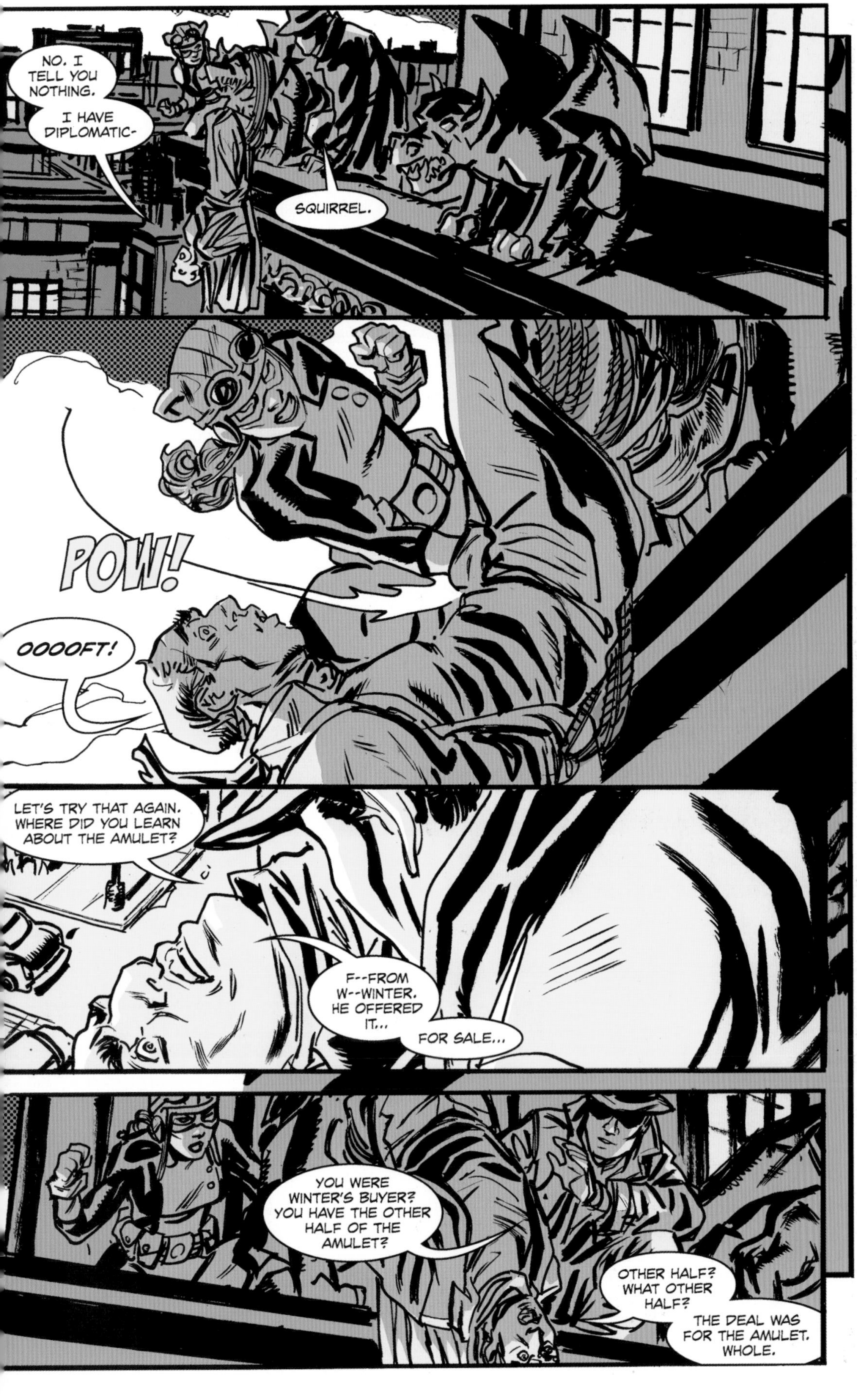
NO. I TELL YOU NOTHING.
I HAVE DIPLOMATIC-
SQUIRREL.
POW!
OOOOFT!
LET'S TRY THAT AGAIN. WHERE DID YOU LEARN ABOUT THE AMULET?
F--FROM W--WINTER. HE OFFERED IT...
FOR SALE...
YOU WERE WINTER'S BUYER? YOU HAVE THE OTHER HALF OF THE AMULET?
OTHER HALF? WHAT OTHER HALF?
THE DEAL WAS FOR THE AMULET. WHOLE.

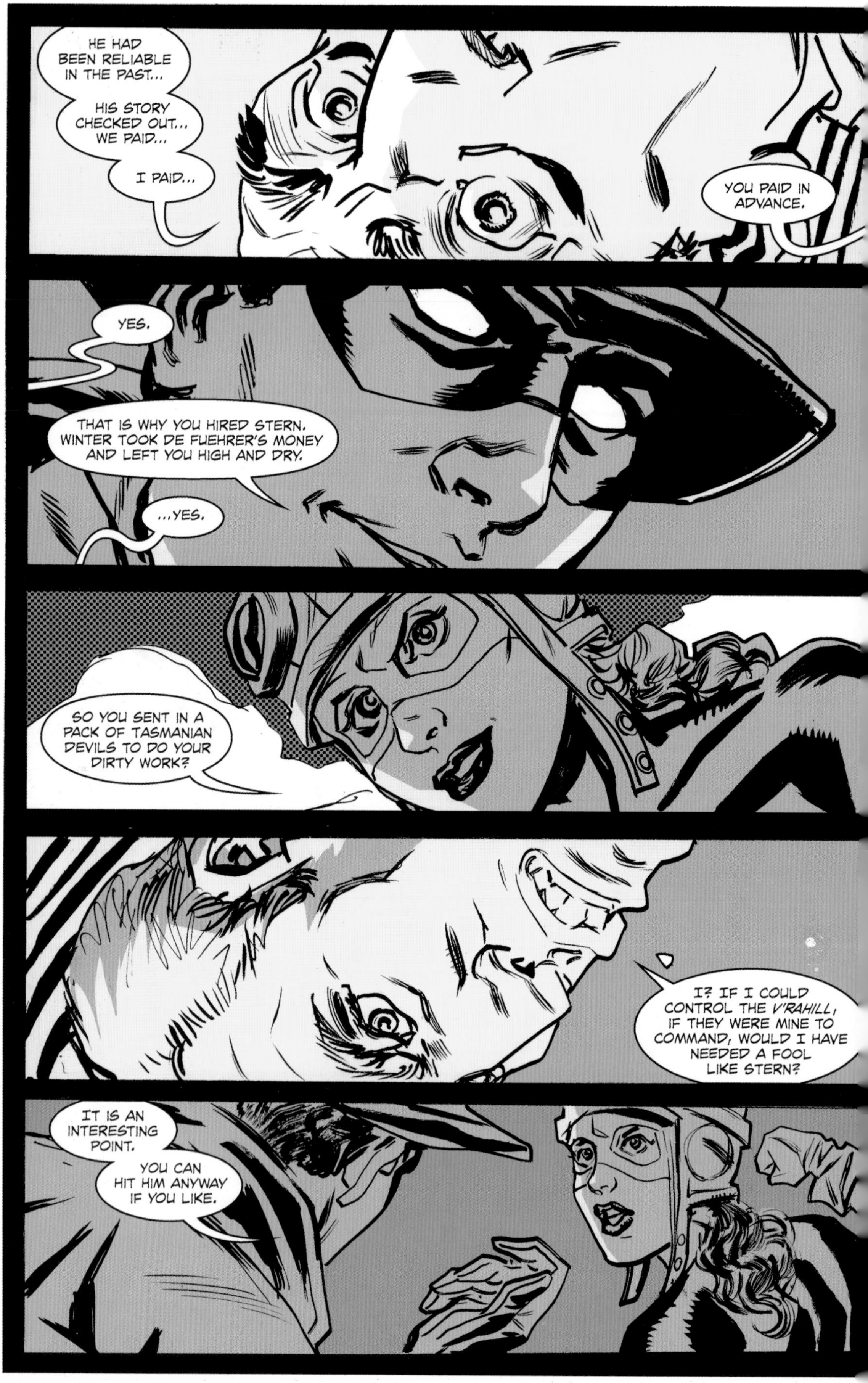
HE HAD BEEN RELIABLE IN THE PAST...
HIS STORY CHECKED OUT... WE PAID...
I PAID...
YOU PAID IN ADVANCE.
YES.
THAT IS WHY YOU HIRED STERN. WINTER TOOK DE FUEHRER'S MONEY AND LEFT YOU HIGH AND DRY.
...YES.
SO YOU SENT IN A PACK OF TASMANIAN DEVILS TO DO YOUR DIRTY WORK?
I? IF I COULD CONTROL THE *V'RAHILL*, IF THEY WERE MINE TO COMMAND, WOULD I HAVE NEEDED A FOOL LIKE STERN?
IT IS AN INTERESTING POINT.
YOU CAN HIT HIM ANYWAY IF YOU LIKE.

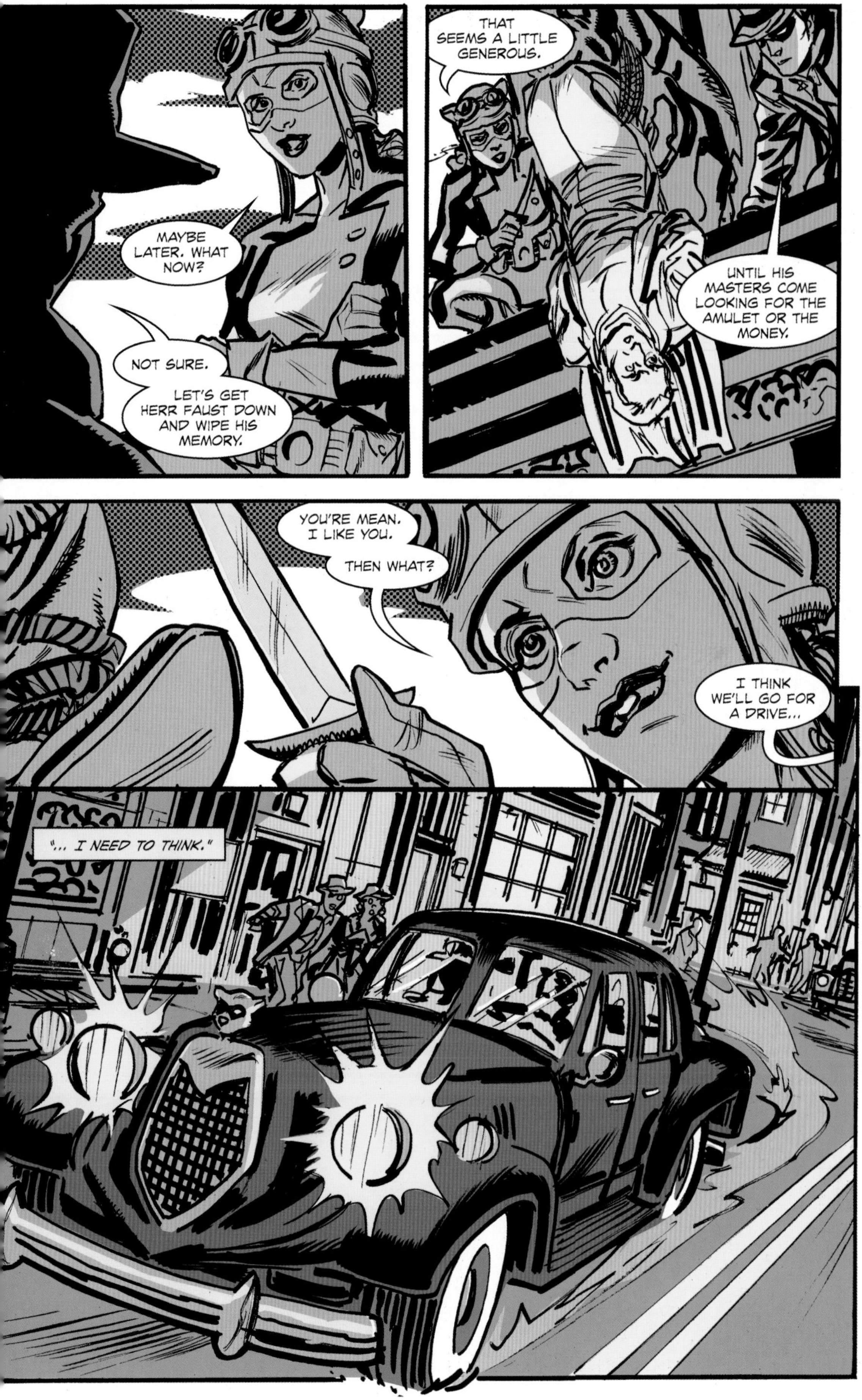
MAYBE LATER. WHAT NOW?
NOT SURE.
LET'S GET HERR FAUST DOWN AND WIPE HIS MEMORY.
THAT SEEMS A LITTLE GENEROUS.
UNTIL HIS MASTERS COME LOOKING FOR THE AMULET OR THE MONEY.
YOU'RE MEAN. I LIKE YOU.
THEN WHAT?
I THINK WE'LL GO FOR A DRIVE...
"... I NEED TO THINK."

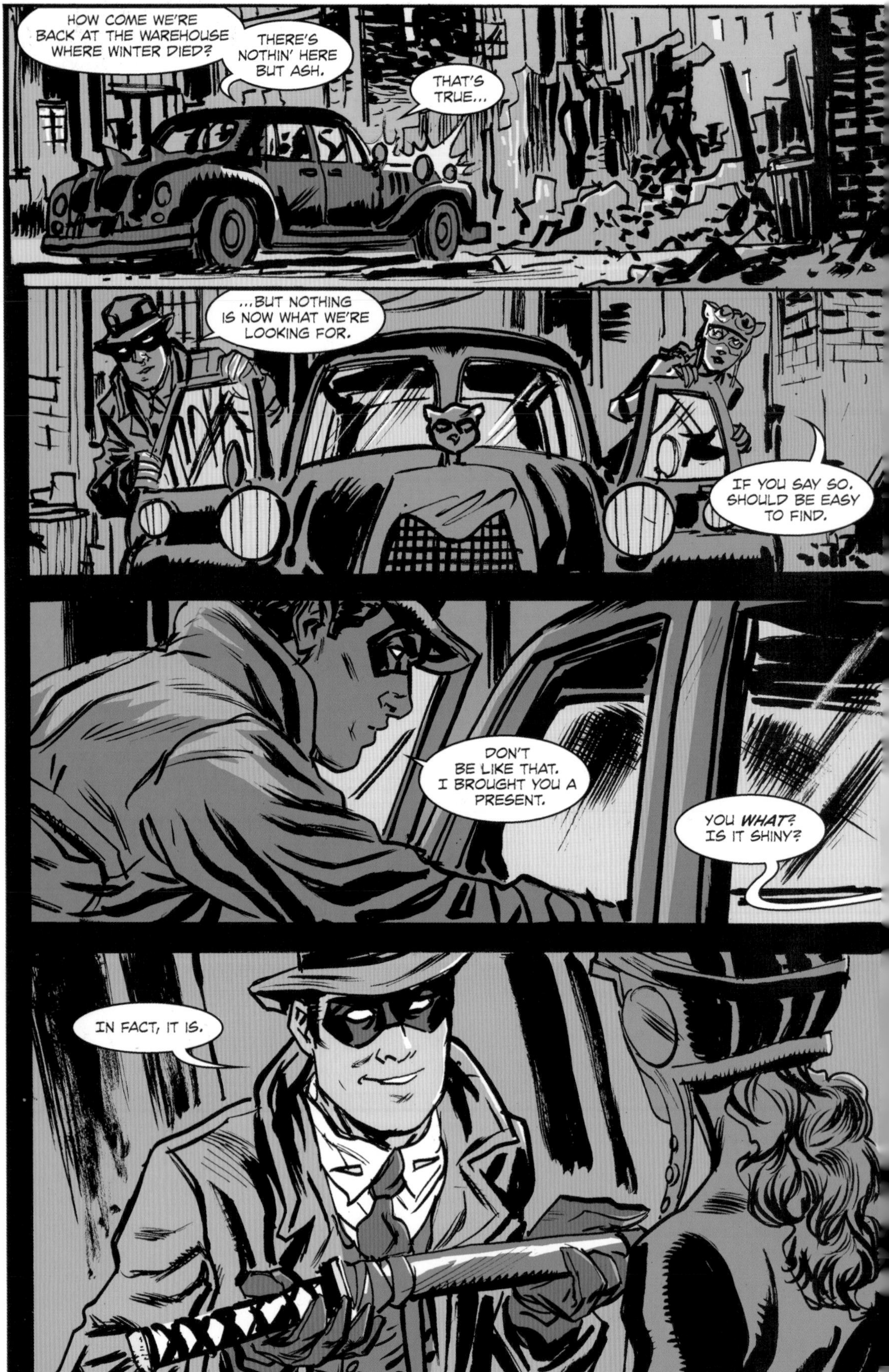
HOW COME WE'RE BACK AT THE WAREHOUSE WHERE WINTER DIED?
THERE'S NOTHIN' HERE BUT ASH.
THAT'S TRUE...
...BUT NOTHING IS NOW WHAT WE'RE LOOKING FOR.
IF YOU SAY SO. SHOULD BE EASY TO FIND.
DON'T BE LIKE THAT. I BROUGHT YOU A PRESENT.
YOU *WHAT*? IS IT SHINY?
IN FACT, IT IS.

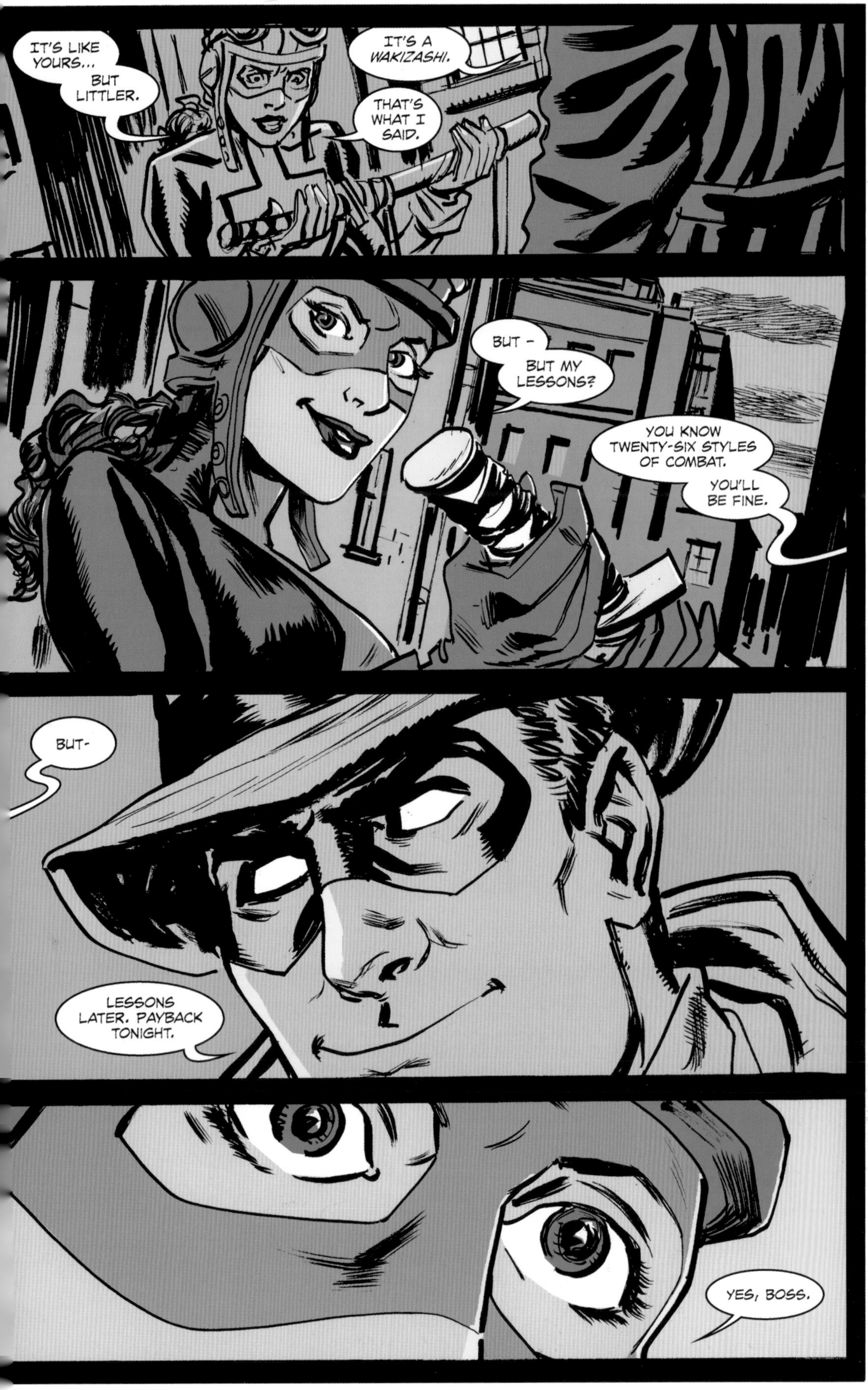
IT'S LIKE YOURS...
BUT LITTLER.
IT'S A *WAKIZASHI*.
THAT'S WHAT I SAID.
BUT -
BUT MY LESSONS?
YOU KNOW TWENTY-SIX STYLES OF COMBAT.
YOU'LL BE FINE.
BUT-
LESSONS LATER. PAYBACK TONIGHT.
YES, BOSS.

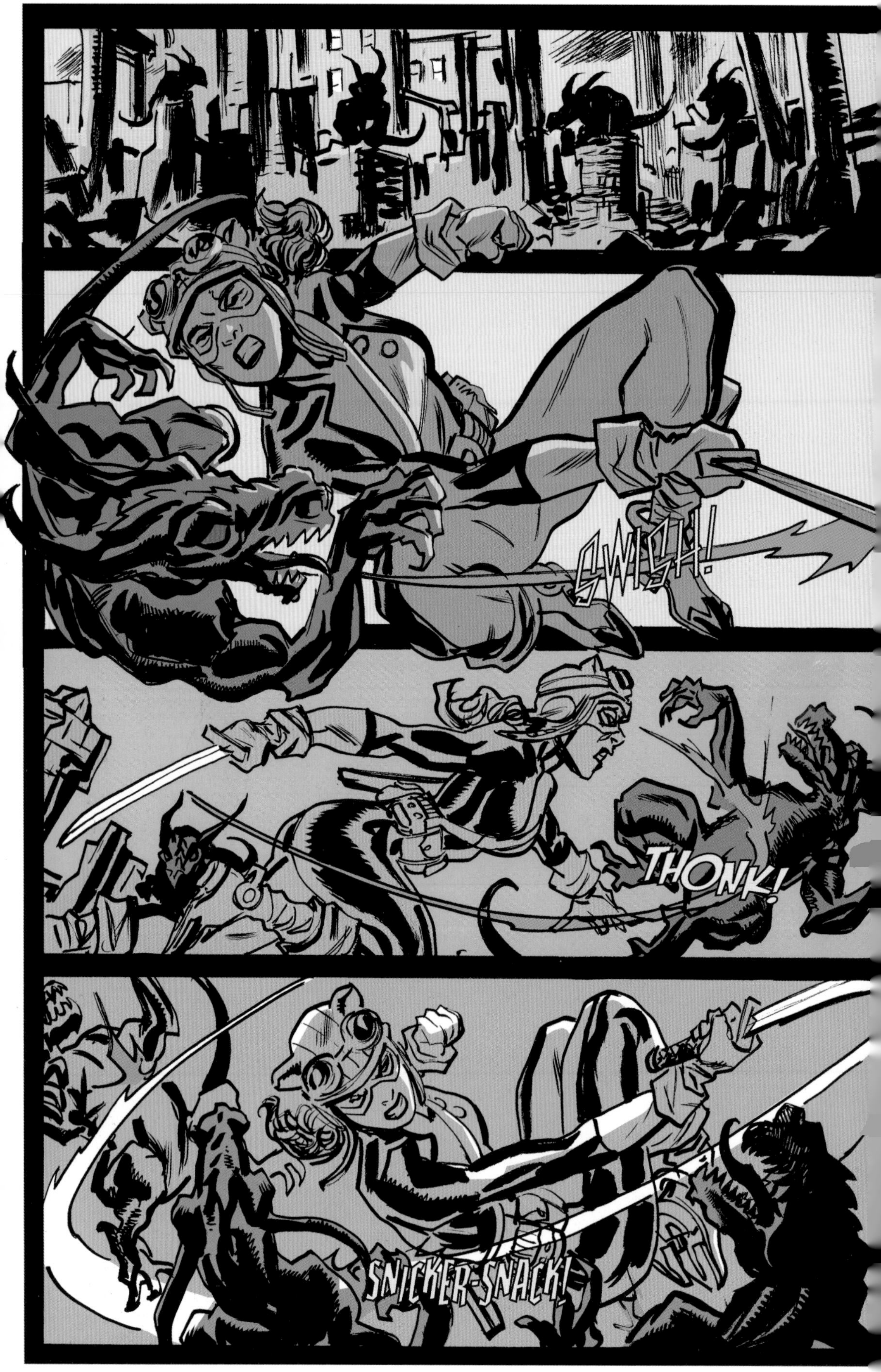
SWISH!
THONK!
SNICKER-SNACK!

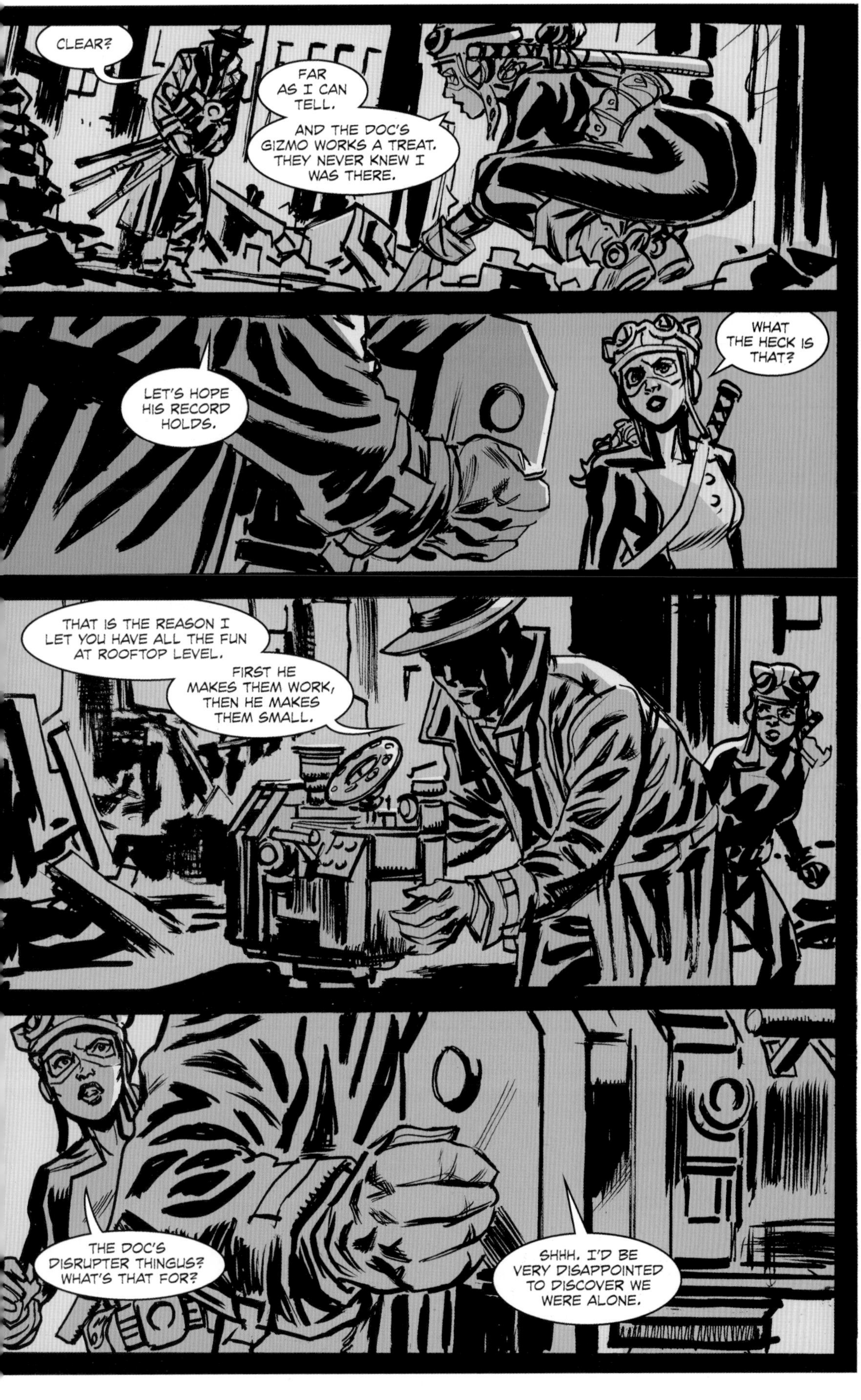
CLEAR?
FAR AS I CAN TELL.
AND THE DOC'S GIZMO WORKS A TREAT. THEY NEVER KNEW I WAS THERE.
WHAT THE HECK IS THAT?
LET'S HOPE HIS RECORD HOLDS.
THAT IS THE REASON I LET YOU HAVE ALL THE FUN AT ROOFTOP LEVEL.
FIRST HE MAKES THEM WORK, THEN HE MAKES THEM SMALL.
THE DOC'S DISRUPTER THINGUS? WHAT'S THAT FOR?
SHHH. I'D BE VERY DISAPPOINTED TO DISCOVER WE WERE ALONE.

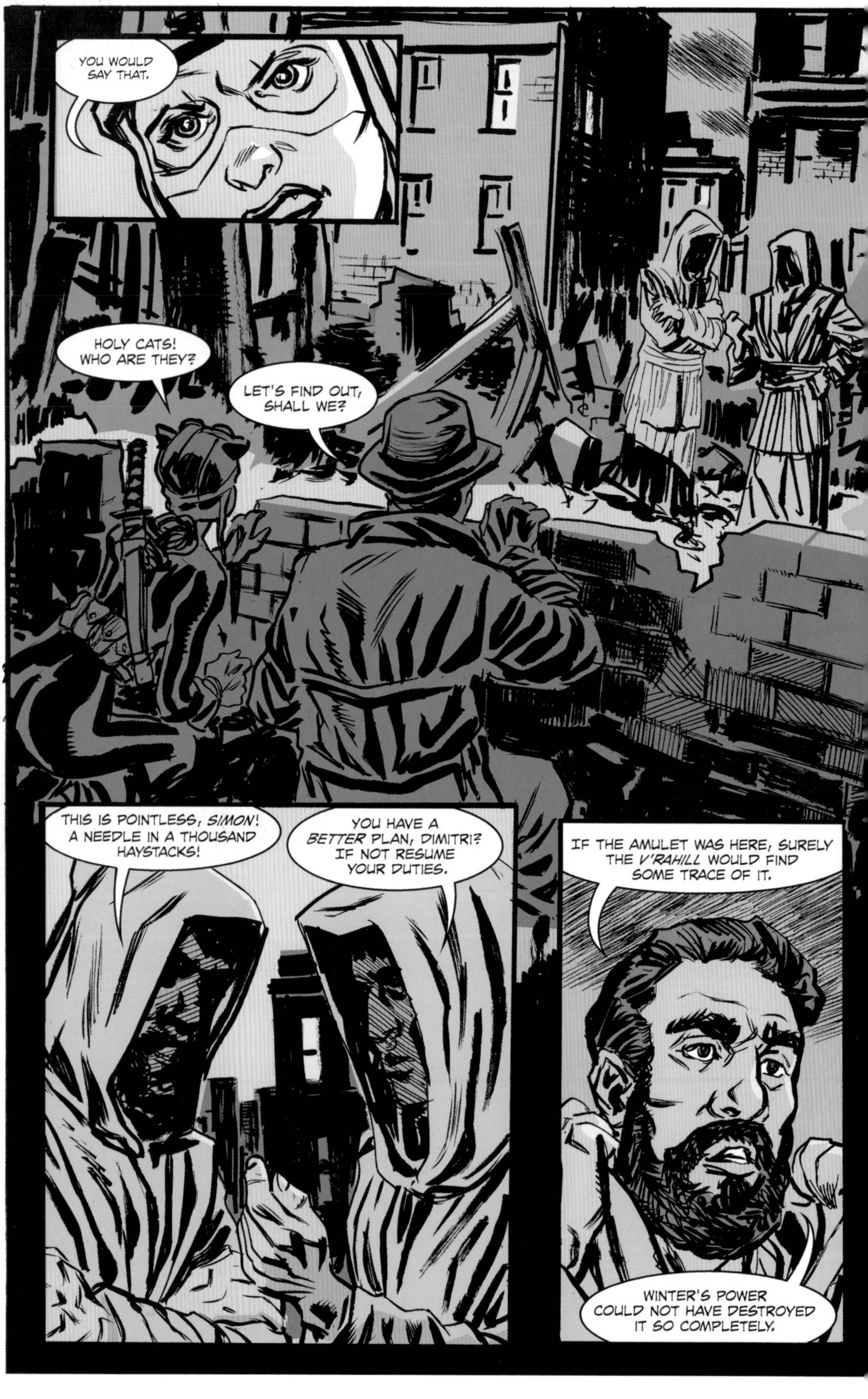
YOU WOULD SAY THAT.
HOLY CATS! WHO ARE THEY?
LET'S FIND OUT, SHALL WE?
THIS IS POINTLESS, *SIMON*! A NEEDLE IN A THOUSAND HAYSTACKS!
YOU HAVE A *BETTER* PLAN, DIMITRI? IF NOT RESUME YOUR DUTIES.
IF THE AMULET WAS HERE, SURELY THE *V'RAHILL* WOULD FIND SOME TRACE OF IT.
WINTER'S POWER COULD NOT HAVE DESTROYED IT SO COMPLETELY.

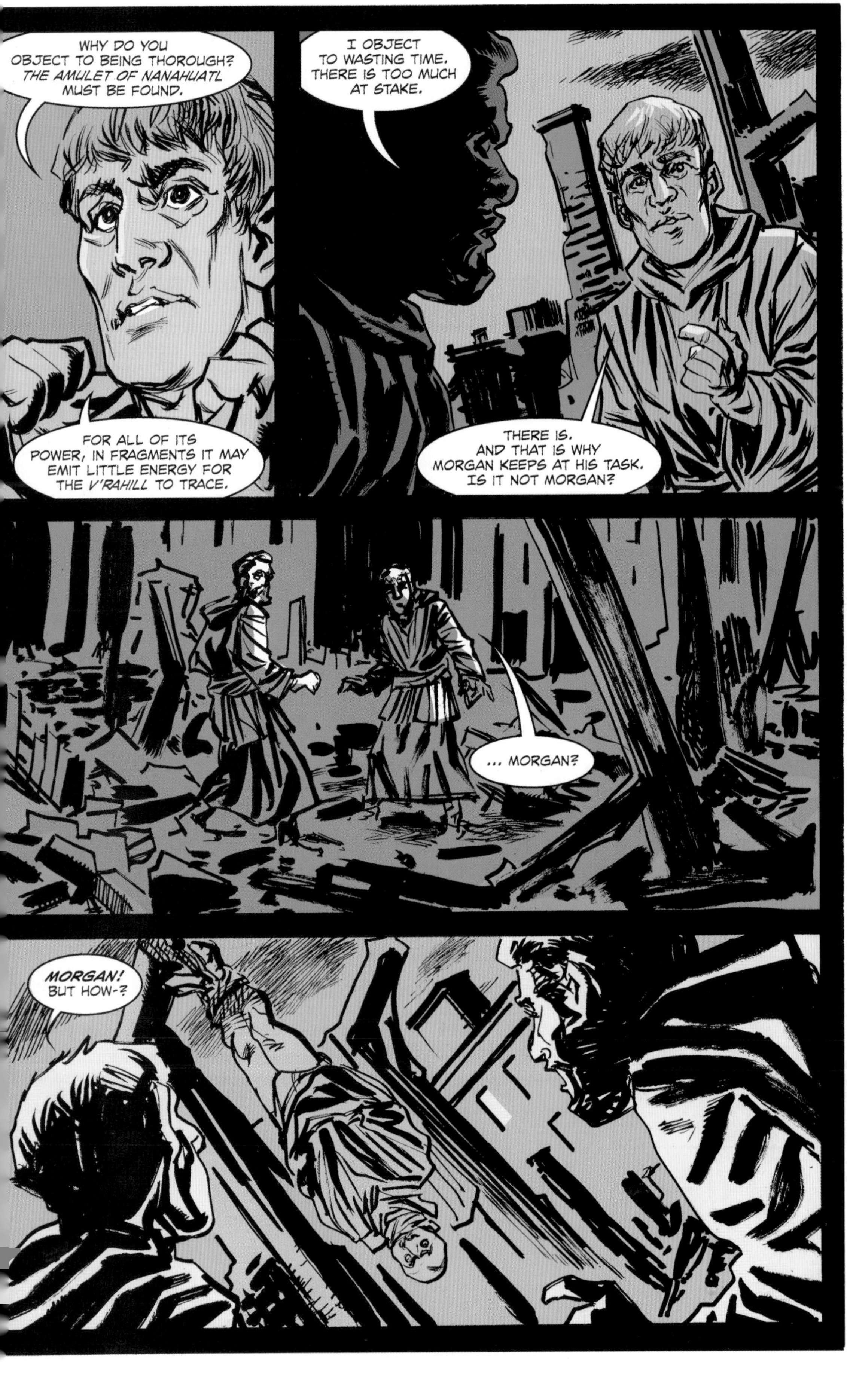
WHY DO YOU OBJECT TO BEING THOROUGH? *THE AMULET OF NANAHUATL* MUST BE FOUND.
FOR ALL OF ITS POWER, IN FRAGMENTS IT MAY EMIT LITTLE ENERGY FOR THE *V'RAHILL* TO TRACE.
I OBJECT TO WASTING TIME. THERE IS TOO MUCH AT STAKE.
THERE IS. AND THAT IS WHY MORGAN KEEPS AT HIS TASK. IS IT NOT MORGAN?
... MORGAN?
MORGAN! BUT HOW-?

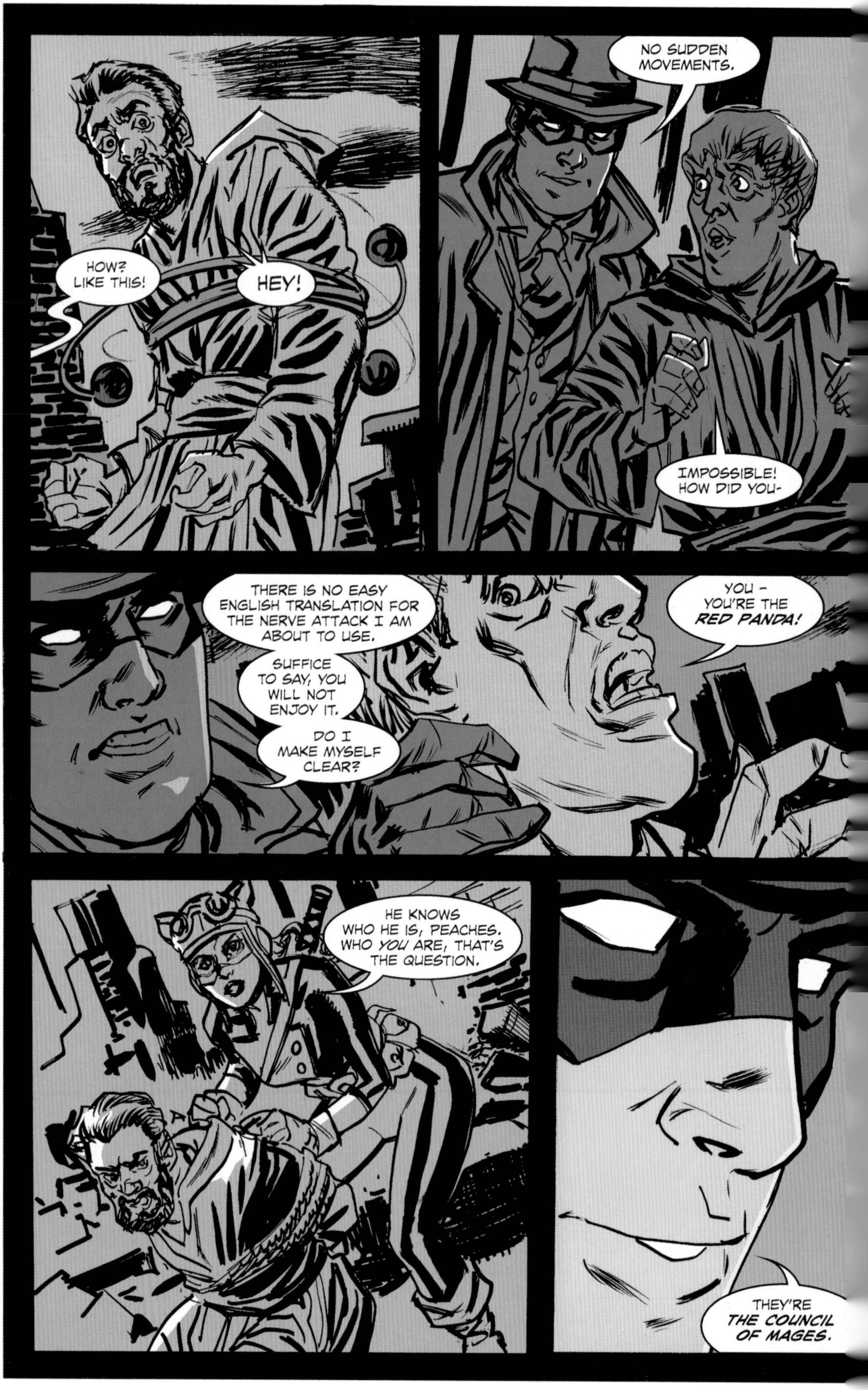
HOW? LIKE THIS!
HEY!
NO SUDDEN MOVEMENTS.
IMPOSSIBLE! HOW DID YOU-
THERE IS NO EASY ENGLISH TRANSLATION FOR THE NERVE ATTACK I AM ABOUT TO USE.
SUFFICE TO SAY, YOU WILL NOT ENJOY IT.
DO I MAKE MYSELF CLEAR?
YOU - YOU'RE THE *RED PANDA!*
HE KNOWS WHO HE IS, PEACHES. WHO *YOU* ARE, THAT'S THE QUESTION.
THEY'RE *THE COUNCIL OF MAGES.*

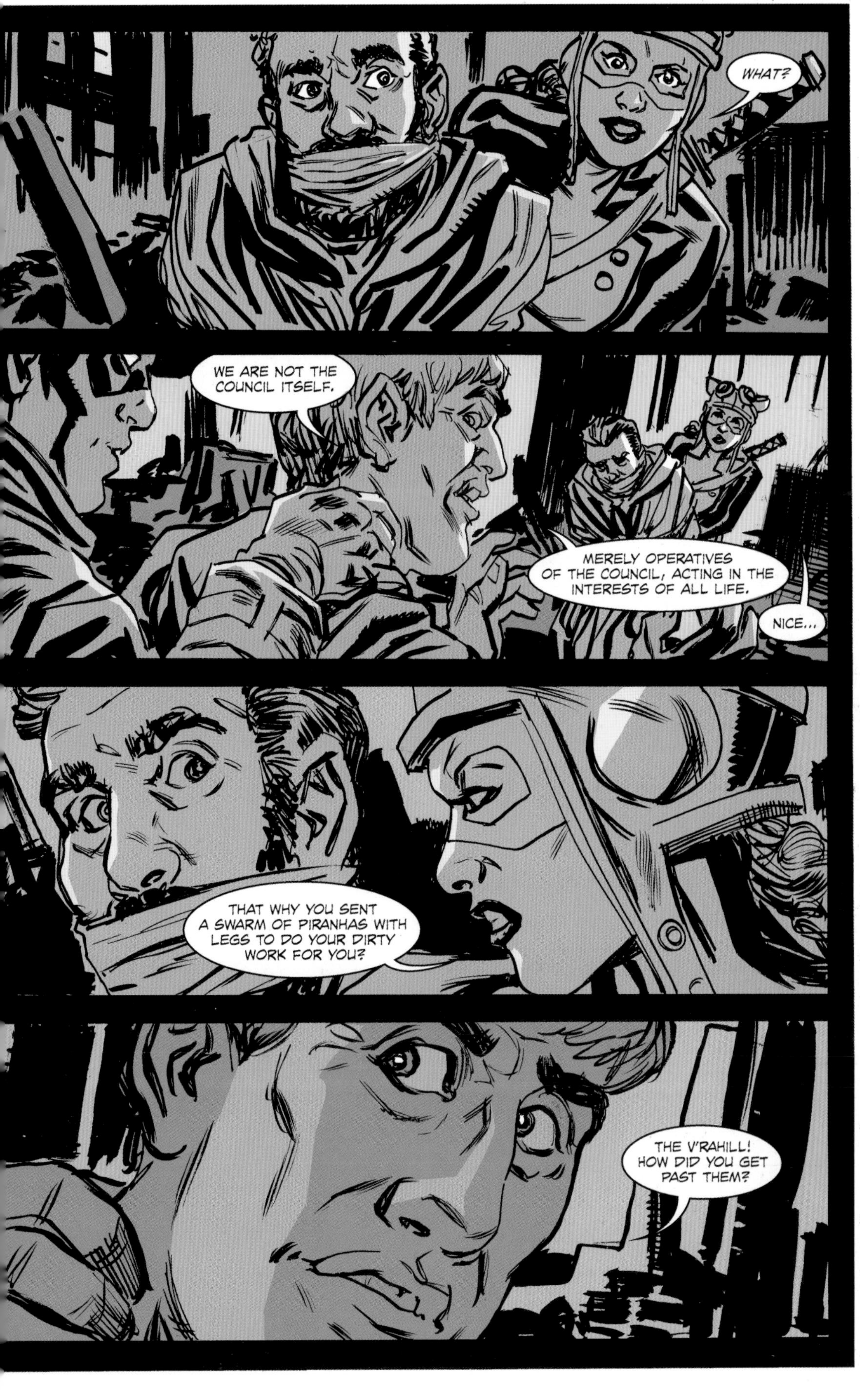
WHAT?
WE ARE NOT THE COUNCIL ITSELF.
MERELY OPERATIVES OF THE COUNCIL, ACTING IN THE INTERESTS OF ALL LIFE.
NICE...
THAT WHY YOU SENT A SWARM OF PIRANHAS WITH LEGS TO DO YOUR DIRTY WORK FOR YOU?
THE V'RAHILL! HOW DID YOU GET PAST THEM?

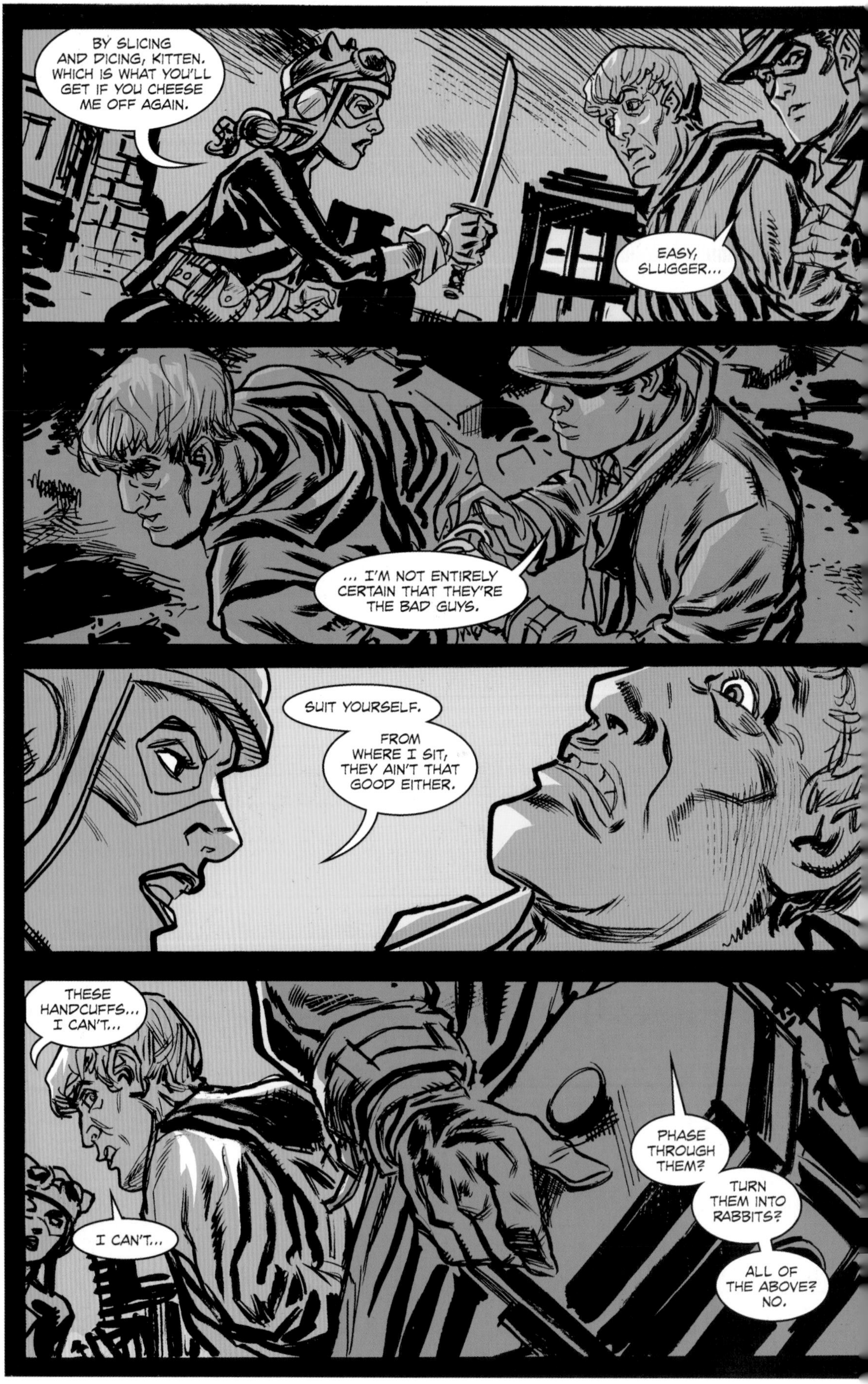
BY SLICING AND DICING, KITTEN. WHICH IS WHAT YOU'LL GET IF YOU CHEESE ME OFF AGAIN.
EASY, SLUGGER...
... I'M NOT ENTIRELY CERTAIN THAT THEY'RE THE BAD GUYS.
SUIT YOURSELF.
FROM WHERE I SIT, THEY AIN'T THAT GOOD EITHER.
THESE HANDCUFFS... I CAN'T...
I CAN'T...
PHASE THROUGH THEM?
TURN THEM INTO RABBITS?
ALL OF THE ABOVE? NO.

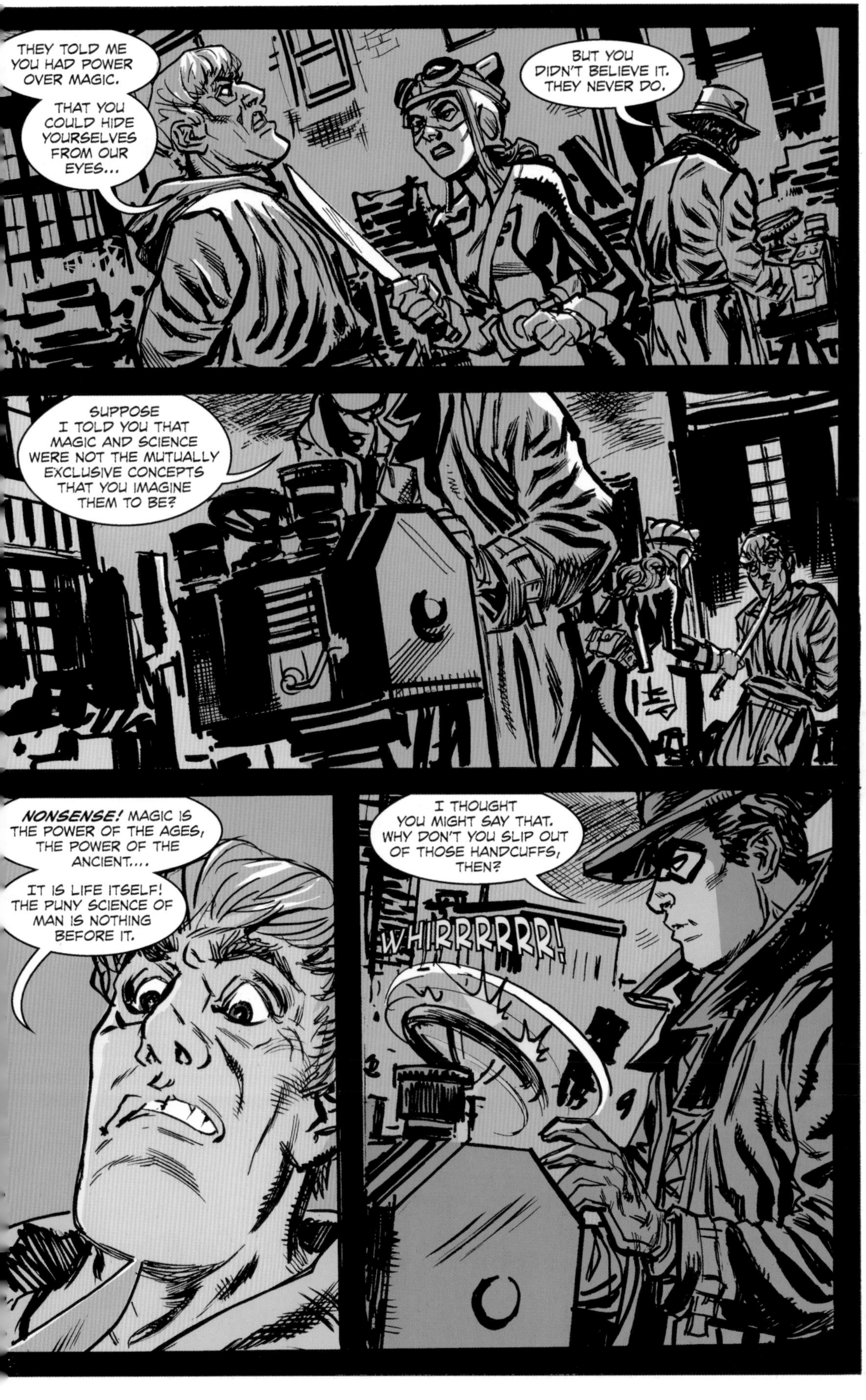

THEY TOLD ME YOU HAD POWER OVER MAGIC.
THAT YOU COULD HIDE YOURSELVES FROM OUR EYES...
BUT YOU DIDN'T BELIEVE IT. THEY NEVER DO.
SUPPOSE I TOLD YOU THAT MAGIC AND SCIENCE WERE NOT THE MUTUALLY EXCLUSIVE CONCEPTS THAT YOU IMAGINE THEM TO BE?
NONSENSE! MAGIC IS THE POWER OF THE AGES, THE POWER OF THE ANCIENT....
IT IS LIFE ITSELF! THE PUNY SCIENCE OF MAN IS NOTHING BEFORE IT.
I THOUGHT YOU MIGHT SAY THAT. WHY DON'T YOU SLIP OUT OF THOSE HANDCUFFS, THEN?
WHIRRRRRR!

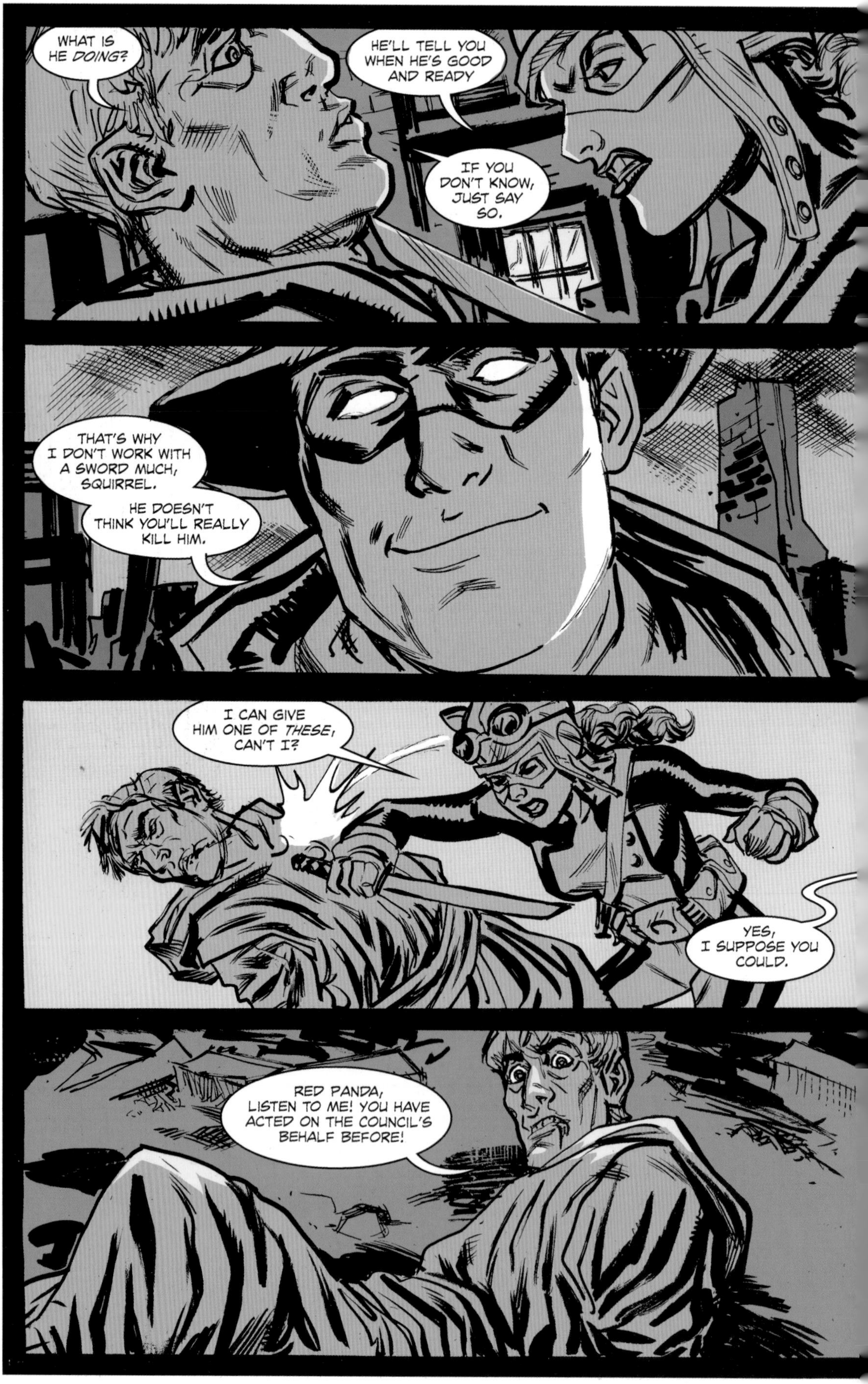
WHAT IS HE *DOING*?
HE'LL TELL YOU WHEN HE'S GOOD AND READY
IF YOU DON'T KNOW, JUST SAY SO.
THAT'S WHY I DON'T WORK WITH A SWORD MUCH, SQUIRREL.
HE DOESN'T THINK YOU'LL REALLY KILL HIM.
I CAN GIVE HIM ONE OF *THESE*, CAN'T I?
YES, I SUPPOSE YOU COULD.
RED PANDA, LISTEN TO ME! YOU HAVE ACTED ON THE COUNCIL'S BEHALF BEFORE!

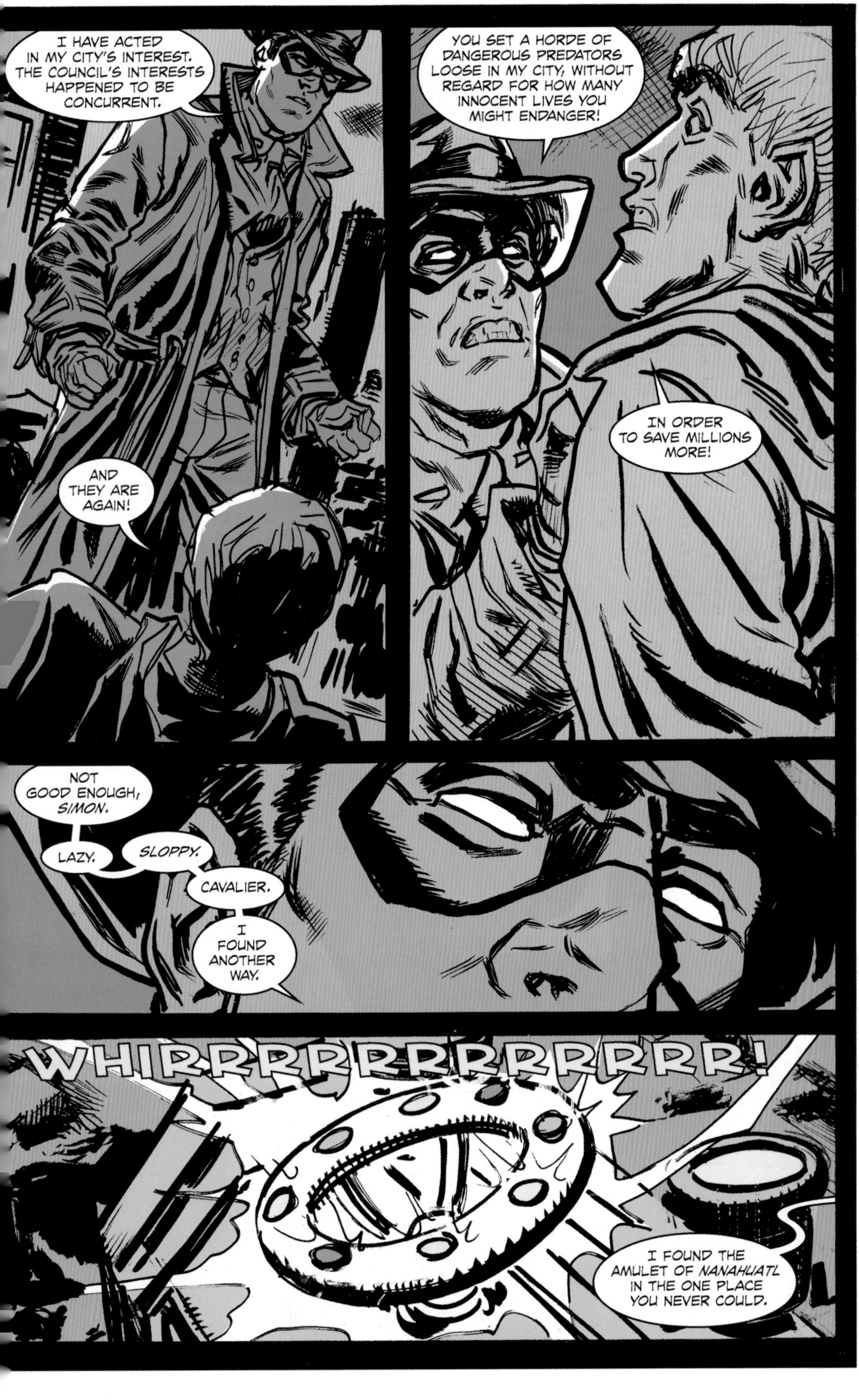
I HAVE ACTED IN MY CITY'S INTEREST. THE COUNCIL'S INTERESTS HAPPENED TO BE CONCURRENT.
AND THEY ARE AGAIN!
YOU SET A HORDE OF DANGEROUS PREDATORS LOOSE IN MY CITY, WITHOUT REGARD FOR HOW MANY INNOCENT LIVES YOU MIGHT ENDANGER!
IN ORDER TO SAVE MILLIONS MORE!
NOT GOOD ENOUGH, *SIMON*.
LAZY.
SLOPPY.
CAVALIER.
I FOUND ANOTHER WAY.
WHIRRRRRRRRRRR!
I FOUND THE AMULET OF *NANAHUATL* IN THE ONE PLACE YOU NEVER COULD.

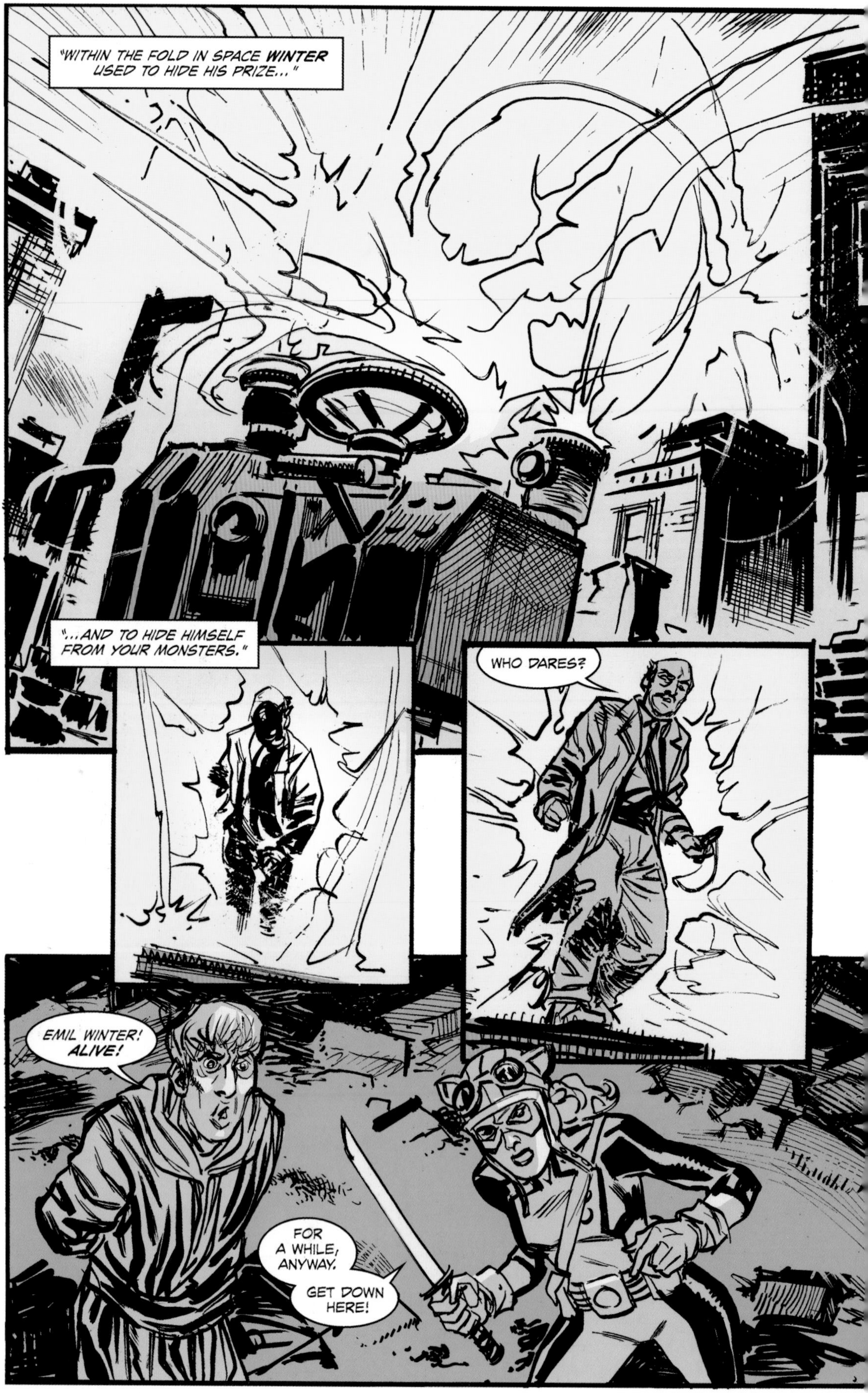
"WITHIN THE FOLD IN SPACE WINTER USED TO HIDE HIS PRIZE..."
"...AND TO HIDE HIMSELF FROM YOUR MONSTERS."
WHO DARES?
EMIL WINTER! ALIVE!
FOR A WHILE, ANYWAY.
GET DOWN HERE!

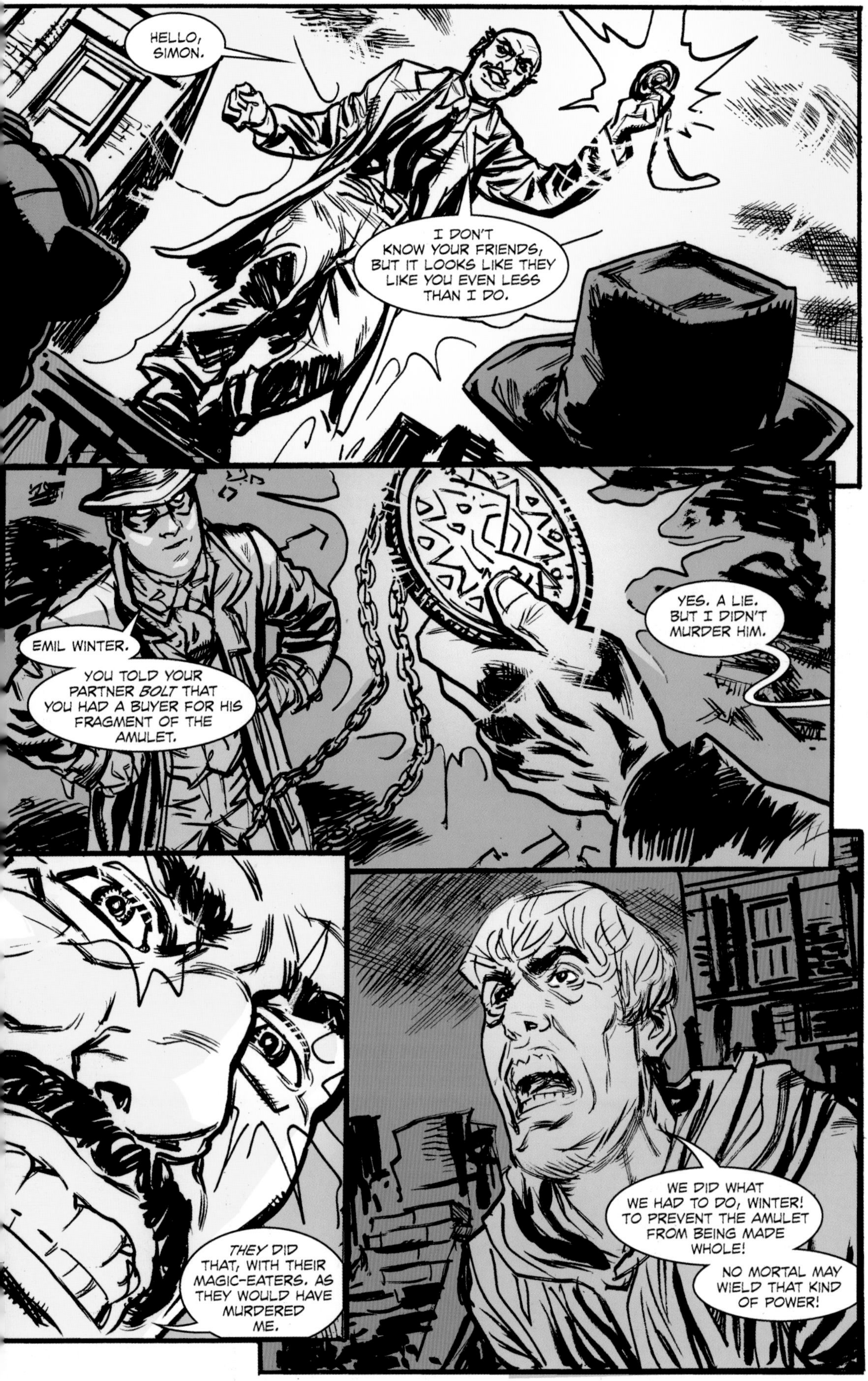

HELLO, SIMON.
I DON'T KNOW YOUR FRIENDS, BUT IT LOOKS LIKE THEY LIKE YOU EVEN LESS THAN I DO.
EMIL WINTER.
YOU TOLD YOUR PARTNER *BOLT* THAT YOU HAD A BUYER FOR HIS FRAGMENT OF THE AMULET.
YES. A LIE. BUT I DIDN'T MURDER HIM.
THEY DID THAT, WITH THEIR MAGIC-EATERS. AS THEY WOULD HAVE MURDERED ME.
WE DID WHAT WE HAD TO DO, WINTER! TO PREVENT THE AMULET FROM BEING MADE WHOLE!
NO MORTAL MAY WIELD THAT KIND OF POWER!

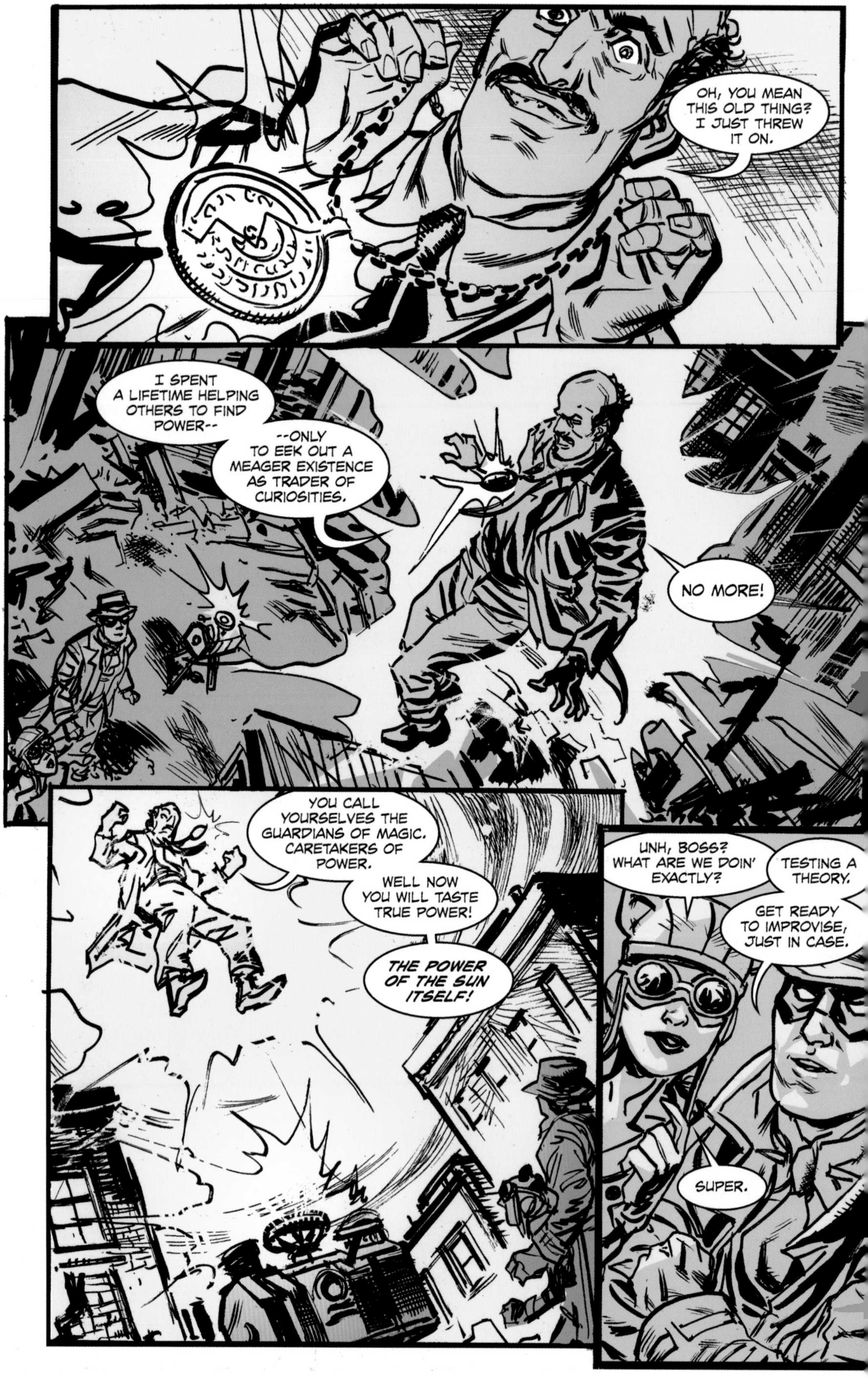
OH, YOU MEAN THIS OLD THING? I JUST THREW IT ON.
I SPENT A LIFETIME HELPING OTHERS TO FIND POWER--
--ONLY TO EEK OUT A MEAGER EXISTENCE AS TRADER OF CURIOSITIES.
NO MORE!
YOU CALL YOURSELVES THE GUARDIANS OF MAGIC. CARETAKERS OF POWER.
WELL NOW YOU WILL TASTE TRUE POWER!
THE POWER OF THE SUN ITSELF!
UNH, BOSS? WHAT ARE WE DOIN' EXACTLY?
TESTING A THEORY.
GET READY TO IMPROVISE, JUST IN CASE.
SUPER.

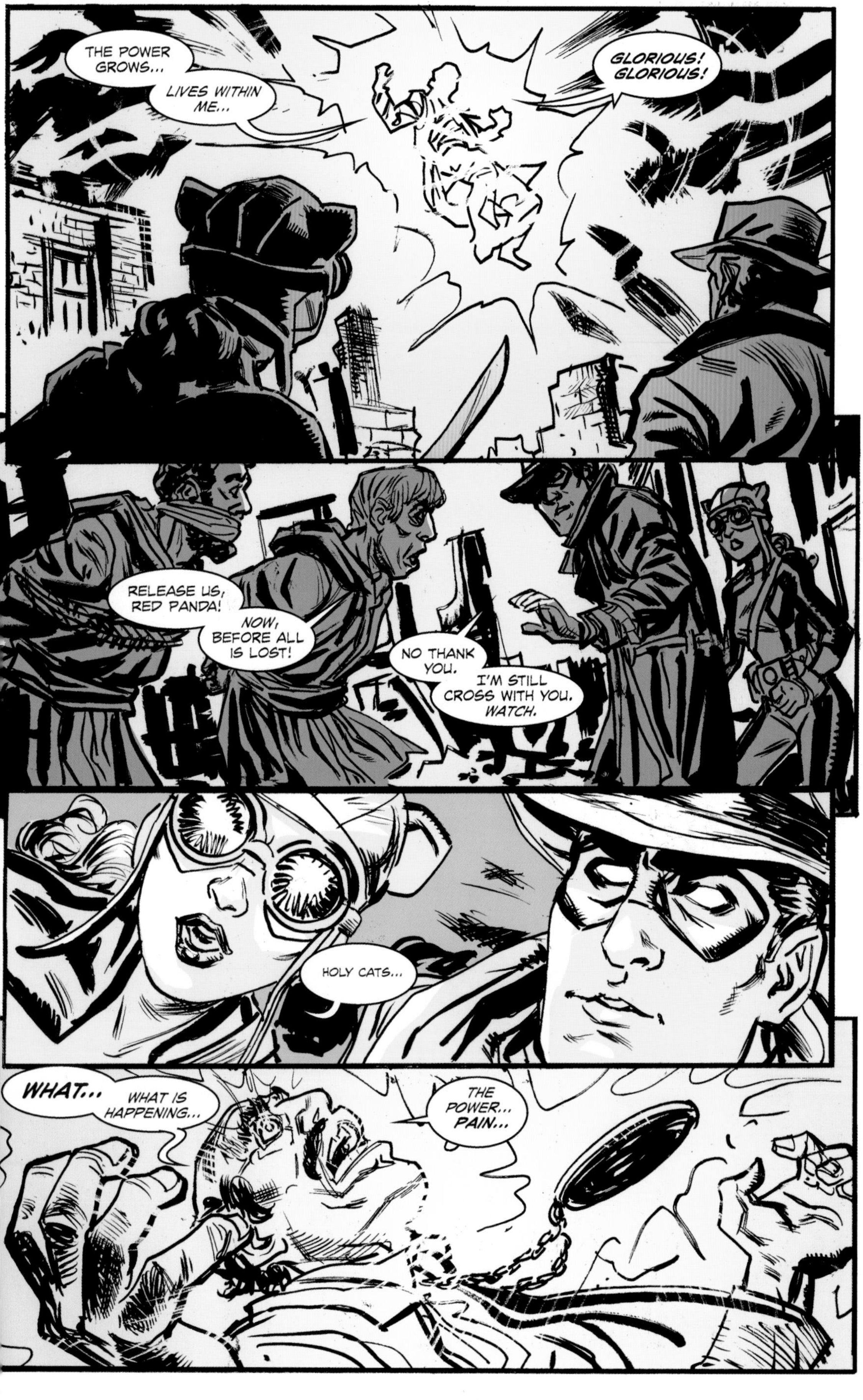
THE POWER GROWS...
LIVES WITHIN ME...
GLORIOUS! GLORIOUS!
RELEASE US, RED PANDA!
NOW, BEFORE ALL IS LOST!
NO THANK YOU.
I'M STILL CROSS WITH YOU. WATCH.
HOLY CATS...
WHAT...
WHAT IS HAPPENING...
THE POWER... PAIN...

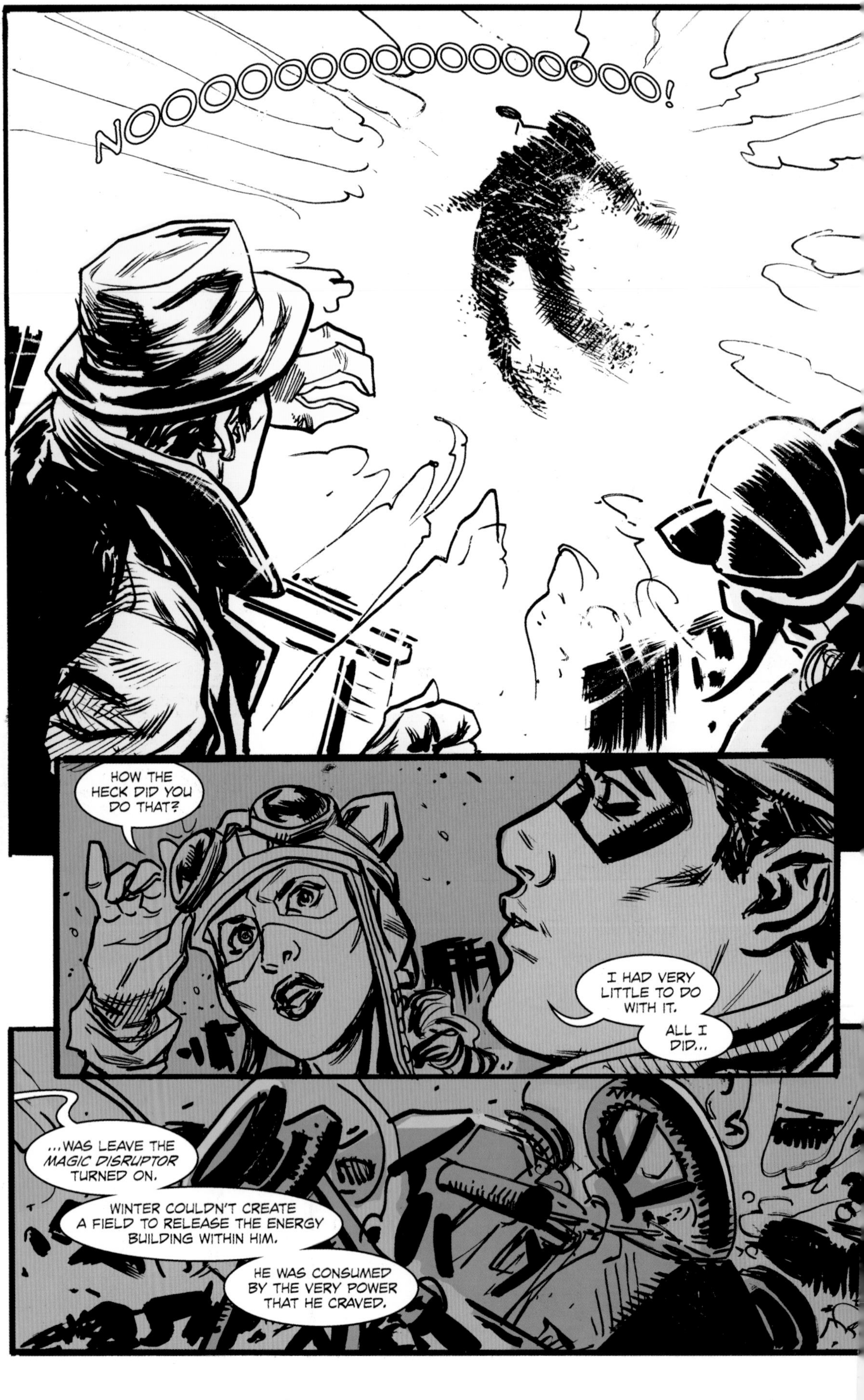
NOOOOOOOOOOOOOOOOOO!
HOW THE HECK DID YOU DO THAT?
I HAD VERY LITTLE TO DO WITH IT.
ALL I DID...
...WAS LEAVE THE *MAGIC DISRUPTOR* TURNED ON.
WINTER COULDN'T CREATE A FIELD TO RELEASE THE ENERGY BUILDING WITHIN HIM.
HE WAS CONSUMED BY THE VERY POWER THAT HE CRAVED.

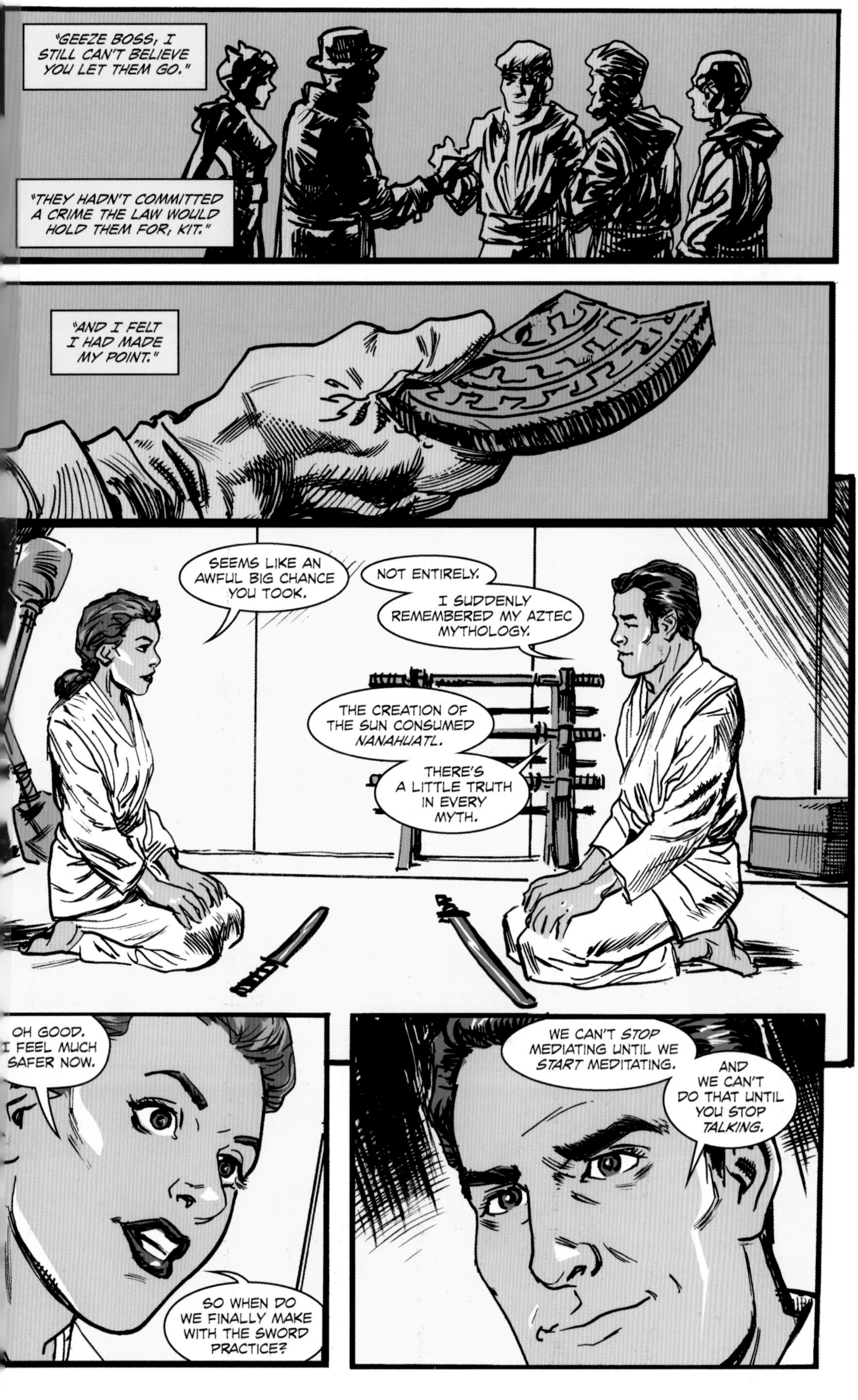
"GEEZE BOSS, I STILL CAN'T BELIEVE YOU LET THEM GO."
"THEY HADN'T COMMITTED A CRIME THE LAW WOULD HOLD THEM FOR, KIT."
"AND I FELT I HAD MADE MY POINT."
SEEMS LIKE AN AWFUL BIG CHANCE YOU TOOK.
NOT ENTIRELY.
I SUDDENLY REMEMBERED MY AZTEC MYTHOLOGY.
THE CREATION OF THE SUN CONSUMED NANAHUATL.
THERE'S A LITTLE TRUTH IN EVERY MYTH.
OH GOOD. I FEEL MUCH SAFER NOW.
SO WHEN DO WE FINALLY MAKE WITH THE SWORD PRACTICE?
WE CAN'T STOP MEDIATING UNTIL WE START MEDITATING.
AND WE CAN'T DO THAT UNTIL YOU STOP TALKING.

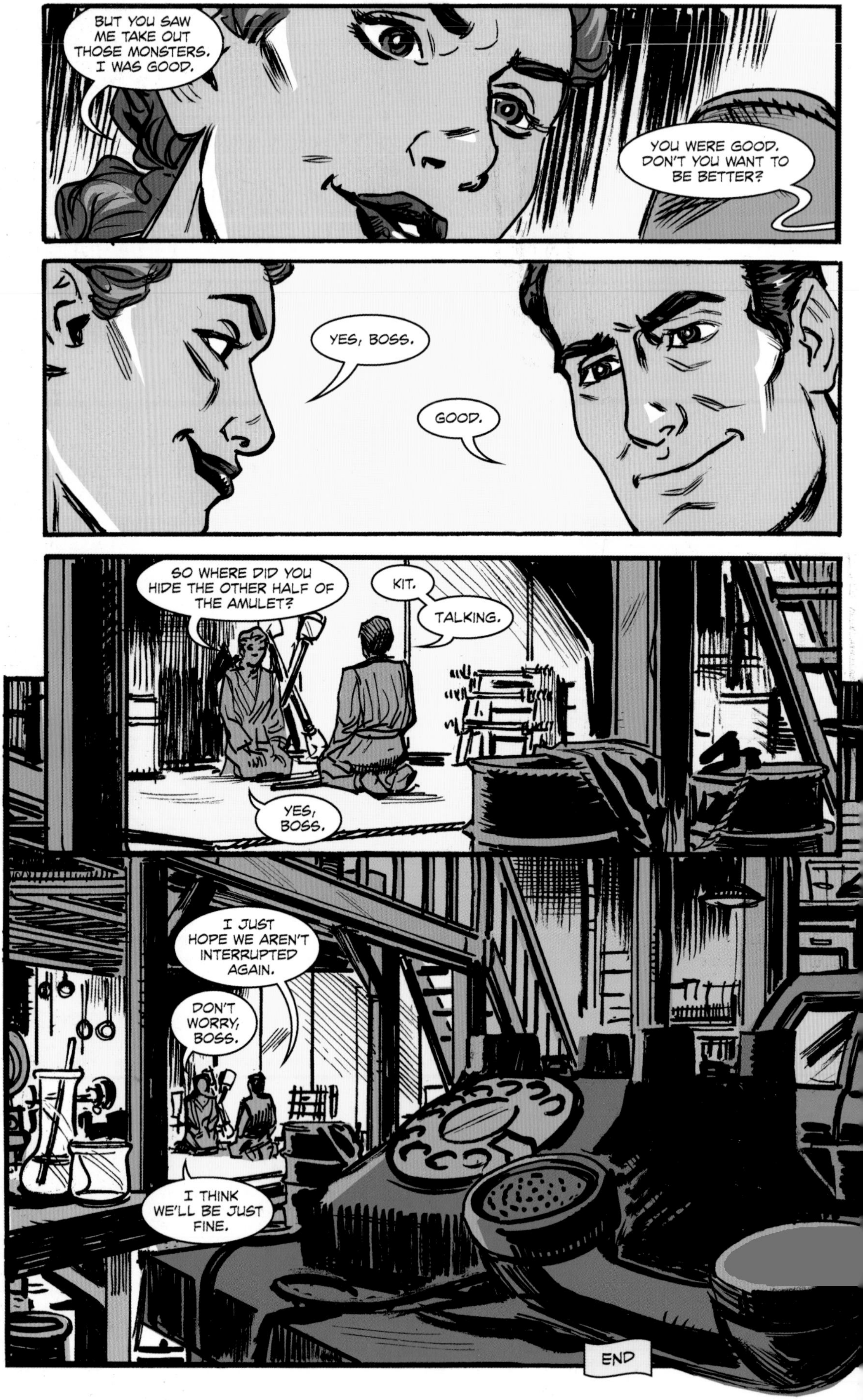
BUT YOU SAW ME TAKE OUT THOSE MONSTERS. I WAS GOOD.
YOU WERE GOOD. DON'T YOU WANT TO BE BETTER?
YES, BOSS.
GOOD.
SO WHERE DID YOU HIDE THE OTHER HALF OF THE AMULET?
KIT.
TALKING.
YES, BOSS.
I JUST HOPE WE AREN'T INTERRUPTED AGAIN.
DON'T WORRY, BOSS.
I THINK WE'LL BE JUST FINE.
END